8/07

# HISTORICAL
# ATLAS
## OF
# The Crusades

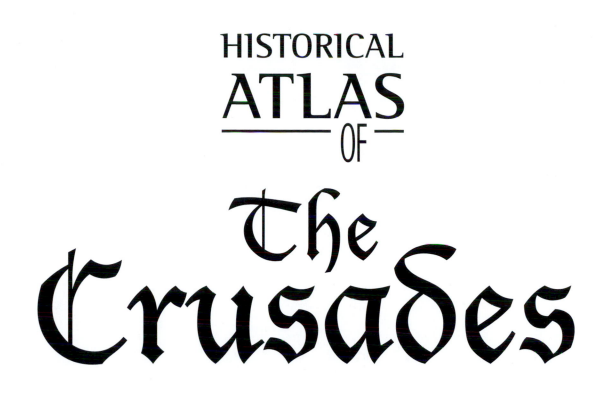

# HISTORICAL
# ATLAS
### OF

# The
# Crusades

### Angus Konstam

Checkmark Books™
*An imprint of Facts On File, Inc.*

## HISTORICAL ATLAS OF THE CRUSADES

**3rd Printing 2003**

Copyright © 2002 by Thalamus Publishing

Checkmark Books
An imprint of Facts On File, Inc.
132 West 31st Street
New York, NY 10001

**Library of Congress Cataloging-in-Publication Data**
Konstam, Angus
    Historical atlas of the crusades / Angus Konstam.
    New York, NY: Checkmark Books, c2002.
      p. cm.
    Includes index.
    ISBN: 0-8160-4919-X
    1. Europe—Historical geography—Maps. 2. Crusades—Maps.
    3. Europe—History—476-1492—Maps. 4. Europe—History—476-1492.
    5. Byzantine Empire—Historical geography—Maps.
    6. Byzantine Empire—History—1081-1453—Maps.  7. Byzantine Empire—History—1081-1453.
    8. Islamic Empire—History—750-1258—Maps.  I. Title.
    D158.K66 2002
    911'.4--dc21                    2002001349

Checkmark Books are available at special discounts when purchased in bulk quantities for businesses, associations, institutions or sales promotions. Please call our Special Sales Department in New York at:
(212) 967-8800 or (800) 322-8755.

You can find Facts On File on the World Wide Web at: **http://www.factsonfile.com**

For Thalamus Publishing
Project editors: Warren Lapworth and Neil Williams
Maps and design: Roger Kean
Illustrations: Oliver Frey
Four-color separation: Michael Parkinson

Printed and bound in Italy

10  9  8  7  6  5  4  3
This book is printed on acid-free paper

**previous pages:**
This 15th-century manuscript illumination depicts the battle of Fons Muratus and the death of Raymond of Antioch at the hands of the Seljuk Turks. It is from *Histoire d'Outremer*, based on the contemporary account of Guillaume de Tyre, Archbishop and chronicler for the princes of Antioch. Raymond was ambushed by the fabled Nur ed-Din's army having encroached into their territory. The prince fought well but was outnumbered. Nur ed-Din had Raymond's head and right arm cut off and sent to the caliph of Baghdad as trophies—and to show his respect for Raymond as a warrior.

# Contents

# The Emotive Legacy

Before the events of September 11, 2001, most Americans and Europeans would question the relevance of the Crusades—a part of world history buried 800 years in the past. After that day the term took on new meaning and long-forgotten history suddenly became more relevant than it had been for centuries.

President George W. Bush used the phrase "this crusade, this war on terrorism." He was using "crusade" in the same way as General Dwight D. Eisenhower used it during the Second World War, when he referred to a "crusade in Europe." To both men the term reflected a great cause, a military and political undertaking against an immoral opponent.

By contrast, the terrorist Osama bin Laden deliberately invoked historic memories of the Crusades, as a means of bringing fundamentalist Muslims to his cause. The Crusades are still an emotive issue almost a thousand years after the knights of the First Crusade scaled the walls of the Holy City of Jerusalem. To many Muslims, the Crusades have long been considered a crime against Islam, and crusading history has become entwined with political and religious rhetoric used by religious hard-liners.

During a video address in front of his Afghan cave, bin Laden made a distinct reference to the Crusading era. He called for "a new battle, similar to the great battles of Islam, like the conqueror of Jerusalem." He was referring to the great Muslim leader Saladin (or more accurately, Salah ad-Din Yusuf), who recaptured the city from the crusaders in 1187, following his victory in the Battle of Hattin earlier that year. Bin Laden was trying to incite

religious unrest by stirring up the past, and in the process likening himself to one of the great military heroes of Islam.

To emphasize his point, he added, "I envision Saladin coming out of the clouds carrying his sword, with the blood of unbelievers dripping from it." For him, Saladin was figuratively riding alongside his Al Qaeda terrorists. His call was an emotive one and met with widespread street level support in the Islamic world. How could a centuries-old historic figure still have such an emotive resonance in the 21st century?

Image was an important factor in the Christian crusade against the Muslim "infidel." The great and gracious of Europe needed to be seen to be fighting for the Holy Cause. No king embodied this spirit more than Louis IX of France (r.1226–70). Chroniclers showed him as a pious man, on his knees before God, or preaching to his flock. His war on Egypt proved to be a disaster, he was ineffective in Acre, and died losing to the Moors of North Africa. He was canonized as a saint in 1296.

## The Crusades

Events such as the attacks on the Pentagon and the World Trade Center have demonstrated how effective this form of historical imagery has been, inciting young Muslims to perform acts in the name of their religion to which the rest of the world attaches the label "atrocity." To understand why this obscure era in world history can still have such a devastating influence over our lives in the 21st century, we need to examine the Crusades in more detail, discovering how tensions between East and West in the late 11th century can still be relevant today.

This book offers a chance to do just that. By understanding the origin of the *jihad* or holy war, and the religious differences which split Islam for centuries, we might comprehend how phrases of the crusading era, such as *munafiquin* (hypocrites or pro-western Muslims), *kuffar* (infidels), and *shahid* (martyr) can have such a powerful meaning for Islamic fundamentalists today. At the same time, the divisive split between the two arms of Islam were echoed by a similar sort of division between the two main arms of the Christian Church, the Latin Church of St. Peter and Rome, and Orthodox of St. Mark and Constantinople. These divisions further heightened religious intolerance and help to provide religious justification for almost any act of barbarity.

It is fortunate that so many documents survived the crusading era to provide us with vivid accounts of the deeds and failures of the great princes and their retinues. Of equal value, many Muslim texts and eye-witness accounts also survived to give a balanced view of events. Often, texts from either side have corroborated each other's viewpoint. In illustrative terms, these contemporary documents were rarely illuminated. The many beautiful illuminations, like this page showing crusaders embarking for the Holy Land, from *Statutes de l'Ordre du Grand Esprit au Droit-Desir*, date to the 14th and 15th centuries. These draw heavily on the chroniclers who visited the Holy Land, but the landscape in which the crusaders campaign more often represents the lush background outside the European monastery where the illumination was probably executed. Nevertheless, among the fanciful there is much detail that is accurate and of historical value.

## Saladin the Hero

Although many Westerners are ignorant of historical facts that are well known in the East, the Islamic world also holds misconceptions. These misconceptions are frequently employed by propagandists. Unique in crusading history, Saladin was regarded as a hero by Christians as well as his own side. The Islamic warrior who recaptured Jerusalem was criticised for not being able to drive the Crusaders from the Holy Land. A shrewd and skilled warrior, he lost two battles against his nemesis, Richard the Lionheart. However, time has been kind to the Muslim warlord. While his critics have been silenced, the historians of both East and West have praised his skill, compassion, generosity and humanity. This is the same Saladin who Osama bin Laden used to represent as a vengeful Islamic warrior, bent on *jihad*, driving the infidels from the Holy City. How can the same figure be a hero to both Christians and Muslims, yet still be used as an icon to incite religious hatred?

Any study of the Crusades will reveal that bin Laden's view of Muslim history is flawed. Saladin is celebrated as a great warrior, but he was also celebrated by both friends and foes for his humanity. Following his victory at the Battle of Jaffa (1192), King Richard fell seriously ill. Saladin promptly sent his opponent gifts of fruit and snow to quell his fever. In the midst of a religiously inspired war, Saladin showed a degree of mercy and tolerance that extremists today would find hard to understand.

Certainly, Saladin committed war crimes, executing prisoners (or having his own *sufis* or holy men do so), but he was always prepared to negotiate, bribe, and reason to achieve his ends. Although locked in a military embrace, the warriors of both sides remained open-minded and aware of non-violent solutions.

## Islam versus Christianity

In 1099, the crusaders captured Jerusalem, desecrated the Dome of the Rock, and wreaked massacre and mayhem. Muslims and Jews alike were murdered until the streets ran with blood. Almost a millennium later, this atrocity against a cultured and tolerant population would be viewed as a war crime. In the Muslim world the crusaders are remembered as brutal, ruthless men who massacred whole populations. However, in their defense it should be argued that they lived in a brutal age and were a small, outnumbered army in a hostile land.

Most historians point out that many Muslim warriors performed similar acts. Ironically, both the Bible and the Koran emphasise love and compassion, but both Christian and Muslim fought and killed for their beliefs.

There is another fascinating aspect to the Crusades. Never since the fall of the Roman Empire in the west had so many people—from the highest to the lowest in the land—been on the move across vast areas of Europe. The Crusades had the same kind of effect on mass numbers that modern package holidays have had in introducing parochial minds to the wonders of foreign places. Alongside the prejudices of the narrow medieval mind that contributed to the atrocities, there was a new flowering of culture and an awareness of something larger outside the confines of a feudal meadow. In time, this would lead to the great socio-cultural rebirth of the Renaissance. As usual in historical eras, the Crusades brought terror, death, and destruction, but also greatness.

## Date systems

Dates in brackets are shown in different ways, depending on the information given. Monarchs are given the dates of their reign, shown like this: (r.1745–67). Papal dates are also the period of the term, shown like this: (p.1590–1615). Birth to death dates are shown without a prefix.

# CHAPTER I

# Jerusalem the Holy:
## Background to the Crusades

Map labels:
FRANKISH KINGDOM c.680
LOMBARD KINGDOM c.680
Venice
VISIGOTHIC KINGDOM before 711
UMAYYAD EMIRATE until 756; then independent of Abbasids
Narbonne
Barcelona
Corsica
Adriatic Sea
Tyrrhenian Sea
Rome
Valencia
Balearic Islands
Seville
Cordoba
Sardinia
Ceuta
AL-MAGHRIB
Sicily
Tunis (Carthage)
IFRIQIYA
Kairouan
Agadir
Tripoli

For centuries, the Romans and then their Byzantine successors controlled Palestine and Judea, the location of most of the events recounted in the Bible. First Persians and then Arabs were held at bay, while cities such as Antioch and Alexandria were among the richest and most prosperous urban centers in the known world. All this changed in the seventh century AD. While a wave of Asiatic invaders threatened to overrun the European heartland of the Byzantine Empire, a religious and cultural revolution took place in Arabia.

The prophet Mohammed proclaimed a new religion. The one God was Allah and salvation lay in *Islam*, the submission to His will. In AD 628, Mohammed and his followers captured Mecca. Within a decade the Arab followers of Allah had conquered Palestine, Syria, and Egypt. As the Arab conquests swept westward along the northern shore of Africa, the Muslims conquered Persia and even reached the borders of India before being halted. The Byzantines lost all of their eastern empire, except the province of Anatolia (Asia Minor).

To the Muslims as well as to Jews and Christians, Jerusalem was a holy city. The Muslims were tolerant of other religions and for centuries holy shrines were kept open to pilgrims of all faiths. This all changed when the Seljuk Turks became the guardians of the Islamic faith. Their defeat of the Byzantines in 1071 forced Orthodox Christians to ask for help from western Europe in reclaiming both their own lands and the Holy Land. The focus of almost all the crusading struggles that ensued was the capture and retention of the Holy City of Jerusalem. For crusaders and Saracens alike, Jerusalem was the ultimate prize.

**Cuman Turks**

THRACE

Cherson

*Danube*

*Sea of Azov*

*Black Sea*

Constantinople

Ancyra

Seljuk Turks 1071–80

**ARMENIA**

**Manzikert 1071**

*Lake Van*

*Lake Urmia*

*Aral Sea*

Samarkand

Bukhara

Balkh

Kabul

Merv

*Oxus*

Seljuks (Ghuzz) 1028–36

Hérat

Nishapur

*Caspian Sea*

**ANATOLIA**

**Seljuks of Rum**

Ephesus

Athens

Bodrum

*Rhodes*

Candia

*Crete*

*Cyprus*

Antioch

Edessa

Aleppo

*Tigris*

Mosul

Nehavend

Samarra

**MESOPOTAMIA**

Baghdad

*Euphrates*

Wasit

Rayy

**SASSANIAN EMPIRE** before c.638

**PERSIA**

Persepolis

Basra

*Persian Gulf*

Tripoli

Beirut

Sidon

Damascus

Jerusalem

Gaza

*Mediterranean Sea*

Barqa

LIBYA

Alexandria

EGYPT

Cairo

*Nile*

Thebes

Aswan

SASSANIAN EMPIRE before c.638

*Red Sea*

Medina

Mecca

**ARABIA**

**OMAN**

San'a

**YEMEN**

Aden

Axum

boundary of Byzantine Empire, 565

boundary of Byzantine Empire, 1100

Arabs practicing Islam, 632

extent of Islamic conquest at fall of Umayyad dynasty, 750

boundary of Great Seljuk Empire, 1100

Turkish migrations

# Land of Judaism and Christianity

**When Rome conquered Judea and made it a province in the first century BC, the empire gained one of the richest areas of the Mediterranean. Renamed Palestine in AD 70, the region retained its great religious importance. Christianity originated there and, following Jesus' death, the new religion survived, then grew. By the start of the fourth century AD, even the Roman emperor was a Christian and Palestine was regarded as a holy land by followers of two of the world's great religions.**

**above:** Judea was not a land running with milk and honey, but careful husbandry brought out the soil's natural fertility and rewarded the Jews who tended it… as well as their masters. First Romans and then Arabs coveted the prosperity of Palestine. These modern grape arbors testify to the continued fertility of Judea, even in its desert regions.

The collapse of the Hellenistic Seleucid Empire in 64 BC created a power vacuum in the Middle East and allowed the Romans to expand their frontiers. Syria was annexed and the following year the Maccabean Jewish dynasty collapsed. The Romans occupied Palestine. The growing threat of the Parthian Persians limited any further eastward expansion, so the Romans consolidated their control over their existing Middle Eastern possessions.

Although occupied by Roman troops, Judea was considered an independent state, but was effectively united with the neighboring provinces of Galilee and Peraea by King Herod, ruler of Judea, to create the larger province of Palestine. Christ was born in this Jewish state, independent yet occupied by Roman troops, who also exerted direct control over the neighboring provinces of Syria and Egypt. In AD 6, Judea and the rest of Palestine was annexed by the Romans, becoming part of the empire.

Almost all our knowledge of Jesus comes from the four canonical Gospels, and we know of the historical times in which he lived. The Jews were allowed a measure of self-government under the Sanhedrin. The preaching of Jesus attracted followers and gradually he became drawn to Jerusalem, the foundation city of the Jewish faith. By challenging the leading Jewish group and entering the precincts of the Temple, the center of the Jewish faith, he incurred the enmity of the Sanhedrin. With Roman support, he was condemned to death c.AD 30. Far from being disillusioned with the death of the Messiah (*Christos* in Greek), his followers remained true to their beliefs. Following the writing of the letters of Paul c.AD 50, the Christian faith blossomed and grew.

## Birth of the Holy City

In AD 66 the Jewish population of Judea revolted against the Romans, and four years later the Romans stormed Jerusalem and destroyed the Temple. By AD 73 Palestine was firmly in Roman control and a second Jewish revolt in 132 led to widespread persecution of the Jewish population and another *diaspora* (dispersion). To both Jews and Christians, Jerusalem became the spiritual home of their faith. Centuries later, it would also become a

but the two faiths became irreconcilably divided following the destruction of the Temple. Christian churches were established during the first century from Anatolia to Italy, and by the early second century Christianity had spread into Roman Gaul, North Africa, and Spain. Alexandrian theologians gave the new religion some intellectual foundation, while Church structures developed as the faith became more stable. Early in the fourth century Roman Emperor Constantine I the Great (r.306–37) became a Christian, ending decades of persecution, and following the Edict of Milan (313), Christianity became the official religion.

Church and state became closely intertwined and the Christian Church used the system of Roman provincial government as its administrative model. When Rome fell in the early fifth century, elements of this Church administration survived, but were unable to prevent the spread of Islam, or even the loss of Jerusalem as a center of the faith. While Rome and Constantinople became the principal Christian centers, Jerusalem became a bastion of the Muslim faith.

spiritual center of Islam. The Holy City had become a place of pilgrimage, veneration, and a symbol of faith.

Christianity proved remarkably resilient. Paul, a Jewish convert to Christianity, who famously saw the light while traveling to Damascus, preached his beliefs throughout Asia Minor, Greece, and Italy. Jewish communities were targeted as potential converts to the new religion,

**above:** "Render unto Caesar what is Caesar's..." said Jesus. This coin of Augustus was found in Jerusalem. Augustus (r.31 BC–AD 14), Rome's first emperor, conquered Judea and ruled the state through its vassal king, Herod. A donkey grazes amid the ruins of Herodian, **below**, Herod the Great's summer palace situated between Jerusalem and Bethlehem.

# The Prophet Mohammed

**At the start of the seventh century AD, the Arabian prophet Mohammed (Muhammad) ushered in a new religion. Islam means submission to the will of Allah (the one God), and His message was spread through Mohammed, the Apostle and Prophet of Allah. By Mohammed's death in 632, the Muslim faith had spread throughout the deserts of Arabia and was ready to emerge as one of the world's leading religions.**

Mohammed was the catalyst of a series of developments that would change the face of the world. Born c.AD 570 in Mecca, a western Arabian trading city inhabited by the Arabic Quraysh tribe, he was orphaned at the age of six. He was brought up by his uncle and grandfather, took up a trade, and eventually married a widow and former employer named Khadija. The couple raised several children and led uneventful lives... until Mohammed was 40. At this point his life changed. According to traditional belief he visited a mountain cave where he was visited by an apparition, the angel Gabriel, who declared that Mohammed would be the messenger of the one God, or Allah. Gabriel forced Mohammed to recite part of what would become the *Qur'an* (Koran; *qur'an* literally means "the book"). Throughout the rest of the prophet's life, Gabriel returned to bring

**right:** This Islamic painting dating from the 18th century depicts the Koran being revealed to Mohammed during a battle.

further passages of the holy text.

Mohammed began to preach to friends and family, then spread his message more widely. Opposition from followers of the existing pantheistic religion in Mecca forced Mohammed and his followers to flee the city on July 16, 622—which later came to represent the beginning of the Islamic era and the date used as the start of the Muslim calendar. He settled in Medina to the north.

The migration (*hijra*) was a turning point for the prophet, because it forced the Muslims to develop their communal organization, with Mohammed as the arbiter of the word of Allah. The local community was predominantly Jewish and prayed facing Jerusalem. Mohammed promptly elected to pray facing Mecca, thereby endowing Islam with a holy center.

## Respecting others' beliefs

In 628, after defeating a series of assaults by the Meccans, the Muslims returned to Mecca. Mohammed cast down the symbols of the local religion and claimed Mecca and the *Kaa'ba* for his own faith. A *kaa'ba* (cube) is a square building, perhaps a fort or a shrine. In Mecca the *Kaa'ba* houses a cube of black stone, which the pre-Islamic priests held to be holy. Mohammed retained this *Kaa'ba*, and reclaimed it as a symbol of the new Muslim faith. By Mohammed's death in 632, the Islamic religion had spread across western Arabia and gained a foothold in Oman, on the Persian Gulf.

At first, Islam was not an aggressive creed that encouraged the conversion of others. Rather, readers of the Koran were encouraged to respect the beliefs of other monotheistic religions, particularly the Jewish and Christian faiths, both of which had shared beliefs with Islam and relied on the same books of scripture. The Koran spoke of Moses, Abraham, and other Jewish Old Testament figures, as well as claiming Christ as an earlier prophet. Recent work by Muslim scholars suggests that the change of facing toward Mecca during prayer may have come after Mohammed's death. Up to that point, then, Jerusalem was a center for both the Islamic and Jewish faiths. In which

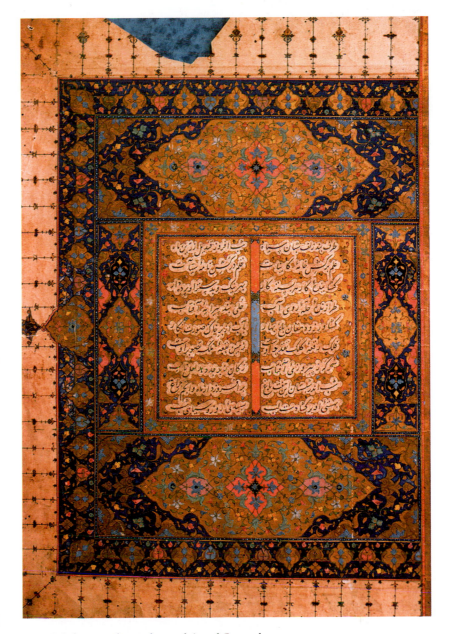

case, Mohammed may have claimed Jerusalem as the spiritual center, with Mecca merely a staging post for Islam.

Mohammed's monotheism was presented as the ancestral faith of his people and therefore transcended tribal or political boundaries, unlike Judaism. For the Arabs, whose shared cultural roots stretched back thousands of years, this homogenous belief was a powerful force and explained how the Arabic conquests in the name of Islam could have been so successful. This unity of purpose, and the Islamic doctrine of all being united as the servants of God, created a unified Muslim world, making the new faith a powerful creed. Whatever the historical roots of the Muslim faith, Mohammed served as a catalyst for a belief that transformed the Middle East within a few generations and would claim Jerusalem as its own.

**above:** An illuminated page from the Koran, probably dating from the 16th century, on display at the Decorative Arts Museum, Tehran, Iran.

# The Arab Conquests

**In AD 634, Abu Bakr the Caliph "successor" to Mohammed, sent Arab armies of conquest northward toward Jerusalem. Within two decades, Persia, Syria, and most of North Africa were in Muslim hands, a dynamic expansion unmatched in history. The frontiers of Islam stretched from the Atlantic Ocean to the mountains of Afghanistan.**

**right:** The decisive actions of Emperor Heraclius in regaining Jerusalem from the Sassanian Persians earned him a place in the growing Christian anthology of inspirational subjects. This detail from the 15th-century altar piece of Santa Cruz de Bleza depicts Saint Helena and the Emperor Heraclius at the Gate of Jerusalem, the latter having retrieved and resurrected the Calvary Cross of Jesus, which had been seized by the Persians. Sadly, possession of this holy relic did not prevent the Muslim Arab armies from taking Jerusalem off the Byzantines only a few years later.

**facing:** The Umayyad dynasty was quick to begin building cities and palaces all along the length of Judea between 638 and 670. This early eighth-century fresco fragment is from the palace at Qasr al Hair.

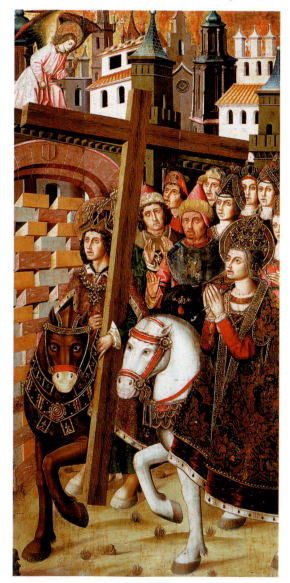

As the successor of Mohammed, Caliph Abu Bakr (r.AD 632–34) was faced with a possible collapse of Islamic resolve. Several regional prophets threatened to disrupt the unity of the Muslim cause but the caliph used military force to bring these rivals into line. He planned to ensure Arab unity by launching a religiously inspired invasion of the Eastern Roman Empire, which by now had adopted its Byzantine appellation.

Following Abu Bakr's death after only a two-year reign, it fell to his successor, Caliph Omar (r.634–44), to launch the *jihad* (holy war) against the Byzantine province of Syria. The Byzantines had just ended a damaging war against the Sassanian Persian Empire and recently recovered their Syrian and Palestinian territories. Emperor Heraclius had restructured the empire and repulsed an Asiatic invasion of the Byzantine lands in the Balkans and Greece.

To the Sassanians and Byzantines, the Arabic army led by Knaled ibn al-Wadid, which stormed out of the desert in 634, was just another group of Arab raiders. However, when the Arabs captured Jerusalem, it became apparent that the Byzantines faced a full-scale invasion. Emperor Heraclius (r.610–41) dispatched an army to deal with the threat. At the Battle of Yarmuk (636) the Byzantine army was destroyed, as was a Sassanian army at Qadisiyya the following year.

With Palestine, Syria, and Mesopotamia in Islamic hands, both the Persian and Byzantine armies were sent reeling northward. Following their defeat at Nihawand (642), the Persian Empire collapsed and its territories fell to the caliph. Persepolis was occupied in 650 and the following year the Arabs reached the River Oxus. The Byzantines retreated into Anatolia (Asia Minor) and tried to reorganize their defenses.

## Muslim divisions

Further to the west, Egypt fell to Islam in 640 and the Arabs continued along the coast of North Africa as far as Cyraencia. Within two decades, the followers of Mohammed had created a new world empire that paralleled what Rome had been in its heyday. Although the first flood of conquests had ended by 651, the borders of Islam continued to expand throughout the rest of the seventh century, although at a far slower rate, partly due to internal divisions. When Caliph Uthman (r.644–55) gained power, Islam came to be ruled by an aristocratic Arab dynasty, the house of Umayyad.

Uthman therefore laid the foundations for a

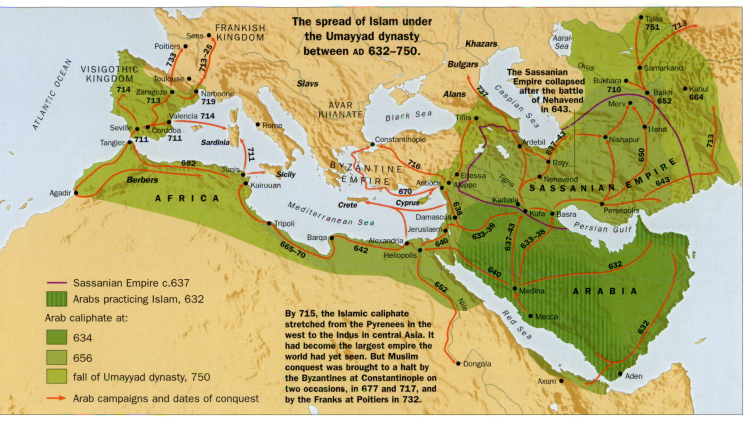

**The spread of Islam under the Umayyad dynasty between AD 632–750.**

*The Sassanian Empire collapsed after the battle of Nehavend in 643.*

By 715, the Islamic caliphate stretched from the Pyrenees in the west to the Indus in central Asia. It had become the largest empire the world had yet seen. But Muslim conquest was brought to a halt by the Byzantines at Constantinople on two occasions, in 677 and 717, and by the Franks at Poitiers in 732.

Sassanian Empire c.637
Arabs practicing Islam, 632
Arab caliphate at:
634
656
fall of Umayyad dynasty, 750
Arab campaigns and dates of conquest

hereditary caliphate. Their dynasty's grip on power was temporarily broken following his assassination when Ali, the prophet's son-in-law, became caliph. The Islamic world faced civil war, since the Umayyad governor of Syria refused to accept Ali, and set himself up as a rival caliph. Following Ali's assassination five years later, the Umayyads regained power but were unable to avoid a religious schism. The followers of Ali (Shi'ites) saw themselves as the rightful heirs of the Prophet's vision and evolved into the Shia Muslims, while the followers of the Umayyad dynasty claimed they represented the Orthodox (Sunni) position. The schism still exists today.

Under the Umayyad caliphs (known as the Caliphs of Damascus), the frontiers of Islam moved eastward to the River Indus, and Kabul and Samarkand became Muslim cities. To the west, Muslim armies reached Tangiers, then crossed into Spain, which they conquered from the Visigoths during the second decade of the eighth century. At first, the native peoples opposed the invaders, but in time they converted and joined the Jihad. With the entire Middle East in Muslim hands, the Byzantines represented a bulwark against Islam. A Muslim raid into Anatolia was stopped at the walls of Constantinople, and by the mid-eighth century an uneasy peace developed between the Muslims and the Christians in Asia Minor that would last for over three centuries.

# The Muslim World

**Muslims who faced the crusaders viewed the Damascus caliphate as representing a golden age, when all of Islam was unified. This was the caliphate represented in *Arabian Nights*, a semi-mythical period of prosperity and happiness. In fact, while the Muslim world prospered during the three centuries before 1095, it also lost its unity, leaving it vulnerable to attack by a dedicated opponent.**

The Umayyad dynasty (AD 660–750) built an Islamic empire that stretched from Spain to Afghanistan. Damascus became Islam's new capital and Arabic became the unifying language for millions of Islamic subjects. In Jerusalem the Dome of the Rock was completed in 692—the first major monument of the Islamic faith. It was built by Caliph Abn-al-Malik on the site of the Jewish Temple, a rock now associated with Mohammed as the site of his ascension to Heaven. Historically, it was the site of a shared Judeo-Islamic heritage involving what Muslims see as the pre-Mohammedan prophet, Abraham. It was also a symbol that the Muslims were no longer occupiers and conquerors, but had become representative of the indigenous converts of the Middle East.

The Umayyads were plagued by Shi'ite insurrections, and in 750 a Hashimite ("family of the Prophet") caliph was enthroned, from the Abbasid rather than the Alid branch of the family. The Umayyad dynasty collapsed and only the Emirate of Cordoba in Spain remained in Umayyad hands.

The Abbasid dynasty moved the capital of Islam from Damascus to Baghdad, where they were closer to their Shi'ite power-base. Under Caliph al-Mansur (r.754–75), some of the former glories of the Persian court were reclaimed by the Abbasids, who have become associated with a cultural golden age of poets, artists, and builders. They also presided over a devolution of central power to the provinces.

The Arab empire was too big to administer without devolution, and a series of regional governors took full advantage of this relaxation of the power of the caliphate. In 777, the first regional dynasty was founded in Africa (the Rustamid house); others were soon to follow. In effect, the Abbasids never established their control over the entire Islamic world. In the ninth century there was further fragmentation, particularly in Africa, Egypt, and the eastern provinces of the Islamic empire.

**right:** Among Arabs, chess was a popular form of exercising mathematical thinking in a relaxing way. The board game's intricate maneuvers captured the interest of Europeans, which the advent of the Crusades extended. This manuscript illumination from the 1282 *Book of Games* by Alphonse Le Sage shows two Arabs playing chess in a tent.

## Fragmentation

In AD 969 Fatimids, leaders of a Shi'ite sect known as Ismailism, seized power in Egypt, establishing their base in the new city of Cairo. By the end of the tenth century, the Muslim world had effectively abandoned its imperial aspirations. Abbasid rule had fragmented the Islamic world, leaving it open to attack by outsiders. The Asiatic Ghuzz tribe known as the Seljuk Turks migrated from the River Oxus into Iran during the third decade of the century, defeating anyone who stood in their way. They also became fervent converts to Islam.

By 1055, Seljuk Turks had captured Baghdad, then continued their expansion west to the shores of the Mediterranean Sea. Unlike the Abbasids, they were Orthodox Sunnis, and following their consolidation of Syria and Persia, the Muslim world became divided between the two sects of Islam. The Fatimid caliphate based in Cairo was Shi'ite, while the Seljuk sultanate based in Baghdad was Sunni. This division weakened the Muslim world at a time when it needed to stand against the crusaders. Instead, the division remained for a further two centuries, and although the two Muslim states would co-operate with each other, each was wary of the other.

This final century before the crusades was a period of political division but also of cultural growth within the Muslim world. Philosophers, scientists, mathematicians,

theologians, doctors, and physicists created a dazzling renaissance that stood in stark contrast to the cultural situation in Christendom. The Muslim world on the eve of the crusades was politically divided, but it retained a vitality and religious belief that transcended the aspirations of its rulers. It was literally a world apart from anything the crusaders had encountered before.

*Abu Zaid's Adventures* is an illustrated book of comic stories about a rogue who pokes fun at the rich and powerful. Created in Baghdad by al-Wasiti in about 1237, it offers an insight into Arab society of the time. In the picture above, Abu Zaid poses as a religious scholar and preaches to an assembled group. In the picture to the left, Abu Zaid confuses a school teacher while his pupils look on. In the background, a servant pulls on a ceiling fan to cool the schoolroom.

# Peregrini Christi

**For centuries,** *Peregrini Christi* **(Pilgrims of Christ) were allowed access to the holy sites in Jerusalem and its hinterland. In 1009 the Holy Sepulcher was destroyed on the orders of Caliph al-Hakim, marking a hardening of attitude to other beliefs. The pope would use the harassment of pilgrims as the major pretext for his decision to launch the crusading movement.**

Of all the major religions that maintained that Jerusalem was a holy city, Islam was probably the most tolerant of other faiths. Jerusalem remained under Islamic control after its surrender to Caliph Omar in AD 638. The Jews and Christians who remained enjoyed a degree of religious freedom, as both faiths were seen to be *ahl al-kitab* (people of the book), religions based on scriptures akin to the Koran. In return for religious freedom, these non-believers were levied a special religious tax, the *jizyah*. The tax also encouraged those who were less than fervent in their beliefs, and could countenance conversion to Islam.

Pilgrimage was an act of supreme faith performed by those with the time, means, and freedom to complete the journey. While many pilgrims had to remain content with journeys to Rome or some of the lesser centers of the Latin Church, the most passionate made their way to the Holy Land. Pilgrims ranged from freemen and simple monks to feudal nobles.

The Count of Anjou made the journey three times, a party of three French bishops made the journey twice. Others never reached their destination at all or never returned from it. Numerous clergymen made the journey, including bishops, prelates, and abbots, and in

**right:** Contemporary manuscripts were full of anti-Islamic propaganda intended to arouse European anger. This frame from a multiple-image illumination in a French manuscript shows a Christian kneeling before a Muslim emir. Behind the pilgrim stands his executioner, scimitar raised to deliver a decapitating blow.

1064, a party of "several thousand" pilgrims (probably only several hundred) joined four German bishops in a mass exodus that predated the crusades by three decades.

Travel was extremely hazardous in early medieval Europe, but the conversion of the Hungarians and Bulgars to Christianity in the 11th century made the journey a little safer. The Battle of Manzikert (1071) led to the collapse of Byzantine rule in Anatolia, but the Seljuk Turks took several years to occupy and police the entire province. Instead, the land became the temporary preserve of lawless bands, working outside either Turkish or Byzantine authority. As this was the main route by which Christians (both Latin and Orthodox) reached the Holy Land, these travelers were prone to attack. Once in the Holy Land, pilgrims searched for the Tomb of Christ and other sites where their savior performed miracles, preached, and died.

## Safety tax

Arab conquests of the early eighth century reduced the flow of pilgrims, but Muslim tolerance soon encouraged travelers again. Indeed, the new Arab masters of the Holy Land found pilgrims a useful source of revenue. Like the *jizyah*, it became common to levy fees, taxes, or safe-conduct passes on the Christian faithful. In theory, the Patriarch of Jerusalem, the senior Orthodox cleric in the Holy Land, safeguarded Christian welfare in Jerusalem and complained about the financial harassment of pilgrims.

The support of both the holy sites and of pilgrims became a suitable beneficial act for the nobility, and following al-Hakim's destruction of the Holy Sepulcher in 1009, Robert II of Normandy sent the Patriarch of Jerusalem money for his restoration. The increasing devotion of secular noblemen in western Europe made the crusades a possibility. The destruction of the Holy Sepulcher and the Byzantine plea for help gave the pope the justification for declaring a holy war.

The Saracens were claimed to be killing and torturing pilgrims, defacing the religious sites in the Holy Land, and even forcing conversion (and circumcision) on pilgrims. The hysterical outpouring had little basis in fact, but it served its purpose and incensed Christendom, resulting in a frenzy of crusading fervor. Crusaders were seen as armed pilgrims and their adornment of a cloth cross marked them as such; *Peregrini Christi*, but armed with swords instead of pure faith.

**above:** The Dome of the Rock was the first great Umayyad monument to be completed after the conquest of Judea. Built by the caliph Abd al-Malik (r.685–705), who also built the Umayyad mosque at Damascus, it became the holiest Muslim place after the Kaa'ba in Mecca. This aerial view shows the Dome of the Rock thronged by hundreds of thousands of Muslim pilgrims on the last Friday of Ramadan, the holy month of fasting.

# The Byzantine Bulwark

**The Eastern Roman Empire survived Rome's fall in the early fifth century AD. It became the Byzantine Empire, with its capital at Constantinople (Byzantium). After safeguarding its borders against a series of barbarian enemies, this great empire continued to play a part in Mediterranean politics for another millennium, retaining traces of the former grandeur of Rome.**

**below:** The writings of the Byzantine John Skylitzes offer a useful contemporary insight into Byzantium's history through two books, the *Byzantine Chronicles* and *Synopsis Historion*. Written at the end of the 11th century, they tended to glorify Byzantine victories and mitigate losses. This illumination shows the Byzantine army taking Syracuse, Sicily, from the Arabs.

Even before the sack of Rome in AD 410, the Eastern Roman Empire was independent, at least for administrative purposes, having been divided by Emperor Diocletian in AD 286. From 330, Constantinople rather than Rome was seen as the capital of the Roman Empire, and the Byzantines of the Eastern Empire saw themselves as the true inheritors of the Roman imperial mantle.

In its new guise as Byzantium, the Eastern Empire weathered the barbarian onslaught and, under Emperor Justinian (r.527–65), even tried to reclaim some of the lost Roman territories. Justinian's reign was the Byzantine Empire's golden age, and his legal and administrative reforms were hailed as visionary. He was also the last truly Latin emperor. His Greek successors lacked any notion of trying to recapture past Roman glories. They were content trying to defend their existing borders against a host of external enemies and defending their own thrones from court intrigues that made the term "Byzantine" synonymous with the convolutions of politics and treachery.

The seventh century was a time of immense external pressure on the empire. It came under attack from the west, north, and east. Inside its borders, trade and the arts flourished and a distinctive Byzantine culture evolved, based on Hellenistic and Middle Eastern rather than Latin roots. While the remainder of Europe struggled to emerge from the period later regarded as the Dark Ages, Byzantium remained a vibrant political and cultural unit.

In the early seventh century the Muslim religion developed in the deserts of Arabia and the successors of Mohammed proclaimed a *jihad* against those who embraced other religions. This militaristic expansion inevitably led to a clash with the Byzantines, who were defeated at the Battle of Yarmuk (634). The Byzantines lost most of their Middle Eastern possessions. Similar victories over the Persians extended Islamic rule as far as India.

## Mistakenly introverted

Although Byzantine armies stemmed the Islamic advance into Anatolia (now Turkey), by the start of the eighth century Byzantium had effectively abandoned all former eastern

possessions, the most fertile portions of the former Roman Empire. Although Byzantium still gave the appearance of being a powerful Mediterranean empire, a succession of military and political struggles left it weak and vulnerable to attack. A fresh wave of enemies threatened from the north, and these Russ (Vikings who had colonized Ukraine), Bulgars, and Magyars forced the Byzantine emperors to devote most of their energies to protecting their northern and western borders. Although Emperor Basil II (r.976–1025) re-established Byzantine control over the Balkans, the process almost bankrupted the empire and left it militarily depleted; quite unprepared to counter a resurgent Islamic threat in the 11th century.

By 1051, the Abbasid Caliphate had fallen, replaced by the more zealous rule of the Seljuk Turks. Under Seljuk leadership, the eastern Islamic world was relatively united and her armies were better trained, equipped, and led. The Seljuks' star was rising in the Middle East and their Muslim troops posed a serious threat to the safety of the Byzantine Empire. By 1067, Seljuk armies had fought their way to the borders of the Byzantine province of

Anatolia, after occupying the Byzantine Christian buffer state of Armenia. Although the Seljuks and Fatimid caliphate were at war, it would have been prudent for the Byzantines to look toward their own defenses. Instead, the empire remained introverted, concerned more with court intrigues than with the Muslim army massing on its eastern border.

Byzantine Empire
under Hercalius I, 628
accession of Basil I, 867
accession of Theodore I, 1204

# Mediterranean Trade

**Regardless of the collapse of the Roman Empire, the rise of Byzantium, and the Arab conquests, trade remained a constant part of life in the eastern Mediterranean basin.**

**below:** Antioch's position at the northeastern end of the Mediterranean put it close to the western end of the Silk Road. Through many centuries, its wealth afforded the best for its merchants. This mosaic is from the tomb of one Amerimnia.

By the 11th century, the principal ports in the Middle East were Antioch and Alexandria, while both Constantinople and Venice retained strong trading links with these Arab ports, regardless of who owned them. The Silk Road ran through Samarkand to Baghdad and caravans brought the precious goods of the Orient across the desert to Damascus, then on to the eastern Mediterranean ports. Spices were shipped up the Persian Gulf from the Indian sub-continent to Basra, then to Baghdad, while a smaller maritime trade linked the ports of the Indian Ocean with Mecca and the head of the Red Sea.

perfumes, sugar, paper, textiles, and grain. To traders from Venice or even Constantinople, they must have seemed the richest places on Earth. Jewish merchants maintained links between Babylonia and Spain, and both Jewish and Muslim vessels sailed the length of North Africa, maintaining a trading link between the two ends of the Muslim world.

There are relatively few accounts of Arab merchants visiting the small ports of western Europe, although the chronicler William of Malmesbury mentions traders from the Arab port of Ascalon visiting the Frankish ports of Languedoc. Compared to the wealth of the eastern Mediterranean, these ports only had raw materials found in their hinterland; timber, wool, and possibly slaves. Much of Southern Italy was still controlled by the Byzantines at the start of the 11th century, but maritime centers such as Bari and Taranto maintained links with Alexandria, Antioch, and Constantinople.

Antioch and Alexandria became bustling commercial hubs and their docks and markets were filled with slaves and spices, cotton, silks,

## Envy of eastern wealth

When Norman adventurers captured the ports, trade still continued. Traders from Amalfi maintained special links with the ports of the Holy Land, and founded a monastery in Jerusalem and a hospice in Antioch. There was also a steady trade in the transportation of pilgrims, which partly explains the generosity of the Amalfians. Palermo also established trading treaties with the Fatimids in Egypt and the Muslim states of North Africa, particularly Kairouan in Tunisia.

Of all the Italian ports who traded with the Middle East before the crusades, Venice was the busiest. Venetians had long been involved in trade with Byzantium, and when Pope Urban II (p.1088–99) proclaimed his crusade in 1095, the Doge of Venice—which up until then had been the main point of entry for luxury goods from the Orient,

such as silks and spices—decided to support Byzantium by forbidding trade with Arabic ports, at least in goods that could be used to wage war.

The various Italian ports contained sizeable fleets of trading vessels and were therefore called on to furnish the transports needed by participants in the First Crusade such as Hugh, Count of Vermandois. What they lost in trade with the Abbasid caliphate they gained through improved trading links with Byzantium and the Crusader States. The Venetians also helped the Byzantines in their war against Norman adventurers in return for a trading treaty, signed in 1082.

Byzantium had no compunction maintaining trading links with Arab ports, even after Manzikert (1071), and following the start of the First Crusade, Constantinople became the principal link between East and West. Compared to the three principal ports of the eastern Mediterranean, Frankish ports were minuscule. When sailors and pilgrims returned with tales of the fabulous wealth of Egypt, Syria, and the Holy Land, it is little wonder that western Europe's feudal rulers cast covetous eyes on the Middle East. There was little doubt that conquest of the Holy Land would bring untold wealth to the crusaders.

**above:** This early 11th-century manuscript illumination depicts merchants on a boat with their goods.

**below:** Antioch became an important trading center for the Roman Empire. The ruins of the once-fine main street are still visible in the Pisidia area.

# CHAPTER 2

# All the Powers in Christendom:

## The Crusaders' World

**Europe and the Middle East, 1025–90**

- eastern extent of Byzantine Empire, 1025
- Byzantine Empire by 1090, after effects of Battle of Manzikert in 1071
- Bulgar Khanate, 963
- Byzantine territory regained from Bulgars under Basil II, 1025
- Byzantine territory regained from Seljuks after 1090
- Holy Roman Empire
- territory controlled by Normans
- territory controlled by Muslims
- direction of Norman expansion
- direction of Seljuk campaigns
- direction of Fatimid expansion

Western Europe in the 11th century was a violent, unstable region. The century had brought invasion by the Norsemen, Magyars, and Moors, near-constant internal warfare between rival nobles, and a population explosion that threatened to bring starvation and disease in its wake. In many regions, the normal order of society had all but collapsed, and an almost anarchical rule by local warlords or brigands had replaced it. In the east, the Muslims were battering down the defenses of the Byzantine Empire—which the West relied on as a protective barrier—while Spain and much of the Mediterranean lay in Moorish hands.

The Church was probably the single most effective form of protection against impending social collapse, but even it was hovering on the brink of extinction. Local priests were often poorly educated or ineffective in preventing the worst excesses of local secular rulers or warlords. At the top of the religious hierarchy the papacy and senior clerics were fighting a losing battle in their attempt to impose some form of political or social control over the rulers and

noblemen who controlled the continent.

For Pope Urban II (p.1088-99), the plea for help from the Byzantine emperor offered a way out for a society in a state of near collapse. If Urban could unite the warring secular factions of Europe in a Holy Crusade, he would not only offer a distraction to the warlords, but he would also be able to impose papal control over a continent that desperately needed spiritual guidance. It also offered the chance to reunite the two halves of the Christian faith—Roman (or Latin) and Orthodox—under one spiritual roof, with the pope as its head. For Urban, it must have seemed as if the Crusade was a heaven-sent opportunity. He could divert the destructive energy of feudal Europe against the enemies of the Christian faith, combining the lust for power of the European nobility with their desire for redemption and salvation. In the process, the Holy See would unleash a tidal wave of human energy that would change the course of history.

In 1025, the Christian part of Armenia joined the Byzantine Empire to gain protection from its Muslim adversaries—a short-lived respite.

The island of Cyprus kept changing hands. Part of the Roman and then Eastern Roman Empire, Arabs seized it in 649. In 746, the Byzantines captured the island from the Muslims and held it until c.826, when it was again taken by Arabs. Not to be outdone, in 965 the Byzantines snatched Cyprus back again and only lost it through treachery in 1191 when the island was captured by Richard I of England during the Third Crusade.

# The Church in the 11th Century

Following the break-up of the Carolingian Empire in the early ninth century, the relative stability enjoyed by Europeans ended. Instead, central power devolved into the hands of provincial leaders, who organized a reasonably effective resistance against the waves of Scandinavian, Moorish, or Magyar invaders. This break-up of centralized control seriously reduced the ability of the pope to control the Church, and local ecclesiastical authorities increased their power at the expense of Rome. The pope was forced to reach an agreement with the Frankish nobility, giving them a say in the appointment of senior clerics within their domains, in return for their protection of Church lands and property.

The monastic movement, which blossomed during the century, was the exception to this parochial Church structure. The Abbey of Cluny was founded in AD 910 and its abbot was directly subordinate to the pope, not to any regional bishop or secular lord. During the late tenth century Cluniac monasteries spread across France and provided impetus for more widespread Church reform during the mid-11th century. These monastic settlements also created a secure basis from which the pope could try to re-establish control over secular Europe.

During the first half of the 11th century the Church was held in widespread disrepute, since its officials were prone to partisan support of their secular sponsors, and the entire organization was considered to be rife with corruption. Apart from the monastic schools, little was being done to improve the education of the priests who provided the main source of contact between Church and people. This began to change under the guidance of Pope Leo IX (p.1049–54), who proved to be a gifted administrator and dedicated Church reformer.

He formed a body of cardinals to assist him in governing the Church and held a series of ecclesiastical Councils, aimed at introducing reforms across Europe and extending papal influence. Clerical marriage was outlawed and any clerics unwilling to fall into line with Leo's wishes were unceremoniously removed from office, regardless of the secular support they enjoyed. While these steps increased the Church's central authority, it also brought it into direct conflict with Christendom's secular rulers.

## Battle of wills

A power struggle between Leo's successors and the Holy Roman emperor (the senior ruler in Germany) led to the emperor's excommunication by Pope Gregory VII (p.1073–85). While the secular rulers of France and England tended to acquiesce to the re-establishment of papal authority over the Church in their dominions, the German emperor challenged any papal attempt to undermine his authority. Church lands in Germany were extensive and rich, and the struggle for their control dominated the relations between pontiff and emperor.

Europe was plunged into a crisis over the right of feudal lords to appoint senior clerics within their own lands that continued for decades. This was not purely a religious matter. These bishops and abbots controlled extensive lands throughout Europe, and land and power were closely related in the late 11th century. This "Investiture Crisis" led to the creation of an alternative pope, the invasion of papal territory, and an undermining of the papal authority that had been won by Leo IX. When Pope Urban II donned the pontiff's crown, he inherited a Church that had increased its authority greatly during the previous decades, but which was nevertheless still locked in a struggle for survival.

Europe was undergoing something of a spiritual revival during the last decades of the century, encouraged by the example set by the monastic communities scattered throughout Europe. Urban saw clearly that if he were to harness this resurgent Christian spirit, it might strengthen his hand against the emperor. By invoking popular support and winning the Investiture Crisis, Urban would regain complete control over Christendom's spiritual affairs. It would also substantially increase the Church's revenues. Much was at stake, and Urban's call for a Crusade was largely influenced by this struggle between Church and State.

**left:** For the vast majority of common folk, the medieval period was not one of great ease or comfort. Unrest was easily provoked by lampoons at the expense of clerics seen to be living in luxury. This illumination for the month of February from the *Breviaire d'Amour* (late 13th century) clearly pokes fun at the monk who toasts his toes over a good blaze, while, undoubtedly, peasants freeze in the nearby fields.

# The Frankish State

**At the start of the 11th century, the Frankish Empire established by Charlemagne (r.768–814) had devolved into two parts. Since its inception in 843, the Frankish Kingdom of France—the western portion—had evolved into a feudal power, a hierarchical system that brought a degree of stability to western Europe. This Frankish realm was the model for the organization of the Crusader States in the Holy Land.**

Unlike the Eastern Frankish kingdom, the Western Frankish state had once been part of the Roman Empire, and apart from Brittany, all provinces within the realm shared a similar cultural background. Faced with a breakdown of order in the Carolingian kingdom due to invasion by Moors and Norsemen, the kings organized their own defenses in what slowly evolved into the feudal system. This was duly exported to England, Germany, Italy, and eventually, the Holy Land. In theory, the king dominated the feudal structure, and each provincial warlord or duke below him was his feudal subject.

Following the death of Louis V (r.986–87), last of the western Carolingian kings, both the Church and the leading nobles of France gathered to choose a successor. They elected Hugh Capet (r.987–96), whose extensive feudal holdings included Paris. One of his leading supporters was the Archbishop of Reims, the primate of the country. Although none of the nobles wanted one of their peers to establish a ruling dynasty, the Capetians retained control of France until the 14th century. Part of this success was the ability of the Capetian monarchs to ensure the succession of their offspring while they were still in power, which ensured an unbroken hold on power.

The Capetians had three roles. They controlled their own duchy, acted as feudal overlords of their more extensive domains, and acted as the feudal superiors of other leading French nobles. Although the French crown was nominally in control, the Capetians were unable to curb the independence of some leading nobles, men like the Counts of Toulouse or Normandy. In this, the feudal structure adopted in the Holy Land was similar, since the king of Jerusalem had little or no authority over the nobles who ruled in Tripoli and Antioch.

## The Church and feudalism

In 1066, William, duke of Normandy, invaded England and conquered the Anglo-Saxon kingdom. In theory, William I the Conqueror (r.1066–87) and his successors owed feudal allegiance to the French king, Philip I (r.1060–1108), a situation that would become a growing source of conflict in coming decades. Pope Alexander II (p.1061–73) and William maintained a close bond, which ensured papal recognition of his seizure of the English throne. In return, the Church received generous grants of English and Norman land.

During Philip I's reign, Capetian France was divided into approximately 15 major feudal domains. The royal demesne (feudal lands of the king) in the Île de France was just one of these. Outside Paris, the king's authority

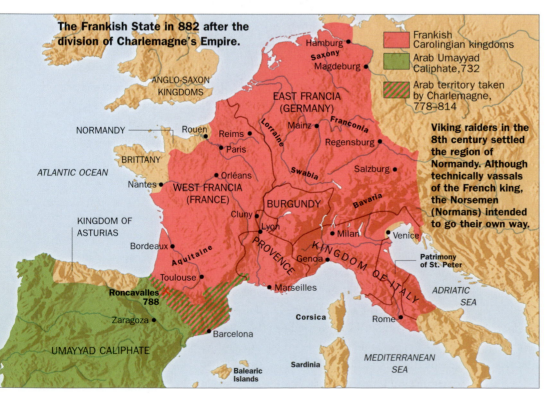

**The Frankish State in 882 after the division of Charlemagne's Empire.**

- Frankish Carolingian kingdoms
- Arab Umayyad Caliphate, 732
- Arab territory taken by Charlemagne, 778–814

**Viking raiders in the 8th century settled the region of Normandy. Although technically vassals of the French king, the Norsemen (Normans) intended to go their own way.**

ANGLO-SAXON KINGDOMS
NORMANDY — Rouen
Reims
Paris
BRITTANY
ATLANTIC OCEAN
Nantes
Orléans
WEST FRANCIA (FRANCE)
KINGDOM OF ASTURIAS
Bordeaux
Aquitaine
Toulouse
Roncavalles 788
Zaragoza
Barcelona
UMAYYAD CALIPHATE
Balearic Islands
Sardinia
Hamburg
Saxony
Magdeburg
EAST FRANCIA (GERMANY)
Mainz
Franconia
Lorraine
Regensburg
Swabia
Salzburg
BURGUNDY
Cluny
Lyon
Bavaria
Milan
Venice
Genoa
KINGDOM OF ITALY
Provence
Marseilles
Corsica
Rome
Patrimony of St. Peter
ADRIATIC SEA
MEDITERRANEAN SEA

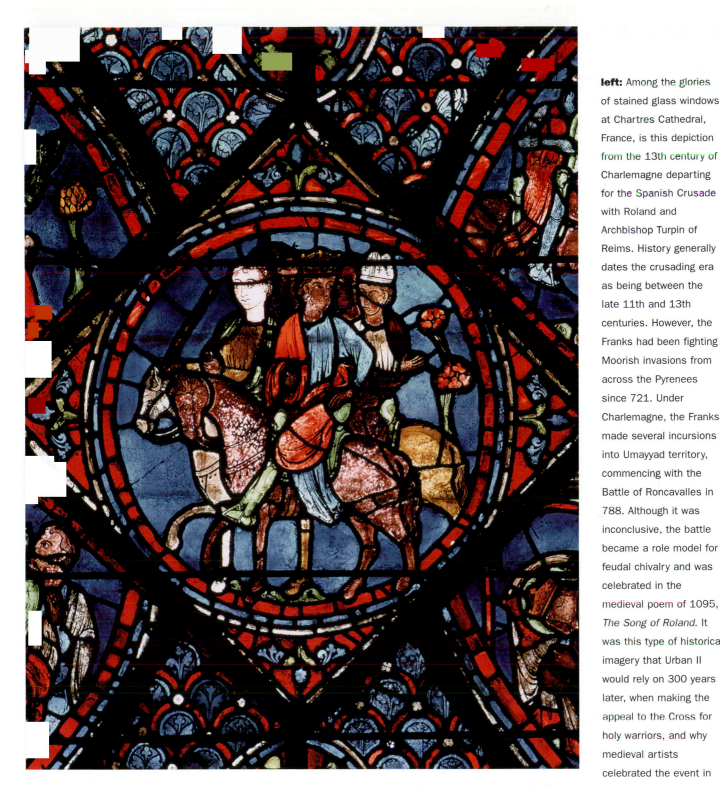

**left:** Among the glories of stained glass windows at Chartres Cathedral, France, is this depiction from the 13th century of Charlemagne departing for the Spanish Crusade with Roland and Archbishop Turpin of Reims. History generally dates the crusading era as being between the late 11th and 13th centuries. However, the Franks had been fighting Moorish invasions from across the Pyrenees since 721. Under Charlemagne, the Franks made several incursions into Umayyad territory, commencing with the Battle of Roncavalles in 788. Although it was inconclusive, the battle became a role model for feudal chivalry and was celebrated in the medieval poem of 1095, *The Song of Roland*. It was this type of historical imagery that Urban II would rely on 300 years later, when making the appeal to the Cross for holy warriors, and why medieval artists celebrated the event in song, poetry, and glass.

was minimal. Before his accession, the royal demesne had been shrinking, but Philip reversed the process, and even added to his own royal lands. His successors would continue this expansion.

The Church was the French king's greatest ally in that, together with the often theoretical bonds of feudal obligation, Church and State exerted some degree of control over the French lords. During the spiritual revival of the mid-11th century, provincial clerical rulers increased their influence, and these bishops and prelates appointed by the pope ensured that their own local secular rulers were subject to supervision.

Papal justice could be harsh, and even Philip was excommunicated for bigamy when he overstepped the bounds of what the pope considered acceptable behavior (*see also page 44*).

Between the Church and the feudal system, 11th century France (and England after 1066) was reasonably well governed, which ensured a relatively stable and prosperous realm. It was natural, therefore, that the Crusader States of Outremer should look to France as a model for their organization. However, while royal authority steadily increased in France, Outremer remained a cluster of states that frequently lacked overall direction or authority.

# The Feudal System

**Developed in response to the threat of invasion by Norsemen, Moors, and Magyars, the feudal system represented a hierarchical social and military structure based on land and rank, while offering protection and stability to society. This tried and tested structure was transplanted into the Middle East.**

Feudalism is a term created by modern historians. In the 11th century, the feudal system was simply the natural order of things. The holding of a portion of land in return for certain obligations was understood in Roman law as the *benefice* system of tenure. During the

warlords in return for martial service, and the structure of the feudal system evolved, so that by the 11th century most of western Europe consisted of various forms of feudal states.

In its most basic form, a farmer or villager who lacked the means or ability to defend his lands sought the protection of a knight. By surrendering his freeholding status the peasant became a serf, almost a slave, the lowest level in the feudal pyramid. His lord took the serf's agricultural produce as payment for protection and returned a small percentage for the peasant and his family to survive on.

**above:** Hard work, if you can get it—the lord giving orders to his peasants from a 13th-century manuscript shows the operation of the feudal system at the lowest level of the pyramid.

subsequent period of barbarian invasions, this developed to incorporate the Germanic tribal tradition whereby vassals swore an oath of fealty to their tribal superiors. Under the Carolingian Franks, this tradition was refined and became closely linked to military service.

The Carolingian army, which relied on armored heavy cavalry, granted these mounted warriors land in return for their assistance in time of war. Effectively this was a military development of the *benefice* system. Following the division of the Carolingian Empire and the instability that ensued, regional warlords offered military protection in return for pay or provisions. Kings gave grants of land to

## Rights and responsibilities

In his turn the smaller knight, unable to protect against large-scale incursions, surrendered his lands to a more powerful nobleman. These were returned to him in exchange for military service and a share of the knight's quota of produce. This system of protection was repeated: the more powerful noble (usually a baron) owed his allegiance to a provincial lord (such as a count), and in his turn he was the vassal of a regional ruler, such as a duke.

In theory this top level of feudal nobleman owed allegiance to the monarch, but during the 11th century royal authority was limited. Many

*above:* In this illumination from a 14th-century manuscript depicting different aspects of feudal life, a knight on bended knee takes orders from his emperor.

powerful western European nobles who participated in the Crusade, such as Raymond of Toulouse and Bohemond of Taranto, felt they owed allegiance to nobody. Senior members of the feudal nobility had the right to levy their own taxes, make their own laws, raise their own armies, and even mint their own money. Some of these were more powerful than the king to whom they owed feudal loyalty, particularly in the case of the Dukes of Normandy, who also became Kings of England while still technically remaining vassals of the French Crown.

If the feudal system was largely based on land and agriculture, urban centers required a different system of government. Towns relied on a surplus of food produced in the surrounding countryside, and presented a market for the produce levied through feudal obligation. By the late 11th century, feudal lords often encouraged the development of towns and offered them protection in return for mercantile revenue. Many other urban centers were administered by the Church, and formed the venue for episcopal centers. The Church, therefore, acted as a form of feudal landowner, administering the town itself, as well as the surrounding rural area.

In the Kingdom of Jerusalem feudal fiefdoms often contained too few peasants to support a traditional feudal system, and urban centers were incorporated into feudal domains, where feudal overlords taxed urban production. Also, in Outremer, unless the Church or a military order ruled them, each vassal was seen as a vassal of the king, regardless of his or her place in the feudal hierarchy. The feudal system represented the best possible method of government, given the rudimentary structure of medieval national administration, both in Europe and in the Middle East.

# Germany and Italy in the 11th Century

**During the two centuries before the start of the Crusade, the Holy Roman Empire emerged as a powerful political entity. The actions of its rulers dominated events in Italy and other surrounding realms, while a succession of emperors and popes became embroiled in a struggle for political supremacy. Italy became a battleground between Church and State, while presenting opportunities for feudal adventurers.**

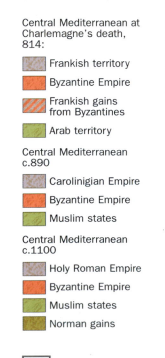

After the division of the Frankish Carolingian Empire, the eastern part consisted of several autonomous states with no effective centralized authority. In order to defend themselves against the Magyar invasions of the tenth century, these states banded together under a high king. Although viewed as merely "first amongst equals" by the dukes who elected them, a succession of high kings gradually expanded their power base through a combination of force and patronage.

Some but not all of these elected kings became anointed Emperor of the Holy Roman Empire, an honor first presented to Charlemagne by Pope Leo III (p.795–816). The imperial title was a former Carolingian appellation that was resurrected by the Germans during the mid-tenth century, when it was awarded to Otto I the Great (r.936–73). However, papal meddling in German affairs led to a clash and Otto created an alternative pope—an antipope—to do his bidding. This friction continued well into the 12th century.

Conrad II (r.1024–39) confirmed Germanic rule in northern Italy by forcing the nobility of Lombardy to guarantee the continued overlordship of the emperor. This was seen as a direct threat to papal lands in central Italy, particularly as pope and emperor were locked into a conflict over the investiture of bishops within Germany. Conrad regarded this privilege as his prerogative, while his ecclesiastical opponent, Pope Leo IX (p.1049–54), a leading Church reformer, was a dedicated opponent of secular intrusion in Church investitures.

A series of synods was held to reform the administration of the Church and safeguard the reforming papal decrees. In 1059, a Church council adopted new rules governing papal elections, a counter to imperial attempts to influence the decision of the newly founded College of Cardinals. Similarly, secularly appointed bishops were suspended if the papacy disagreed with their selection.

**Central Mediterranean at Charlemagne's death, 814:**

- ◻ Frankish territory
- 🟧 Byzantine Empire
- ▨ Frankish gains from Byzantines
- 🟩 Arab territory

**Central Mediterranean c.890**

- ◻ Carolinigian Empire
- 🟧 Byzantine Empire
- 🟩 Muslim states

**Central Mediterranean c.1100**

- ◻ Holy Roman Empire
- 🟧 Byzantine Empire
- 🟩 Muslim states
- 🟢 Norman gains

The carving up of Italy, 814

Milan · Venice · Ravenna · Pisa · Rome · Naples · Otranto (Taranto) · Corsica · Sardinia · Sicily · Tunis · Syracuse · Malta · KINGDOM OF THE LOMBARDS · Croats · Serbs · UMAYYAD CALIPHATE

The carving up of Italy, 890

Milan · Venice · Ravenna · Pisa · Patrimony of St. Peter · Rome · Naples · Otranto (Taranto) · Corsica 846 · Sardinia 846 · DUCHY OF BENEVENTO · Sicily 827 · Tunis · Syracuse · Malta · KINGDOM OF ITALY · CROATIA · Serbs · AGHLABID EMIRATE

## Italy is carved up

While it became increasingly rare for the kings of France or England to appoint senior clergymen, German emperors forced the issue. Henry IV (r.1054–1106) saw his selection of German bishops as crucial if he was to limit the influence of his leading nobles. In 1075, Pope Gregory VII (p.1073–85) excommunicated the emperor in response to

his meddling. Henry promptly had his bishops declare Gregory a usurper. The crisis lasted a year, until the emperor met the pope as a penitent at Canossa in 1077 and begged forgiveness. With his title restored, Henry returned to the offensive, appointing an antipope and invading Rome.

German political aspirations in Italy resulted in imperial influence extending as far south as Rome. During this same period, a group of Norman adventurers were busy campaigning in Southern Italy, driving the Byzantines from the region and carving out their own series of feudal fiefdoms. In 1060 the Normans invaded Moorish Sicily, a conquest that was completed in 1091. Among the Norman warlords was Prince Bohemond of Taranto, one of the principal participants in the First Crusade.

The Italian peninsula had been used as a battleground by both land-hungry Norman adventurers and a German emperor who wished to extend his influence over the rich Lombard provinces of Northern Italy, its growing urban centers making it one of the richest regions in the continent. Pope Urban's appeal at Clermont was largely motivated by a desire to end this political instability that plagued 11th-century Italy and to ensure his position of authority in the conflict with the Holy Roman Emperor. European politics were therefore as much an influence over the decision to call a Crusade as were the external problems of Byzantines and Muslims.

**The carving up of Italy, 1100**

- Milan
- Venice
- Ravenna
- Pisa
- KINGDOM OF ITALY
- Corsica
- Rome
- Papal States
- Naples
- 1060
- Taranto
- Sardinia
- KINGDOM OF SICILY
- Sicily 1091
- Tunis
- Syracuse
- ALMOHAD CALIPHATE
- Malta

**facing:** Detail from the statue of Otto I the Great at Magdeburg Cathedral, Germany.

**above left:**

A Byzantine relief of St. George on horseback. The saint is revered as the patron saint of England, yet his story is associated with Byzantine Capadocia in Anatolia. It is unlikely that Anglo-Saxon England would have known about him, but some legends say he showed himself to King Richard the Lionheart during the Third Crusade, and St. George's adoption by the English may stem from that visitation.

**above right:**

A manuscript illumination from the 13th century depicting a man on a falcon hunt, from Alphonse Le Sage's *Las Cantigas*.

# The Reconquista

**In the year before Pope Urban II's call to Christendom to rescue the Holy Land, a Spanish knight nicknamed "The Chieftain" by his enemies captured the Spanish city of Valencia from the Muslims. It was the start of the Christian reconquest of Spain, a campaign that would take centuries to complete.**

Few buildings echo the transition from Muslim to Christian culture during the *reconquista* of Spain as well as Cordoba's magnificent *Mezquita*. The huge rectangular mosque, started in 785 on the site of an earlier Visigothic church, was returned to Christianity after its capture from the Moors in 1236. The huge exterior and internal Muslim spaces remain largely unchanged, but in the center there now sprouts the tall nave of Cordoba Cathedral.

In 711, a Muslim army crossed from Africa and landed on the southern coast of Spain at Jebel al-Tariq (Gibraltar). The invasion was mounted by people of mixed Arab and Berber descent from Mauritania, the *Maurus*, or Moors, under Umayyad leadership. The Visigoths who occupied the Iberian peninsula were defeated, and within a decade the Moors occupied most of Spain. Asturias, a Basque region on the northern coast remained as the sole surviving Christian enclave. The Moors continued over the Pyrenees to invade the Frankish kingdom beyond, but they retired after their defeat at the Battle of Tours (732).

Umayyad rule brought unity and peace to Spain, and trade thrived between Toledo, Seville, and the markets of Africa and the Middle East. During the next century, while the Abbasid dynasty seized power in the rest of the Muslim world, the Umayyads retained control of Spain, the land of Al-Andalus (Andalusia). A century later they survived the expansion of the Fatimid caliphate and its seizure of the Middle East. By this time, Spain had become a separate Muslim state, although it retained close trading links with the rest of the Mediterranean world.

By the start of the 11th century the Kingdom of Galicia had evolved into the Kingdom of León, named after its new capital, while the Basques formed their own Kingdom of Navarre. During this period there was little open animosity between the Christian and Muslim states in Spain, and each avoided full-scale attacks against the other. Inside the Umayyad caliphate, Christians (known locally as *mozarabs*) were given freedom of worship, as was the sizeable Jewish community. Moorish Spain was noted for its tolerance, prosperity, artistry, and learning. All that was swept away by the religious revival in 11th-century Europe.

In 1035, the southern portion of the Basque homeland of Navarre broke away to create the

Kingdom of Aragon, while further east the Catalan region around Barcelona formed its own autonomous region. Together this strip of small independent Christian states formed a continuous front that would be used to launch a Christian *reconquista* (reconquest) of the whole peninsula. The collapse of the Umayyad Caliphate of Cordoba in 1034 acted as a catalyst for Christian expansion. The caliphate was divided into 20 small states, each ruled by petty Moorish nobles who were unwilling to set aside their differences in order to repulse Christian invaders.

## Advent of the crusading era

The *reconquista* began in earnest around 1070, the Spanish Christian kings gradually pushed their borders further south. The Spanish were assisted by French crusading expeditions that crossed the Pyrenees almost every year to help fellow Christians. Among these crusaders was Raymond of Toulouse, who would play a leading part in the First Crusade.

Under King Alfonso VI of León and Castille

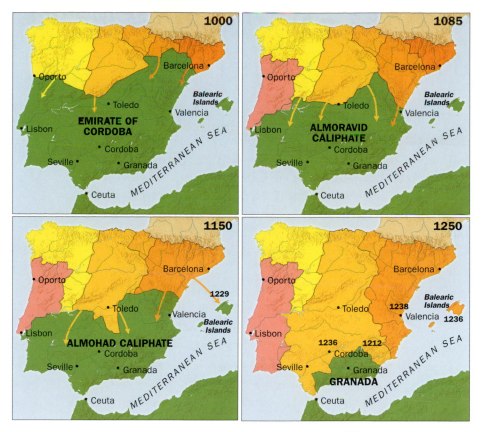

(r.1065–1109) and King Sancho of Aragon and Navarre (r.1063–94), the various Christian forces combined into two powerful, unified Spanish armies. While the Castillians pushed south through central Spain, the Aragonese drove south down the Mediterranean coast.

In 1085 the Moorish capital of Toledo was taken, prompting the Moors to appeal for help from the Berber Almoravid dynasty of North Africa. Christian momentum slowed when the Africans defeated the Castillians, and the Moors, now under Almoravid dominion, recaptured Andalusia. Then, a Christian hero arose, an Aragonese nobleman named Rodrigo Diaz de Vivar.

He became better known as *El Cid,* a nickname that means "The Chieftain," bestowed on him by his Arab enemies. In 1094 *El Cid* captured Valencia, and although he died four years later defending the city against the Almoravids, his efforts blunted the Moorish counterattack. The frontiers stabilized and the stalemate continued for nearly a century.

Spain was the first region of Europe occupied by the Muslims, and the *reconquista* continued for almost two centuries after the Crusades in the Holy Land came to an end. The Iberian peninsula, rather than the Holy Land, was the real and lasting battleground between Christian and Muslim during the medieval period, and the stand-off would not be settled until the last Muslim stronghold was overrun in 1492.

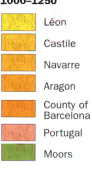

**The *reconquista*, 1000–1250**

- 🟨 Léon
- 🟨 Castile
- 🟧 Navarre
- 🟧 Aragon
- 🟧 County of Barcelona
- 🟥 Portugal
- 🟩 Moors

# Two Churches

**While the Byzantine Empire followed its Orthodox Christian beliefs, the people of western Europe adopted the Roman (Latin) form of Christianity. For a brief moment at the end of the 11th century, it seemed that the two Churches might combine in the face of the Islamic threat. To the papacy, the opportunity to unite Christendom must have seemed irresistible.**

Following the collapse of the Western Roman Empire in the early fifth century AD, Constantinople became the prime seat of the Christian Church. For nearly a century, this portion of the empire, which became Byzantium, served as a bulwark against a wave of pagan invaders. By the end of the century, both the Frankish Kingdom and the western Christian Church emerged from the chaos of the barbarian invasions as tangible entities in their own right. The ecumenical Patriarchy based in Constantinople now had a rival Christian institution in Rome.

In the Byzantine Empire, the emperor was head of both Church and State. By contrast, in the Roman Church the pope saw himself as the successor to St. Peter, and therefore raised above the secular world of emperors and princes. During the seventh century, the Roman Church established its own system of regional ecclesiastical centers in the Frankish Kingdom. Under Charlemagne the Latin version of the Christian faith became the accepted religion across most of what would become Italy, Spain, France, and Germany.

Early attempts to reunite the two Churches were unsuccessful, but the Byzantine emperors of the seventh and early eighth centuries were too busy defending their provinces from a wave of Arab invaders to concern themselves unduly with theological debate. During the eighth century, the Isaurian dynasty of emperors stabilized the situation. Leo III (r.717–41) stemmed the Muslim invasion, which allowed him and his successors to return to the religious divide that had split Christendom in two.

Over the centuries, the Byzantine Church had adopted a version of Monophysitism, a view at odds with the Latin stance. (Monophysites asserted the existence of a single nature in Christ; their opponents the co-existence of a divine *and* a human nature.) Byzantines eventually moved away from Monophysitism, but at this time the divergent theological views led to the Iconoclastic Controversy that first emerged c.730, when Leo III tried to limit the spread of what he saw as the excessive veneration of holy images by sections of the Byzantine Church. The Greek, or Orthodox, religion became split between *iconodules* and *iconoclasts* (image breakers) with the emperor favoring the latter group.

The controversy aroused considerable popular feeling, and the Roman Church became embroiled in the debate when it

The Roman Church began to eschew iconic representations after 1000, but for the Orthodox Church, icons were a means of emphasizing the pre-eminence of the emperor as head of both State and Church. John II Comnenus (r.1118–43), second of the Comnenian dynasty, appears here in this contemporary mosaic flanking the Virgin Mary and Christ child with his wife, the Empress Irene.

supported the iconodules. When, in 730, a council of the Orthodox Church formally condemned the veneration of icons, Rome established a contrary position.

## Christianity embattled

A similar argument over the nature of the Holy Spirit kept the Churches apart, but the final and seemingly unbreachable schism took place in 1054, when pope and patriarch excommunicated each other during an argument over the nature of the Eucharist.

The schism of 1054 proved to be a permanent division between Roman and Orthodox Christianity, but a succession of popes, patriarchs, and emperors held onto the hope that Christendom could still be united. By the 11th century iconoclasm was abandoned, leading to a thawing of hostility.

The establishment of diplomatic links between the Churches in 1094 and the Byzantine plea for help offered an opportunity for rapprochement. Pope Urban II thought he had been granted the opportunity to unify Christendom. In fact, all that the Byzantine emperor Alexius I Comnenus (r.1081–1118) wanted was military aid. Any talk of religious unification was firmly avoided. When the popes and crusaders recognized that the Byzantines had no intention of surrendering control of their Church, relations between the two groups plummeted. In either camp, the other branch of Christianity was the dissident group. By the time the First Crusade was over, Romans and Orthodox Christians viewed each other as the enemy of the faith, and hated each other almost as much as the Muslims.

# Disaster at Manzikert

**Enemies surrounded the Byzantine Empire during the 11th century. Bulgars massing along the Danube were a serious problem, but the realm's greatest threat came from the east, where the Seljuk Turks were the rising power in the Middle East. In 1071, a decisive victory altered the balance of power in Muslim favor.**

In the 11th century, the Bulgars, Russ, and Magyars on the northern borders of the Byzantine Empire had coalesced into the Bulgar Khanate (kingdom), which covered much of the Balkans. Emperor Basil II (r.976–1025) of the Macedonian dynasty campaigned so successfully against the Bulgars that he drove them back from the frontiers and earned himself the nickname Bulgar Slayer. It was the highpoint of Byzantine military prowess.

The empire remained relatively stable until the death of Constantine IX (r.1042–55), when problems of succession led to a period of instability, military coups, and untimely death.

In four years three rulers came and went until the Byzantine court nominated Constantine X Ducas (r.1059–66). He was an intellectual who spurned the military in favor of courtly delights. At a time when Seljuk Turks were establishing their control over Persia and neighboring Syria, the Byzantine court did nothing to prepare for a clash that wiser heads saw as being inevitable.

For decades, Armenia—a Christian province in the mountainous region to the east of Byzantine Anatolia—had served as a buffer zone between Byzantines and Muslims. Alp Arslan became the Seljuk sultan in 1063, and in the following year launched an invasion of Armenia, capturing its capital, Ani. By 1067 he had conquered the whole country and the Turkish army stood on the borders of the Byzantine Empire.

Following the death of Constantine, his widow married a handsome young officer, Romanus Diogenes, who became Romanus IV.

**right:** A Seljuk bas-relief of two Turkish warriors. Manzikert was a victory over the Byzantine rulers of Anatolia, but it also completed the establishment of Turkish control over most of the Islamic Middle East, with the exception of Fatimid Egypt (which had generally good relations with Byzantium and Europe). In Turkish Syria, militarism was everywhere on the eve of the First Crusade, as the writer Ibn Abu Tayyi wrote: "There was no person in Aleppo who did not have military attire in his house, and when war came he would go out at once, fully armed."

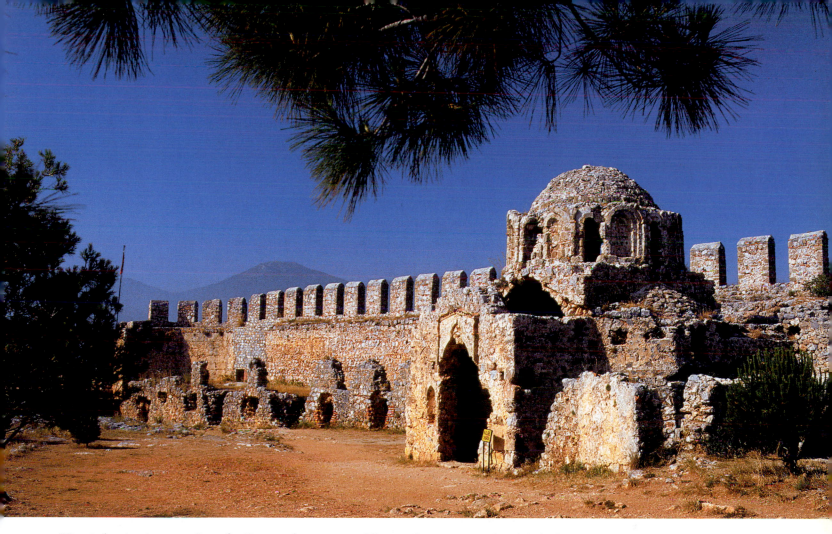

He tried to institute a policy of military reform and worked on strengthening the eastern borders of Anatolia, but it was too little, too late. Recognizing the logistical problems, he set about raising additional troops and re-equipping existing ones. By May 1071 he had 60,000 men on the Armenian border and was ready to take the war to the enemy. His polyglot army included native Byzantines, mercenaries (including some Frankish knights), and auxiliaries from the Balkans and the steppes. Romanus needed one decisive battle to buy the time for his reforms to be carried out and for the Byzantines to organize proper defenses.

## End of an emperor

Because the Seljuks were locked in conflict with Egyptian Fatimids, it was hoped that Seljuk forces would be divided. Romanus crossed the border in two columns and captured the Armenian frontier fortress of Manzikert. For some reason, the column commanded by General Tarchaniotes took no part in the coming battle and it is possible that for political or military reasons Tarchaniotes decided to stay on the sidelines. The emperor was left with about 30,000 men at Manzikert to face a smaller force of Turks, commanded by Alp Arslan himself.

The two forces met on the plain before Manzikert. At first, the battle seemed to go in the Byzantines' favor. The Turks retreated, drawing the emperor's troops forward. Fearing a trap, Romanus gave the order to turn back, but it was too late. Seljuk cavalry attacked and broke through the Byzantine ranks. Bewildered, some Byzantines escaped while others, including the emperor, found themselves surrounded. While his mercenaries fled, the remaining troops were cut down and the emperor captured. Released by the sultan to return and raise funds for a ransom as part of a negotiated peace treaty, Romanus suffered treachery at home. He was replaced in another coup and then murdered by his own soldiers.

Considering the Byzantines to have broken the treaty, the Seljuks invaded and occupied Anatolia. In the words of the historian Sir Steven Runciman, the Byzantines "forfeited on the battlefield their title as protectors of Christendom." Manzikert was clearly one of the most decisive battles in history, and it would end with Muslim settlers occupying half of the undefended Byzantine Empire. It was a Muslim triumph and set a series of events in motion that would bring two centuries of religious conflict to the Middle East.

**above:** Once the Roman city of Coracesium, Alanya on the coast of the Mediterranean above Cyprus became an important Seljuk stronghold ringed with powerful fortifications on its rocky perimeter.

# The Emperor's Plea

**The Manzikert disaster cost the Byzantines half of their empire. The once-great realm plunged into a period of political chaos and civil war. The weakened emperor who emerged from this period of instability had little option but to appeal to Rome for help. It was a decision that ultimately cost the Byzantines dearly.**

August 19, 1071 was a black day for the Byzantine Empire. Not only had its only effective army been decimated, it had also lost its emperor, Romanus IV. Without an army to defend it, the rich province of Anatolia (Asia Minor) fell into Seljuk Turkish hands. In

Arslan was no longer bound to honor the peace treaty agreed with Romanus. However, full-scale occupation of Anatolia was slow at first, due to preoccupation with the war against the Fatimid caliphate. However, a series of nomadic Turkish settlers moved westward into the province from 1073. Seljuk leader Suleiman ibn Kutulmish began to formally annex parts of Anatolia and the Byzantines seemed powerless to stop him. Others followed him and, by 1080, Alp Arslan's son Malik-Shah controlled much of the province. As an acknowledgement that it once formed part of the Roman Empire,

Constantinople, Michael VII Ducas (r.1071–8) seized power in a coup and captured and killed the ransomed Romanus.

Deprived of payment, Seljuk Sultan Alp

Anatolia was renamed the Sultanate of Rum.

The Byzantines were left holding a narrow coastal fringe on the eastern shore of the Sea of Bosphorus. By 1081, a decade after Manzikert, the Byzantines had lost half their empire, half their source of grain, and half their available manpower. It was a blow from which they would never fully recover.

Michael VII's reign proved to be disastrous. He was unable to prevent the loss of Anatolia and Byzantine holdings in the south Italy, or to prevent Norman adventurers from invading Albania and Greece. The Balkans were in a state of revolt, inflation was rising, and rebellion within the court was a constant threat. His reign ended in rebellion, mass rioting, and abdication. His rivals fought for the imperial mantle, but in 1081 an aristocratic young general named Alexius Comnenus seized power and ended a decade of disorder and decline.

## Fateful appeal

Alexius I Comnenus (r.1081–1118) made his first move against the Normans, whose numbers included the future crusader Bohemond of Taranto. Although Alexius was defeated at the Battle of Durazzo (1081), his campaign was ultimately successful. He retained a healthy respect for the martial abilities of Frankish knights, however. Over the next decade, he quelled any attempts at revolt, settled disturbances in the Balkans, and ejected

Norman adventurers from his Adriatic possessions. His limited military resources may have been sufficient in the west, but were unequal to the task of reclaiming Anatolia.

In late 1094, Alexius received an embassy from Pope Urban II, who was trying to improve relations between the two branches of the Christian Church. Alexius had recently reopened the Latin churches in Constantinople as a conciliatory gesture, and after years of hostility both Churches were willing to talk. The papal legate invited Alexius to send representatives to address the Council of the Roman Church, due to be held at Piacenza in the following March. Alexius accepted and saw the move as an opportunity to seek help in his war against the Muslim Turks.

During the winter of 1094–5, Alexius, together with his ministers and clerics, drafted an appeal for help. It spoke of the suffering of Christians in the east, the threat to Christendom, and the opportunities offered by conquest. It also hinted at a possible union of the two Churches. After hearing the plea at Piacenza, Pope Urban and his cardinals had much to think about. Little did Alexius know that he had just opened Pandora's Box.

**facing:** Byzantine altarpiece with Virgin and Child, flanked by two saints. Despite the differences between the two arms of the Christian Church, the emperor was able to call on the pope for help by appealing to what they had in common.

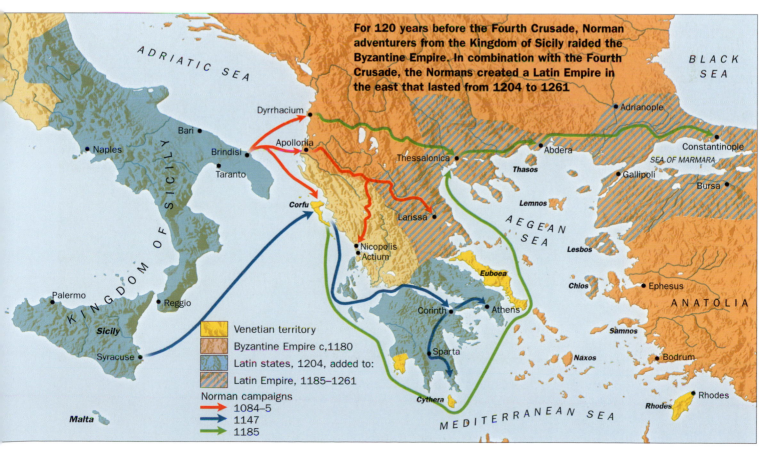

For 120 years before the Fourth Crusade, Norman adventurers from the Kingdom of Sicily raided the Byzantine Empire. In combination with the Fourth Crusade, the Normans created a Latin Empire in the east that lasted from 1204 to 1261

ADRIATIC SEA

BLACK SEA

Dyrrhacium

Adrianople

Bari

Naples

Brindisi
Apollonia

Constantinople

Taranto

Thessalonica

Abdera

SEA OF MARMARA

Thasos

Gallipoli

Corfu

Bursa

Larissa

Lemnos

AEGEAN SEA

Nicopolis
Actium

Lesbos

Euboea

Chios

Ephesus

Palermo

Corinth

Athens

ANATOLIA

Reggio

Sicily

Samnos

Syracuse

Sparta

Naxos

Bodrum

Venetian territory
Byzantine Empire c.1180
Latin states, 1204, added to:
Latin Empire, 1185–1261
Norman campaigns
1084–5
1147
1185

Cythera

Rhodes

Rhodes

Malta

MEDITERRANEAN SEA

KINGDOM OF SICILY

# The Pope's Dilemma

**The Byzantine plea for help came at an opportune moment for a papacy desperately looking for a way to strengthen Rome's influence over Christendom and the troublesome kings of Europe. Pope Urban II had to decide how to respond.**

**below:** This 11th-century illumination depicts the various aspects of rural work from a manuscript titled *Cynegetica*. After decades of war between the many barons and princes of Europe, it was the peasantry who had suffered the most. The papal call to arms for a holy war would relieve the pressure on the feudal serfs as their lords turned their attention to weightier matters abroad.

Before his ascension to the throne of St. Peter, Urban II was known as Odo of Langery, a monk who rose to prominence as prior of the Abbey of Cluny. This monastery, founded in 910, was the centerpiece of the monastic movement. Secondary monasteries of the Clunaic order were established across France, England, and parts of Germany, but Cluny remained the center of monastic and Church reform. During the mid-11th century the movement joined forces with the pope to push through a series of reforms that re-established the control of the Church, but which also led directly to the Investiture Crisis between late-11th century pontiffs and the Holy Roman emperors. Odo was known for being honest and, following his investiture in 1088, he took a critical look at both his position and the Church itself.

Contemporary clerics record that Urban was "admirable in life and habit, always striving to raise high the honor of the Church." This indicates that he was well aware of the problems the Investiture Crisis was causing to papal authority. In 1088 there were two popes, the second "antipope" being a puppet of the German emperor, Henry IV (r.1056–1106). Henry was still locked in a struggle with Rome over the issue of investiture to high ecclesiastical offices. Bluntly, this meant that he wanted to reserve the right to place his own supporters into German bishoprics, in return for a share of the revenues. For Urban, the emperor was only one of his worries.

## A ravaged Europe

King Philip I of France (r.1060–1108) had recently been excommunicated on the grounds of bigamy and there was a chance that he would rebel against ecclesiastical authority within his dominions as a means of fighting back. Western

Europe had been ravaged by decades of war. In 1066, Duke William of Normandy had invaded England and conquered the country. Other Norman adventurers were carving out their own feudal territories in southern Italy, Sicily, and Greece, while Spanish and Frankish knights engaged in a bitter religious struggle for control of Spain. Across Europe, petty barons, feudal overlords, and mercenary adventurers fought to extend their own power at the expense of each other. In almost all cases, the real victims were the peasants tied to the land, whose revenues were needed to keep both Church and State functioning.

For years, Urban had looked for a way to harness the latent martial energy of the feudal nobility and channel it in a way that could benefit the Church. Emperor Alexius's plea offered a means to do just that. It also might be used to consolidate his spiritual authority over Christendom, by uniting all Christian secular nobles under the banner of a common cause.

For years, Urban had preached that violence was abhorrent. Killing was a grave sin, even if it took place as an act of war. It placed the soul of the slayer at risk unless he performed penance to the Church. By introducing the notion of a "just war," Urban made the killing of the "enemies of Christ" a penance in itself, an act of piety and devotion. This theological twist ensured the interest of many of the knights and warlords who ravaged Europe. The initial offer required expanding to appeal to the universal desire for land and power, but at the same time the Church needed to maintain control over any crusading venture.

Urban decided to grasp the opportunity. By calling for a campaign against the unholy Muslims, he felt he could benefit both Europe and the Church. He also naïvely believed that he would be able to control the crusaders once the expedition got underway.

# The Pope's Address at Clermont

**On November 27, 1095, Pope Urban II addressed a council of bishops and senior clergy in Clermont, central France. Since a major announcement was expected, thousands of laymen and clerics flocked to listen and the dais had to be moved into an adjacent meadow, so that everyone could hear Urban's words. It was a speech that would alter the course of history.**

At 53, Urban was a robust, healthy figure and spoke with the passion of a man many years his junior. The address was well prepared and copies had even been written out beforehand for distribution to secular and ecclesiastic leaders. The appeal had been meticulously planned. There was even to be a papal tiara, and spiritual leader over the whole world, have come here in this great crisis to you, servants of God, as a messenger of divine admonition." His words were aimed directly at the secular kings and nobles, including the German emperor. He continued, "Above all, keep the Church in all its orders entirely free from the secular power of princes."

He outlined the sins of those who "seizes monks, or priests, or nuns, or pilgrims, or traders, to despoil them." Most noblemen who heard or read the speech were guilty to some extent, but his words were directed at another target. He reminded the noble listeners that they had promised "to sustain the rights of

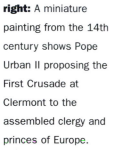

**right:** A miniature painting from the 14th century shows Pope Urban II proposing the First Crusade at Clermont to the assembled clergy and princes of Europe.

**facing:** The papal word was meant for the ears of the powerful and wealthy, but within weeks, the message had been taken up by Peter the Hermit who appealed to the masses (*see pages 54–55*).

tour of France to repeat the speech and to exert continued influence on the feudal nobility of Christendom.

He began, "Dearest brethren. I, Urban, invested by the permission of God with the

Holy Church" and that "there still remains for you a very necessary work. For you must hurry to aid your brethren in the East." He outlined the attacks made by the Muslims against Christians, and in reference to the Byzantine loss of Anatolia he claimed they had "devastated the kingdom of God." He was ready for the clarion call.

"So I exhort you with earnest prayers, not I, but God, that as heralds of Christ you urge men of all ranks, rich as well as poor, knights as well as foot soldiers, to hasten to exterminate this vile race from the lands of your eastern brethren. I call on those present here. I proclaim it to the absent. Moreover, Christ commands it!"

## Soldiers of Christ

He outlined the sins of the Turks in detail, listing torture, desecration, human sacrifice, robbery, and a catalog of other horrors. His aim was to incense his audience—and he succeeded admirably. These heathens were clearly the enemy. War against them was also a just one, he argued, and the killers of Muslims would not only be absolved, but they would be blessed! To fight them was an act of piety.

He urged his listeners, "Enter upon the road to the Holy Sepulcher, wrest that land from the wicked race and make it subject to yourselves. Jerusalem is the navel of the world." He was appealing to the power-hungry nobles, encouraging them to seek out new territories beyond the lands of fellow Christians. He urged the knights to face their sins, then to become the "soldiery of Christ." Death in battle would be rewarded by salvation and, if successful, "the possessions of the enemy will be yours." He knew exactly how to appeal to his audience, who were wooed with a heady mixture of treasure, land, martial challenge, and immortal blessing.

the Cross on their body, marking them as "Soldiers of Christ." Those who wore the emblem would become "crusaders" (the term derives from *cruciare*—"to mark with a cross").

In an hour, Urban had achieved his goal. Christendom was united; any opposition by

Victory was assured, as "Christ will be your inseparable standard bearer." He absolved all who would heed the call of their sins, and ended by demanding that all who undertook the venture should wear an emblem in the shape of

secular powers was now inconceivable. The violent nobles and their retainers who threatened the stability of Europe would become Soldiers of Christ. Pope Urban had set the Crusades in motion.

# CHAPTER 3

# God Wills It:

## The First Crusade

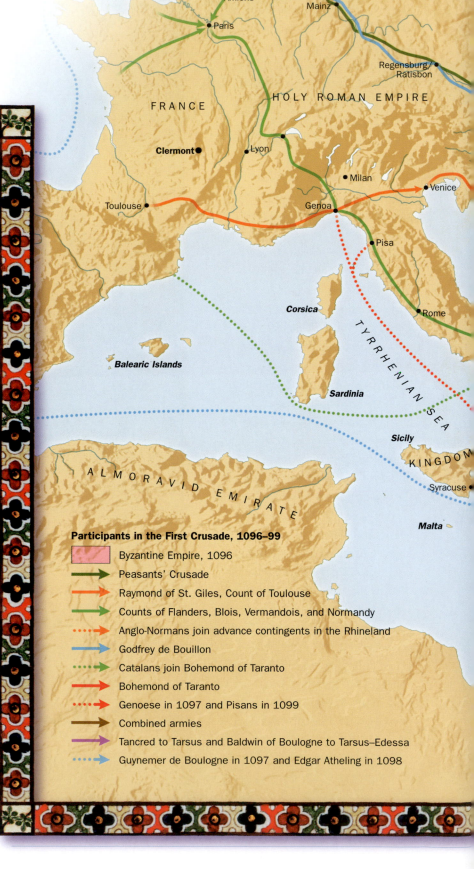

Pope Urban II's appeal for a crusader army to recapture Jerusalem resulted in a movement that exceeded all his expectations. He promised that service in his holy army "to liberate the Church of God can substitute this journey for all penance." The leaders of the first crusader army were the nobility of Europe and their retainers. The Turks would be beaten back by western European—Frankish—tactics in which mounted knights were key to military success.

Even before the main army gathered in Constantinople, the fervor created by the papal call unleashed a wave of unofficial crusaders. These marched east, leaving destruction in their wake. This movement—known as the Peasants' Crusade—would end in disaster, but it reflected the incredible popular appeal that the crusading ideal engendered.

For Alexius I, the ensuing chaos created a climate in which the Byzantine emperor was able to avoid Pope Urban II's desire to bind the Orthodox Church to the Roman and unify the two. Instead he unleashed the crusaders on the Turks who had defeated his own army. As the army marched through Asia Minor toward the Holy Land, the Byzantines followed in their wake, reclaiming the empire they had lost to the Turks. Everyone was able to benefit from the crusading movement, apart from those who stood in its way, or who held different beliefs. As instruments of God's will, the crusaders were about to change the course of history.

**Participants in the First Crusade, 1096–99**

- Byzantine Empire, 1096
- Peasants' Crusade
- Raymond of St. Giles, Count of Toulouse
- Counts of Flanders, Blois, Vermandois, and Normandy
- Anglo-Normans join advance contingents in the Rhineland
- Godfrey de Bouillon
- Catalans join Bohemond of Taranto
- Bohemond of Taranto
- Genoese in 1097 and Pisans in 1099
- Combined armies
- Tancred to Tarsus and Baldwin of Boulogne to Tarsus–Edessa
- Guynemer de Boulogne in 1097 and Edgar Atheling in 1098

Map labels: Cologne, Amiens, Mainz, Paris, Regensburg/Ratisbon, HOLY ROMAN EMPIRE, FRANCE, Clermont, Lyon, Milan, Venice, Toulouse, Genoa, Pisa, Corsica, Rome, TYRRHENIAN SEA, Balearic Islands, Sardinia, Sicily, KINGDOM, Syracuse, ALMORAVID EMIRATE, Malta

Bedouin woman herding camels, from an Arabic manuscript of 1237 by al-Wasiti. The everyday lives of many Muslims would soon be thrown into chaos by the arrival of Frankish knights on their holy quest. But it was the common folk whose efforts would be needed by the European invaders to maintain their imported feudal way of life in the Holy Land. The initial disruption the First Crusade created among Muslim peasants made this a difficult proposition.

Vienna

HUNGARY

Belgrade

Nish

ADRIATIC SEA

Scutari

Philippolis

Adrianople

Dyrrhacium

SEA OF AZOV

BLACK SEA

Sinope

Trebizond

Bari

Taranto

OF SICILY

Thessalonika

Constantinople

Civetot

Nicaea (Iznik)

Dorylaeum 1097

Ancyra

Caesarea

AEGEAN SEA

Philomelium

ANATOLIA

Mara'

Edessa

**The Peasants' Crusade was wiped out near Nicaea on October 1, 1096.**

Iconium

Heraclea

Cilician Gates

Tarsus

Syrian Gates

Antioch

Rhodes

Crete

Cyprus

MEDITERRANEAN SEA

Tripoli

Beirut

Sidon

Damascus

Acre

Jaffa

Ascalon 1099

Jerusalem 1099

Damietta

Alexandria

Cairo

FATIMID CALIPHATE

**An army of the Fatimid Caliphate marched north to counter the crusader threat. The two forces met near Ascalon on August 12, 1099 where the crusaders were victorious. The Fatimids left the field to Christendom, but only for a short while.**

# Crusading Fervor

**After addressing Europe's nobility at Clermont, Pope Urban II went on a campaign tour of France. Other clerics spread the message across the breadth of Europe. During the first half of 1096, a host of lords, knights, and their retainers answered the call. So too did thousands of commoners who wanted to serve God and play their part in what had become a mass movement.**

**facing:** Crusading fervor aroused passions in the common people that frequently overflowed in disastrous ways, and the first victims were not the Muslim enemy but other Christians. This medieval illumination depicts the incident on Peter the Hermit's Peasants' Crusade when unruly German elements set fire to some houses outside the Bulgarian city of Nish. As the crusaders made their way along the river bank, the governor of Nish ordered his army to attack the rearguard and take hostages. Those captured were put to death, which further inflamed the Germans. A battle ensued, in which as many as ten thousand of Peter's army was massacred before the Byzantine emperor intervened with his governor to help Peter calm the situation.

Urban's intention was to encourage the nobility of Christian Europe to join together in a movement under the authority of the Church. He appointed Adhemar of Monteil, the Bishop of Le Puy, to be the crusading movement's religious figurehead. As Urban's personal representative, he was to ensure papal control of the expedition. While he lived, Adhemar managed to hold the crusaders together in a reasonably cohesive unit. His real problem, however, was that the motivation of the princes and leading nobles was not exclusively spiritual.

While there is no doubt that piety played its part, and that most would have fervently believed in the pope's promise that all sins would be forgiven and a place in heaven assured, nevertheless the more earthly promise of adventure and a chance to carve out new feudal domains was a more heady combination. At a time when hundreds of minor nobles were locked in a struggle for feudal territory in France, Italy, and England, an important second consideration was the holy promise that the lands back at home of those who participated in the crusades would be protected. These promises of salvation and protection were welcome. For many, crusading fervor was closely linked to a desire to hold onto land and to find more land. In an era of deep religious belief, the chance to claim feudal domains while serving the cause of righteousness was a heaven-sent opportunity.

Papal couriers relayed Pope Urban's message to other parts of Europe, where bishops and priests urged their regional nobles to participate in the crusade. In southern Italy, Norman adventurers had recently carved out their own feudal territory by capturing land from the Byzantine Empire. Although the Church viewed the seizure of land from fellow Christians with displeasure, doing so against the infidel was seen as an act of devout penance. Holy slaughter brought spiritual as well as territorial rewards.

The nobility who led the First Crusade came from four areas: southern Italy, Normandy, Flanders, and southern France. These nobles and their retinues were exactly the people Urban had in mind when he spoke at Clermont. Tough experienced soldiers such as Bohemond of Taranto and his nephew Tancred or Robert, Duke of Normandy were intended to bring a level of military professionalism to the enterprise and prove more than a match for the Turkish armies who had defeated the weakened Byzantines. They were the same Normans who had conquered Anglo-Saxon England, or the French nobles who had held the Moors of Spain at bay. Now they would fight under papal direction, in an army protected by God, and would kill as a demonstration of their belief.

## Out of control

Urban never intended that his crusading message would result in peasants, women, and even children joining in his great venture. The economy of feudal Europe was tied to an agrarian system where peasants and freeholders were needed to support the knights and nobles on the upper rungs of the feudal system. When tens of thousands of peasants became enthused with crusading fervor, the economy of Europe was temporarily disrupted, particularly in Germany and northeast France.

These commoners wanted to benefit from the same promises of eternal glory as their betters. They became caught up in the wave of popular enthusiasm that turned Urban's appeal into a mass movement. All of Christendom was now united in the crusading spirit to reclaim the Holy Land, or *Outremer* (Overseas). It was a reaction that exceeded Urban's wildest expectations. However, it was also a movement that the pope was virtually powerless to control. The forces that would be unleashed on the Turks were beyond the control of any individual.

preschier des le mois de Nouembre. dxs. m°l°. vb. Touteffois po° les hants apuieis que pour pir souttnir tant dāngtereuse ↄ tāmt besoūgne conuentoit le gencrals pir tement kētarda grānt temps et aussi vuir la predication dille. dꝰus reftu Gauttier sans sca noir. ↄ ses gens qui furent les premiers Comme sap dit. se dep tirent du sieu ou ilz auotent en trepnis eulx assembler le vnf. sour du mois de mate auant pasques. Lan a vii ml°. vb. ↄ comnnetcer sam apres la bene dition du Saint E ietrebenit e lnsi que se fait ou pusement de puie. Lesquelz passerent

# Pogrom and Massacre

**The first victims of crusading zeal were the Jewish communities of Germany, not the Muslims of the Holy Land. Although the persecution of the Jewish population was no new phenomenon, the widespread massacres that took place at the start of the crusading era amounted to Europe's first genocide.**

**below:** Medieval Europe's relationship with Jews was uncertain; toleration varied enormously from country to country and from time to time. For a largely ignorant population, it was easy to forget that Jesus had been a Jew, and on many occasions the peasantry was driven to anti-semitic fervor through the simple device of pointing out that it was the Jews who had crucified Him. This illumination from the 1023 *De Universo* equates Jews (left) with heretics as being unable to hear the word of God.

German Jewish communities, economically separated from the rest of feudal Europe, relied on the protection of feudal, or more usually ecclesiastic, landowners in return for taxation. Most were clustered in the cities of the Rhine and Danube rivers, where their development of regional trade was a useful source of civic income. The system of protection in return for trade benefited both parties, until Pope Urban stirred up religious resentment.

In 1096, the Jewish communities in towns and cities along the Rhine were slaughtered, often with the consent of their feudal protectors. Mainz, Speyer, Worms, Trier, Xanten, Metz, and Cologne were all turned into charnel houses, as were dozens of smaller settlements. Some churchmen tried to protect the Jews, but to little avail. In Speyer, the local bishop saved hundreds of Jews by hiding them in his church, but in Worms crusaders stormed the bishop's residence and massacred the Jewish families secreted there.

These crusaders were not the courtly leaders of the First Crusade. Many were peasants, petty knights, and brigands for whom the First Crusade presented an opportunity for profit. Count Emich of Leiningen was by far the worst. He encouraged his followers to sack Worms, then continue up the Rhine. As one chronicler noted: "Just at that time there appeared a certain soldier, Emich, a count of the lands around the Rhine, a man of very ill-repute because of his tyrannical way of life…. He usurped to himself the command of almost 12,000 bearers of the cross. As he led them through the cities of the Rhine, the Main, and the Danube, they utterly destroyed the hateful race of the Jews wherever they found them."

## Old hatreds

The reason for this carnage was suggested by a Jewish author, who placed these words into crusading mouths: "Look now, we are going to a distant country to make war against mighty kings. Our lives will be in danger to conquer these kingdoms who do not believe in the crucified one, when actually it is the Jews who murdered and crucified him…." To encourage them along this path, a man known as either Dithmar or Folkmar swore that he would "not depart from this kingdom till [he had] killed at least one Jew." Folkmar has been named as the

instigator of the massacre in Prague.

Although some communities managed to evade their attackers, or pay a bribe to be left in peace, ringleaders such as Count Emich encouraged violence. Even though protection payments were made, the pogrom continued. In Bavaria, the crusading leader Gottschalk killed Jews in massacres at Regensburg and Ratisbon. After a summer of violence, Emich and his "crusading" band crossed Germany and entered Hungary, where the local feudal overlords were less sympathetic.

Following Folkmar's massacre in Prague, the Hungarian royal army attacked and scattered Emich's band, while another group led by Gottschalk was captured and promptly executed to the last man. Surviving bands galvanized into the movement known as the Peasants' Crusade. The religious zeal of these lowly crusaders was more akin to the revivalist or "born-again" Christian movements of today than any contemporary religious doctrine. Their zeal was only matched by the ignorance and blind bigotry that led them to genocide.

These roving bands provided ammunition for critics of the crusading ideal, many of them in Germany, which had been devastated by the marauders. But the tumultuous religious fervor drowned their arguments as the Church continued preaching Urban's message. However devastating the human cost, the crusade would continue.

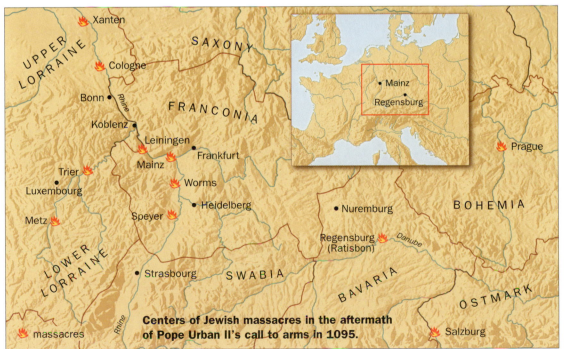

**Centers of Jewish massacres in the aftermath of Pope Urban II's call to arms in 1095.**

🔥 massacres

**above:** Crusaders pillage a Jewish ghetto, from a 19th-century illustration by Gustave Dore. The word "ghetto" comes from the Venetian *gheto*, which means "metal casting." Jews were originally welcomed to the Republic of Venice but were required to live in a separate community. A disused city foundry isolated on its own island was given to the first Jewish settlers, and they were literally said to be living in the *gheto*.

# The Peasants' Crusade

**Of all the unsanctioned crusaders who set off for the Holy Land, Peter the Hermit was the most significant. The small eccentric monk turned Urban's appeal into a mass movement. His commoner sympathizers followed him across Europe, encountering hardships that would have challenged all but the most faithful.**

**above:** Two peasants plowing, from the 1028 manuscript *De Rerum Naturis*.

**below:** A similar scene of plowing from *Cynegetica*. Peter's appeal was to hit home.

Peter the Hermit (or Cucu Peter, which probably meant "Cowled Peter") was a pilgrim whose charismatic personality enthused thousands with crusading zeal. A contemporary, Guibert of Nogent, said of him that "whatever he did or said was regarded as little short of divine, to such an extent that hairs were snatched from his mule as relics." In March 1096, he left Amiens in northern France, bound for Jerusalem via Cologne in Germany.

Peter was accompanied by a growing host of the faithful; people of all ages and backgrounds of both genders. The majority were French, but he attracted disciples from all over Europe. While most were peasants, Peter's crusaders included several knights, and one, Walter Sans-Avoir, became the expedition's *de facto* military leader.

The Peasants' Crusade consisted of several columns. Walter Sans-Avoir led around 10,000 men in a first group, and a larger body led by

Peter himself followed him some weeks later. Both groups left Cologne and followed the Rhine and the Danube into Hungary. Walter convinced King Coloman of Hungary that the crusaders offered no threat and both groups were given leave to traverse the kingdom. Walter's band crossed Hungary without serious incident.

Peter's group was less fortunate. Their lack of discipline led to a full-scale battle between one of his columns and Hungarian troops. Astonishingly, the peasants won, and were left to go on their way. Later bands of peasants and isolated groups were deemed a threat to Hungarian authority and massacred.

## Christian against Christian

Walter crossed the border into the Byzantine province of Bulgaria during the early summer of 1096, with Peter's band a few weeks behind. Denied food by the alarmed governor of Belgrade, the rag-tag army ran amok. But the governor rounded up a group of looters in a church and burned them before sending the crusaders onward. When Peter's crusaders reached Belgrade, they set fires and did great damage before order could be restored. Worse came when a straggling band of German crusaders burned houses near the city of Nish, and were promptly set upon by the city's garrison. Almost 10,000 crusaders were killed or led into captivity in a three-day massacre before Peter could defuse the situation, aided by the emperor. Alexius forgave the "pilgrims" their excesses and offered escorts to gather them near Constantinople. When the various bands were amalgamated in August, the peasants were ferried across the Bosphorus into Asia Minor, before they could cause any further trouble.

Around 30,000 men, women, and children were now on the Asian continent, wondering what to do next. Peter the Hermit pleaded for caution and to wait until the main crusading army arrived. He was ignored. The crusaders were divided into two groups, one French and the other mixed German and Italian. The latter elected a man called Rainault as their leader, and both groups promptly marched on the Turkish city of Nicaea, looting and killing indiscriminately on the way. The Turkish garrison, led by Sultan Kilij Arslan, decimated the Frankish column.

The Germans avoided the city and occupied a fortress called Xerigordon, where the Turkish army caught up with them. The fortress fell in late September, and all who were unwilling to convert to Islam were massacred. The surviving crusaders regrouped at Civetot (near modern Adapazari), in Byzantine Asia Minor and, under the leadership of Geoffrey Burel, they renewed their offensive. Two hours later the Franks were ambushed and slaughtered. While a few women and children were kept as slaves, almost all the remaining crusaders were killed. Only a handful escaped the disaster, including Peter the Hermit, who was in Constantinople when the massacre took place.

The Peasants' Crusade ended in disaster, but within days of the massacre, a more professional army arrived in Constantinople. The Turks would find these real crusaders far tougher opponents.

**below:** Peter the Hermit leads the First Crusade, from a 14th-century manuscript. The man—who may or may not have actually been a monk—proved to be an incompetent leader, yet he remained an inspiration and a legend in his own time. After the debacle of 1096, Peter led a peasant militia all the way to Jerusalem, and was among the first to enter the Holy City.

# A Motley Gang of Princes

**Pope Urban II had not selected a commander. Instead, he relied on the participating nobles—united in one common purpose—to work together. Each, with his own feudal contingent, was wary of submitting to the leadership of the others. This lack of leadership was to have a profound effect on the crusaders and on the political development of the conquered territories.**

Adhemar of Monteil, Bishop of Le Puy, the pope's representative, was charged with providing spiritual leadership to the crusaders. A member of the nobility himself, he proved to be a gifted military commander, a capable politician, and a diplomat. He exerted a significant influence over the crusade's secular leaders and, until his death at Antioch, he managed to control their more excessive political aspirations. Those he was dealing with represented some of the most headstrong and spirited young princes of Europe.

Robert, eldest son of William the Conqueror, and Duke of Normandy was closely allied with his cousin, Robert II, Count of Flanders and his brother-in-law, Stephen of Blois. Nicknamed *Curthose* (short pants), Robert was likeable and gregarious, but lacked the natural leadership qualities of some of his fellow crusaders.

Another group formed from the retinues of three brothers: Godfrey of Bouillon, the Duke of lower Lorraine; Eustace, the Count of Boulogne; and Baldwin of Boulogne. Godfrey, who claimed to be the direct descendant of Charlemagne, was tall, handsome, and the empitome of medieval aristocracy; but his younger brother Baldwin proved to be the more able military commander.

Raymond IV, the Count of Toulouse and of St. Giles, had lost an eye fighting the Moors in Spain. To him, the crusade was merely a continuation of this struggle. His feudal domain in southern France was the richest province in the kingdom, and consequently he commanded the largest retinue in the expedition. Raymond was 56 when he embarked on the crusade, and felt he had to make one last service to God before he died. Of all the crusaders, he was the most committed to fulfilling the Urban's religious goals. He shared the diplomatic skills of Bishop Adhemar, who he accompanied on the journey to Constantinople. Of all the crusading leaders, Raymond of Toulouse developed the closest relations with the Byzantines, and consequently became able to rely on their political support. Emperor Alexius regarded him as the most intelligent of all the crusading leaders.

**right:** Godfrey of Bouillon embarks on the Crusade. This whimsical version of the great prince's departure for the Holy Land appears in the *Chronicle of the Jerusalem Empire,* created for Philip the Good of Burgundy in 1467.

## Cruel and pompous

Bohemond, Prince of Taranto (Otranto) was a Norman adventurer from southern Italy who had carved out a feudal principality from territory formerly held by the Byzantines. He was besieging Amalfi when news of the pope's appeal reached him. He decided to join the crusade, and of all the crusaders, he was the most in need of the protection offered to his domains by Pope Urban. His nephew Tancred, who was destined to become one of the leading figures of the expedition, accompanied him, along with a retinue of poor and land-hungry Italian Norman knights. Like their leader, these men had already developed a reputation for unscrupulousness and cruelty. They were about to be unleashed on the unsuspecting Turks.

Henry, Count of Vermandois was the younger son of King Henry I of France. Anna Comnena, the daughter of the Byzantine emperor, considered him a pompous upstart, and she records that he described himself to her father as "king of kings, and the greatest of those under heaven." His arrival at the Byzantine court failed to match his lofty pretensions, however. He was shipwrecked on the eastern coast of the Adriatic and cast ashore on Byzantine soil half-naked and barely alive. Grievously, almost all of his followers were lost in the wreck. Alexius's envoys clothed him and took him to Constantinople. Henry became the first of the crusading princes to arrive at the Byzantine court. Although the chronicler William of Tyre called him "Hugh the Great," most contemporaries agreed with Anna Comnena.

**above:** The crusader army of Raymond of Toulouse makes its way through a fantastic Balkans landscape on its way to Constantinople. Raymond represented the best of the First Crusade and remained the most responsible of the princes.

## CHAPTER 3 — GOD WILLS IT

# On the Banks of the Bosphorus

**Constantinople was fast becoming the central focus of the crusading effort, and contingents of crusaders arrived by a variety of routes during the summer of 1096. The fact that they arrived in Constantinople was a miracle in itself, in an age when most men rarely ventured further than the next town or village.**

Having arrived first, Hugh of Vermandois was showered with gifts... and guarded closely. Hugh swore a feudal oath of loyalty to Alexius, promising to return to the emperor any former Byzantine lands he recaptured. He then waited for his fellow crusaders to arrive.

In August 1096, Godfrey of Bouillon led his retinue across northern France and into Germany, following in the wake of the Peasants' Crusade. He followed the route known as the Charlemagne Road, the path supposedly taken by the emperor on his pilgrimage to Jerusalem. Charlemagne had actually never made any such pilgrimage, but the name remained. In October, Godfrey entered Hungary, sending emissaries ahead to convince King Coloman that he had no hostile intentions. Escorted by Hungarian troops, the crusaders passed through the country without incident, a testimony to the discipline Godfrey imposed on his men.

They entered the Byzantine Empire and were met by another armed escort, finally arriving before the walls of Constantinople two days before Christmas. Here, the army remained for another four months, waiting for the other contingents. Unlike Hugh, Godfrey and his men refused to swear allegiance to the emperor, and Alexius cut off their food supplies. Their response was to ravage the countryside until the supplies were resumed. In March 1097, after an uneasy truce, Alexius cut off the supplies again, in an effort to force Godfrey to swear fealty to him. This time Godfrey attacked the city, which proved to be a tougher proposition than the unresisting countryside. The attack was repulsed and Godfrey was obliged to take the oath in order to get his army fed.

In April, three days after Godfrey's contingent stepped onto Asia Minor, Bohemond of Taranto arrived, after crossing the Adriatic Sea then marching through Byzantine Greece. A former enemy of the Byzantines, Bohemond was well versed in their protocol, and without demurral promised to swear an oath of loyalty he had no intention of keeping. In doing so, the wily prince avoided any trouble that might delay him getting his hands on a piece of the Holy Land that the emperor would never see.

## A mixed blessing

Days later, Raymond of Toulouse arrived, with the largest contingent of all. His men had marched from Lyon in the company of Bishop Adhemar, and reached Constantinople via Italy and Serbia. Confronted by two skilled diplomats, the emperor was forced to revise his oath-swearing policy. A modified version was agreed upon, where Raymond swore only to safeguard Byzantine property and restore her lost provinces. The relationship between Raymond and Alexius was founded on mutual respect, and both men would profit from the friendship that developed.

The last crusaders to arrive were the Normans, led by Robert, Duke of Normandy. They had traveled through Italy, then followed the route taken by Bohemond. Robert had no hesitation in swearing the full oath, and together with Raymond and his contingent, the Normans were duly ferried across the Bosphorus.

To the Emperor Alexius I Comnenus, these crusading contingents were a mixed blessing. On the one hand, they were allies in his war against the Turks; on the other, they were themselves a latent threat to the realm's stability. By getting their leaders to swear oaths of allegiance, he hoped to mitigate against the day when the cure might prove to be worse than the affliction. While such forces remained encamped about Constantinople, there was bound to be continual trouble. By ferrying them into Asia, he managed to distance these land-hungry adventurers from his opulent capital. By the end of April 1097, the crusading army was gathered together at Pelecanum and was preparing to advance into Asia Minor. The coming battle would test the effectiveness of two completely different military styles.

PERA

Sautari

Turquia

porta del meso

Scs demet?

Scs geor gius

CONSTAN=
TINOPOLIS.

chiramos

palacij Impaus

portus olim
palacij im
pator16

porta

Scus loci? de p̃

pdronia

Scus toffe? d
andri

olangu

Calchidona

portus fed deftruit
excepto teutrorii

# Nicaea and Dorylaeum

**The crusaders who gathered on the fringes of Asia Minor in the summer of 1097 were a polyglot force, comprised of contingents from most European countries. Divided by language, background, and even motive, they were united solely by their common desire to defeat the infidel.**

To Sultan Kilij Arslan, the crusaders were no more a threat to his forces than the ragged participants of the People's Crusade. This was a serious error based on assumptions that the *Ifranj* (Franks; the word came to cover all "foreigners") were still the primitives who had made up isolated bands of mercenaries in the region for some time. The error was about to become apparent. The leaders elected to advance on the sultan's regional capital of Nicaea. The city stood on the eastern side of Lake Iznik, some 50 miles southeast of the crusaders' camp.

The Christian army advanced and laid siege. However, Arslan was away from his capital at the time and returned with his army, intent on defeating the besiegers. He attacked the portion of the circle of crusading troops commanded by Raymond of Toulouse, who repulsed the attack with ease. The Seljuk army had no troops

**below and right:** The relief force of Sultan Arslan was defeated by the crusaders outside Nicaea. The Turkish captives were then decapitated. These two illuminations from the 13th-century manuscript *Les Histories d'Outremer* show the crusaders advancing on Nicaea with the heads of their captives and then using a trebuchet to catapult them over the city's walls at the defenders.

capable of defeating the heavily armored knights in close combat.

Alexius assisted the siege by supplying several boats, which were transported overland and then floated on the lake. The city was completely cut off. The Byzantine emperor also sneaked a diplomatic embassy into the city by water, and on June 19, just before the crusaders launched an assault on its walls, Nicaea surrendered. Denied the spoils of the city, the crusaders were furious, but any confrontation was diverted when the emperor lavished gifts on the crusade's commanders.

## Unexpected reinforcements

With a secure base at Nicaea, the crusaders continued marching to the southeast, pursuing Sultan Kilij Arslan and his Seljuk army into the mountains. Stephen of Blois expected it would take them five weeks to reach Jerusalem. Instead, it took a full year to reach the Holy Land, and yet another year to reach Jerusalem.

The delay was not entirely due to the enemy. Between the crusaders and their goal lay some of the most inhospitable terrain in the Middle East. The crusaders divided their force into two columns to speed their progress, one commanded by Prince Bohemond of Taranto, followed by a second group led by Raymond of Toulouse. Four days after the crusaders left Nicaea, Arslan's army fell upon Bohemond near the city of Dorylaeum. Mounted knights held the enemy at bay while the defenses were prepared and Bohemond dispatched messengers down the road to find the second column of crusaders. Meanwhile, the Norman drew his baggage wagons into a circle and his men defended their makeshift fortification against the swarms of Muslim horse archers who surrounded it. The crusaders lacked any means to respond and over several hours their numbers were steadily depleted.

Just when defeat seemed inevitable, Raymond of Toulouse arrived with his own column of fresh troops. Assuming that they were faced by the entire crusading army, Raymond's arrival threw the Turks into confusion. Inspired by reinforcements and the enemy's confusion, Bohemond's knights charged and routed the Turks. Victory was assured when Raymond's rearguard, commanded by Bishop Adhemar, arrived behind the reeling Turkish army. The cost of the victory was high—almost 4,000 crusaders were killed or wounded in the battle. Turkish losses were significantly higher.

The battle of Dorylaeum broke Seljuk resolve and the crusaders faced no further serious opposition as they marched through the rest of Anatolia. Nature would prove to be a more implacable enemy than the Turks. The first battle between crusaders and Muslims demonstrated the armies' opposing tactical methods. While the Christians relied on the shock power of a charge of mounted knights to break their enemy, their opponents tended to avoid contact and use missile power. Like the children's game of rock, scissors, and paper, each method had its advantages.

**above:** Nicaea (now the modern town of Iznik) was a formidable target, surrounded by the massive concentric walls built by Byzantine architects that now afforded the Seljuk Turks protection. Fortunately, the besieging Christian army never had to assault the fortifications. Today, a small road runs through the three gateways that make up the Lefke Gate.

61

# Through Asia Minor

**It was determined that the fastest route to the Holy Land lay through the center of Asia Minor (Anatolia). It meant crossing an inhospitable desert at summer's height and climbing over the Anti-Tauran Mountains as winter approached. A journey expected to take a month would become a year-long ordeal, pitting crusading zeal against the extremes of nature.**

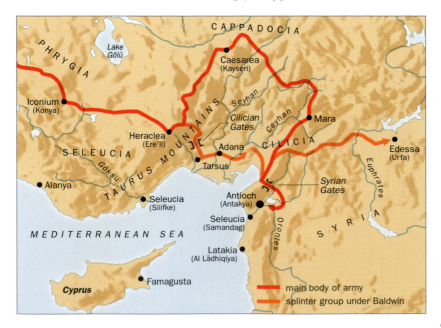

**right:** Although the major contingents of the First Crusade took the land routes through Europe to Constantinople, there were also sailors. Guynemer de Boulogne sailed around Spain and the length of the Mediterranean to join the army in Antioch. Once the Syrian ports were in crusader hands, maritime traffic increased, bringing provisions, military materiel, and new recruits to Outremer. This illumination shows a ship laden with knights under the ecclesiastical care of the priest at the rudder.

Heartened by victory at Dorylaeum, the crusaders buried their dead, then continued their journey, heading southeast through the foothills of Phrygia to Iconium (now Konya), then east across the desert to Heraclea (Ere'li). The cleric Fulcher of Chartres recalled the nightmare of the journey: "We suffered such extreme thirst that many men and women died from its torments. We often lacked bread and other food in these places, for the land was ravaged and devastated by the Turks."

The midsummer sun blazed down on the crusaders' backs. The arid deserts of central Anatolia must have appeared endless. Used to the gentler climate of western or southern Europe, the crusaders were pushed to the very limits of their endurance in a struggle between physical torment and spiritual faith.

The heat increased throughout August. Another cleric, Albert of Aix, described how women gave birth by the roadside, then abandoned their desiccated babies, and how hundreds simply dropped from heat exhaustion and thirst. When the columns reached rivers, many drank too much water and died from the effects. It took a month of this torment before the foothills of the Anti-Taurus Mountains were reached. The direct path to the Holy Land lay through the cluster of mountain passes known as the Cilician Gates, but mounting Turkish opposition forced the leaders to consider a change of route. It was feared that fighting through mountain passes while facing enemy troops of superior number would be too dangerous. Instead, the army turned northeast toward Armenia, nominally a Christian province.

## Dissent

The aim was to find a crossing through the mountains in friendly territory, then descend into Syria and approach Antioch from the east rather than the north. It was at this stage that

the princes began to disagree. The main body of the army took the Armenia route but two of the contingent leaders decided to make their own ways to Antioch. Baldwin of Boulogne, Godfrey of Lorraine's younger brother, managed to bluff his way through the Cilician Gates and arrived in front of the southern Anatolian city of Tarsus, close to the Mediterranean Sea. Tancred, nephew of Prince Bohemond, had already separated from the main body and reached Tarsus. He was obliged to hand the city over to Baldwin, who commanded the larger force. The two groups of crusaders continued eastward, skirmishing with each other as much as with the Turks.

The main body of crusaders marched through Cappadochia into Armenia but encountered a "diabolical mountain which was so high and steep that none of us dared to step before another through the pass... there horses fell headlong, and one pack animal pushed over another." The march through the desert and the mountain crossing caused far more casualties

than had been inflicted by the Turks, and it was an exhausted, ragged, and diminished crusading army that emerged from the Anti-Taurus Mountains near Marash (Maras).

Baldwin caught up with the army only to discover that his wife was dying, and with her, his chance of inherited wealth. He decided to find his own fortune and set off with a hundred knights and their retainers to the east, bound for the Christian Armenian city of Edessa. The remaining crusaders were reunited with the Norman Italian force commanded by Tancred in the Syrian Gates, a pass through the low mountains that separated Syria and Anatolia. Beyond them, a mere ten miles to the south, lay the rich port city of Antioch, the gateway to the Holy Land. After almost a year in the Anatolian wilderness the crusaders were nearing their destination.

**above:** Muslim battalions scattered by victorious crusaders, from a 19th-century engraving by Gustave Dore.

# The Siege of Antioch

**Third largest city in the Roman Empire, Antioch was still a rich, vibrant city six centuries later. Protected by formidable fortifications, in the space of one year it endured two sieges and the massacre of its population. This city, the gateway to the Holy Land, was the first real prize of the First Crusade, and the most costly.**

"When we had crossed that accursed mountain, we came to a city called Marash, and so at last our knights marched more easily, and came into the valley which contains the royal city of Antioch, capital of Syria." So recorded the *Gesta Francorum* (The Deeds of the Franks), which formed the "official history" of the First Crusade. After a year of travel, the crusaders were standing before the city where Christ's followers had first been labeled "Christians." Although its defenses were formidable, the crusaders had high hopes that they would be able to take the city, then press on toward Jerusalem before the month ended. That was in mid-October 1097. More than seven months later, they had advanced no further.

Before being surrounded, Yaghi Siyan, Antioch's Turkish governor, gathered supplies in preparation for a siege and sent word to Mosul for help. Food was not a problem for the crusaders, who had captured a Turkish supply convoy on nearing the city. With Antioch besieged, the Christian leaders argued over what to do next. Prince Bohemond wanted Antioch for himself, while Raymond of Toulouse argued that it should be handed back to the Byzantines, as agreed in Constantinople.

The discussion remained academic in the face of their failure to breach the walls. Provisions, too, were now running short. A brief respite came in November when Simeon, former Patriarch of Jerusalem, arrived in Antioch's port of Seleucia (now Samandag)

with 13 ships bearing supplies from Cyprus. The port—renamed St. Symeon—provided the army with a link to the rest of the Christian world. But by Christmas the supplies had been used and by late January morale was low.

Both sides tussled continually over the road to the vital port. In February, a Turkish relief attempt on the road was thwarted and a sortie by the garrison repulsed. These victories raised morale, and when fresh supplies arrived from Constantinople, the crusaders became increasingly confident. News that a huge relief army commanded by Kerbuqua Atabeg of Mosul was on its way soon changed that. Stephen of Blois deserted after an argument with his fellow commanders and took his men with him. Those who remained were at risk of being caught between two enemy forces. It became crucial that Antioch be captured before the Muslim army arrived, so the leaders decided to storm the city.

## Crusaders invade Antioch

Bohemond had spies within the walls. One, Firouz, "a certain amir of the Turkish race," who commanded three towers, offered to betray the city. During the night of June 3, 1098, a party of 60 crusaders scaled the walls unopposed using a ladder provided by Firouz. Then they opened the closest gate and their Christian colleagues flooded into Antioch.

Fulcher of Chartres recorded what happened next: "When the Turks saw the Franks running through the streets with naked swords and wildly killing people… they began to flee. The Greek and Armenian Christians in the city joined in and the city became a bloodbath as the Christians massacred every Turk trapped within the walls. By nightfall it was all over, and all the streets of the city on every side were full of corpses… nor could one walk in the paths and

alleys except over the bodies of the dead." The governor was killed by an Armenian shepherd and his head presented to Bohemond.

Apart from its main citadel, Antioch was in Christian hands, and just in time. Within days the besiegers were the besieged, as Atabeg's army surrounded the city. Provisions were low, the streets were full of bloated corpses that threatened disease, and the crusaders lost control of the harbor to Atabeg. Short of food and cut off from aid, the Christian host was left to its own devices. Any aid Emperor Alexius might have offered fizzled out after hearing Stephen of Blois' story and he decided any relief attempt was futile. As the *Gesta Francorum* recorded, "those profane enemies of God held us so enclosed that many died of hunger." The First Crusade looked like ending in Antioch.

**both pages:** The siege and taking of Antioch by Christian forces is documented in this French manuscript without favor. The crusaders surround the city, **facing, above,** and then sack and pillage, **frame below.** The frame above depicts the massacre of the infidel citizens, whose naked, slaughtered bodies were hung up, **below,** for all to see. This massacre would lead to wholesale Muslim retribution.

# The Capture of Edessa

**As the crusaders fought around Antioch, Baldwin of Boulogne invaded Christian Armenia. Leading a force of less than 80 knights, his target was the prosperous desert city of Edessa. The first conquest made by the crusaders on their own behalf in this "overseas" land was achieved at the expense of fellow Christians.**

**below:** "Crusaders Amazed at the Luxury of the Orient", 19th-century engraving by Gustave Dore. To Frankish eyes, used to a far lower level of sophistication, the splendor of the Muslim culture was often overwhelming. Over time, crusaders would become assimilated into the customs they observed.

Edessa (now Urfa) lay to the east of the Euphrates in the province of Mesopotamia. Armenia's richest and most prestigious city, it was a prize recently taken back form the Turks by an Armenian force. Reputed to be the birthplace of Abraham, the city had a large Christian population, who welcomed first their Christian Armenian liberators and then what they thought was a reinforcing column of western Christians, led by Baldwin of Boulogne, who had broken away from the main body of crusaders around Antioch (*see page 63*).

Captured in 1096, the Armenian garrison expected a Muslim army to attack them at any moment and their commander Prince Thoros needed Baldwin's help to defend the city. The crusaders were welcomed as liberators. Fulcher of Chartres recorded that "when we passed by the villages of the Armenians, it was astonishing to see them running toward us with crosses and standards, kissing our feet and garments most humbly for love of God, because they heard that we would defend them from the Turks."

Thoros was old, childless, and an Orthodox Christian. Baldwin insisted that Thoros adopt him as his son and heir, as security for both parties, to which Thoros agreed. A little over two weeks after the adoption ceremony, Thoros was killed during a riot, torn to pieces as he tried to escape through a palace window. Baldwin did nothing to protect the prince.

Almost certainly, Baldwin recruited the mob; Armenian and crusading chroniclers provide different versions of what happened. Fulcher of Chartres claimed the revolt was caused by a disagreement between the Greek Orthodox elements of the Christian population and those who wanted to retain their independence from the Byzantine Church and State. The majority of the Armenians were Monophysites and were therefore at odds with both the Orthodox and Catholic churches. Baldwin became the sole ruler of Edessa and its hinterland.

## Siding with the natives

In theory the Armenians owed a nominal allegiance to Byzantine Emperor Alexius, but Baldwin turned his back on this political nicety and proclaimed himself Count of Edessa. In effect he was his own man, independent of both his fellow princes and the Byzantines. Because Armenia was broken up into several petty states, all vying for power, Baldwin's position now became similar to that of the region's other Christian rulers.

The crusader force consisted of a mere 80 knights and perhaps 200 foot-soldiers—not much to hold a large city and state. To ensure his hold, Baldwin married an Armenian princess and used the vast treasury inherited

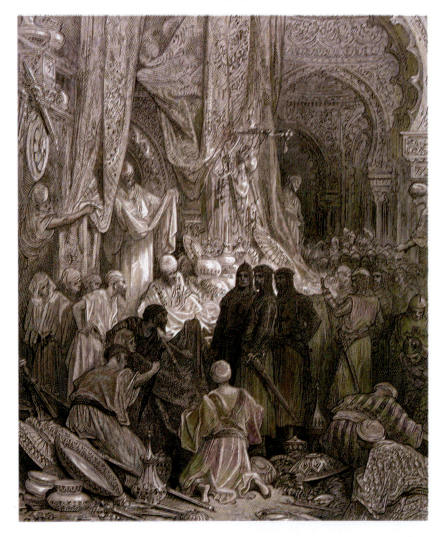

from Prince Thoros to bribe the nearest Muslim ruler. Although Edessa's independence would cause problems in the future, for the time being Baldwin's borders were secure.

His troops had won a kingdom. They had also penetrated further into Asia than any other Europeans since Alexander the Great. Baldwin of Boulogne became the first crusader to fulfil his dream of establishing a feudal realm. He was also the first prince to abandon his mission of recapturing Jerusalem. In his rich city astride the caravan routes into Persia, Baldwin ruled a population of Armenians, Jews, and Muslims with a religious tolerance that was at odds with his fellow crusaders. The new Count of Edessa had "gone native" and become assimilated into the local population. He supported the Armenian Church and he and his retinue adopted eastern ways. Strategically, both the Armenians and the County of Edessa would play a significant part in the development of the Crusader States. For both Byzantines and crusaders, Edessa provided a secure northern flank, a bulwark against their Muslim enemies. As such, the County would survive as a Crusader State for another half-century.

# The Holy Lance

**Trapped by their Muslim foe, the crusaders in Antioch saw little hope of survival. With their fortunes at their lowest ebb, a lowly crusader had a vision that an important relic was buried within the city. When the Holy Lance was found, crusader fervor was rekindled and the Christian army seemed invincible.**

When the Christians took Antioch, the city was already bereft of food and the crusaders had little enough of their own. According to the *Gesta Francorum*: "There was such a famine in the city that a horse's head without the tongue was sold for two or three solidi, the guts of a goat for five, and a hen for eight or nine." Around 20,000 crusaders and a surviving Christian populace of a similar size slowly starved. It was commonly held that to surrender would invite a massacre similar to the one they had inflicted on the Muslims only days

previously. The siege continued.

And then a peasant from Provençe named Peter Bartholomew had a vision. A servant in the southern French contingent, he was known for his unruly behavior and claimed to have had visions for the past month. This one was different. St. Andrew, he claimed, appeared to him in a dream to reveal that the Holy Lance, which had pierced Christ's side as he hung on the cross, was buried beneath the Church of St. Peter, within the walls of Antioch.

Bartholomew sought an audience with his lord, Raymond of Toulouse, and convinced the prince that he spoke truly. Raymond's colleagues doubted the vision's accuracy and Bartholomew's integrity, but when a respected priest also had a similar vision, it appeared that the story might have merit. Antioch buzzed with nervous anticipation while the church was cleared of

everybody but 12 men, including Peter Bartholomew and Raymond of Toulouse. Another member of the group, Raymond of Aguilers related that, "After we had dug from morning to evening and found nothing, some began to despair.... Then, when the youth Peter Bartholomew saw that we were worn out, he disrobed... and jumped into the pit in his shirt.... At length, the Lord was minded in His mercy to show us the Holy Lance.... What great joy and exultation that filled the city I cannot describe."

## A false relic?

The Muslim version of events was different. The Arab historian Ibn al-Athir wrote, "There was a holy man, a man of low cunning, who proclaimed that the Messiah had a lance buried.... Before saying this he buried the lance in a certain spot and concealed it." Whatever its provenance, the holy relic galvanized the crusaders and gave them a renewed belief in their own spiritual righteousness.

Days later, Peter Bartholomew had another vision. This time, St. Andrew urged the crusaders to fast for five days, then to ride out and attack the Turks. No further encouragement was required. With the Holy Lance in their possession, the troops would be invincible. On June 28, 1098, after a period of fasting in penance for their sins, the army emerged from Antioch to give battle.

With Raymond of Toulouse taken to his bed ill, Prince Bohemond commanded the crusaders. He divided them into six lines of battle, inspired by Bishop Adhemar who carried the Holy Lance. According to the *Gesta Francorum*: "when all our men were outside the city... we called upon the true and living God and charged against them... and with God's help we defeated them. The Turks ran in terror, and we pursued them, more eager for the chase than for the plunder."

The crusaders were unstoppable and Kerbuqua Atabeg's besieging army disintegrated. Internal political divisions had already weakened it and many of the Muslim sub-commanders refused to fight on behalf of Atabeg. To the crusaders, their victory was nothing short of a miracle. A rusty spearhead had been used to open the gateway to the Holy Land.

# On to Jerusalem

**An epidemic swept through Antioch as the Christian army prepared to leave. Bishop Adhemar was one of its victims. With his death, the princes became further disunited. Their disorganization delayed the Crusade's advance on Jerusalem for a further six months.**

While the army rested in Antioch, its leaders considered their next move. Prince Bohemond (as its captor) refused to relinquish his *de facto* control over the city and on August 1, 1098 Bishop Adhemar of Le Puy died of disease, probably typhoid. The epidemic that swept through the city encouraged several of the princes to launch raids into surrounding Muslim territories in a simultaneous search for healthier climes and profit. These territories included the rich city of Marra (now Ma'arrat), which fell on December 11.

Bishop Adhemar had been the one man capable of maintaining some degree of unity among the crusading leaders. When the various contingents returned to Antioch to celebrate the feast of Michaelmas (Christmas), unity of purpose seemed impossible. Raymond contested control of Antioch with Bohemond, and they also disagreed over their vows to the emperor.

The arrangements of their superiors were in disarray, but among the rank and file there was unity of purpose. As Raymond of Aguilers recorded: "Since the princes… are unwilling to lead us to Jerusalem, let us choose some brave knight in serving whom loyally we could be safe and, if it is the will of God, we will arrive in Jerusalem with this knight as our leader. If this great dispute about Antioch is continued longer, let us tear down its walls."

The pressure from below had its effect by forcing Bohemond and Raymond to settle their differences and present a unified front together with the other remaining princes. A deal was agreed and, in January 1099, Raymond of Toulouse led the Crusade onward southeast from Antioch toward Marra, while Bohemond of Taranto remained behind, undisputed ruler of Antioch and its environs. The second Crusader State had been forged. Bohemond's fiefdom would become known as the Principality of Antioch, but the crusaders were no closer to Jerusalem than they had been a year before.

## Holy City in sight

On January 13, Raymond burned Marra, after which there could be no turning back. "Invoking the compassion of God and the protection of the saints," Raymond led his men

**below:** Ruins of an ancient Roman aqueduct on the coast near Caesarea, Israel. As the crusaders moved south along the Mediterranean coast, they would have seen constant reminders of Roman dominion from earlier centuries.

south in bare feet, traveling as a pilgrim. It was 300 miles to the Holy City. The crusaders moved inland to capture the fortress of Hosn al-Akrad (Citadel of the Kurds), which would later become the site of the great crusader castle of Krak des Chevaliers. From there they marched to the port of Tripoli, joining up with a Norman contingent that had followed the coastal road from Antioch.

United again, the crusaders continued to Beirut, then south past the ports of Acre (Arqua) and Jaffa. They had now entered Fatimid Egyptian territory. Each city welcomed and feted the crusaders as they passed through. The Fatimids, who had held cordial relations

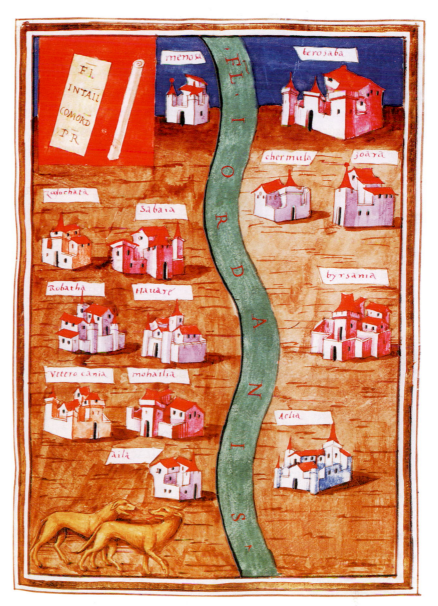

with Constantinople, even hoped to forge an alliance with the crusaders against their hated foe, the Seljuk Turks. It was a neutrality doomed to failure as the determination of the crusaders to take Jerusalem from the Fatimid Caliphate became clear.

The Crusade was finally nearing its goal. As they marched inland toward Jerusalem, Christian messengers arrived from Bethlehem, asking the crusaders to liberate the birthplace of Christ. "The following night a hundred of the truest soldiers mounted their horses… and hastened all the way to Bethlehem." The next day, Mass was said in the town. On June 7, 1099 the crusaders reached the top of a hill they named Montjoie and saw the Holy City of Jerusalem. After years of marching, they had arrived at the destination to which Pope Urban has dispatched them. All they had to do now was capture it.

**above:** A medieval map of Palestine shows the major crusader towns dotted in the landscape and the River Jordan bisecting Judea vertically.

# Jerusalem Besieged

**Of those who began their march to the Holy Land, less than 12,000 remained to stand before Jerusalem. The crusaders, although outnumbered by as much as five to one, laid siege around the extensive walls. With few provisions and plagued by summer heat, the task should have been impossible.**

The Fatimid Egyptian Governor of Jerusalem, Iftikhar al-Daula (Pride of the State) had done his job well. Warned of the crusaders' impending approach, he had gathered provisions into the city, filled the cisterns, and prepared his garrison of Arab and Sudanese infantrymen to resist any assault. The countryside around the city had been stripped of crops and livestock, farms and villages had been razed, and all the wells, pools, and streams had been deliberately poisoned or polluted.

The Fatimids had captured Jerusalem from the Seljuk Turks only the previous year. Now, the walls first laid down by the Roman Emperor Hadrian were repaired and strengthened. These defensive measures were of little concern to those on Montjoie hill. When the crusaders first saw the Holy City, there was "rejoicing and exulting, and they began to besiege the city in a marvelous manner."

It took little time, however, to realize the immensity of the task before them. Raymond of Aguilers reported that "according to our estimate and that of many others, there were 60,000 fighting men within the city…. At the most we did not have more than 12,000 able to bear arms, for there were poor people and many

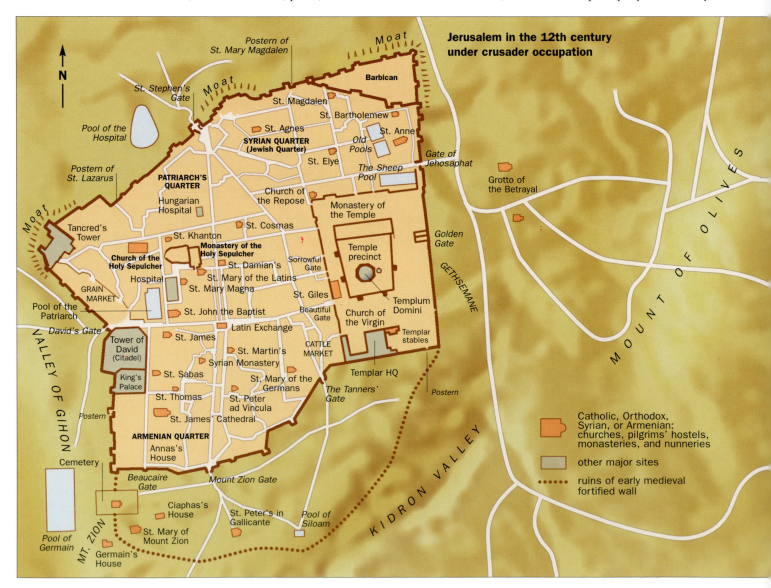

Jerusalem in the 12th century under crusader occupation

sick. There were 12 or 13 hundred knights in our army, as I reckon it, not more. I say this that you may realize that nothing, whether great or small, that is undertaken in the name of the Lord can fail." His blind faith was typical of the views held by the crusaders. After traveling so far, it seemed inconceivable that they would fail. This self-belief was to win them a kingdom.

## A makeshift assault

The siege of Jerusalem began on June 8, 1099, the day after the crusaders arrived in front of the city. Antioch had taken over seven months to capture. Jerusalem fell in five weeks. First, siege lines were established. Duke Godfrey and the Counts of Flanders and Normandy besieged the city from the north side, Count Raymond approached on the west. The crusaders then pondered their next move. With the land about laid to waste and over-extended supply lines, it was impossible to sustain the army for several months outside the walls. The princes agreed that there was no option but to launch an assault.

Raymond of Aguilers recounts, "It happened one day that some of the leaders of the army met a hermit on the Mount of Olives, who said to them: If you will attack the city tomorrow till the ninth hour, the Lord will deliver it into your hands." The crusaders had no siege towers or ladders but they considered the hermit's pronouncement an omen and prepared to attack the following morning. Ladders were hastily constructed during the night and at dawn on June 13 assault began. Against overwhelming odds, the crusaders gained a foothold on the top of the outer walls and the defenders were forced back. However, Fatimid forces rallied and repulsed the attack. Demoralized, the crusaders retreated to their camps.

The Christian army's low morale improved when a squadron of ships sailed into Jaffa with supplies and siege materiel. A column was sent to Jaffa and the supplies were brought to Jerusalem, together with the sailors, their ropes, and tools. Wood was gathered and the crusaders set to work to build real siege ladders, siege towers, and trebuchets; all the paraphernalia needed to conduct a proper assault.

When news of the imminent arrival of a relieving Fatimid force reached the crusaders, Raymond of Toulouse, who understood only too well what it would take to keep an army in the field with doubtful supply lines, realized they had one last chance to assault the city before the army would have to retreat to the coast to avoid being attacked from behind. This final assault was set to begin on July 13.

**above:** The Tower of David stands against Jerusalem's western wall of the Old City. A citadel (city fortress) had stood here since Roman times. Although the crusaders faced formidable defenses at Jerusalem, their weakest point was the citadel, which had been allowed to fall into disrepair during the peaceful period of Arabic occupation. It was rebuilt and considerably strengthened by the crusaders and then further enlarged by the Mamluks.

# Fall of the Holy City

**By July 1099, the crusaders were short of men and supplies… and almost out of time. A large Egyptian relief army was on its way and the crusaders had to assault the city or retreat to the coast. Drawing on their last reserves of faith and strength, they prayed, fasted, and then stormed the walls. After two days of heavy fighting, Jerusalem fell into Christian hands.**

you do not, all the evils that you have suffered will be multiplied by the Lord." Ever willing to accept divine guidance, the crusaders complied. The fasting began immediately.

On July 8 the defenders were amazed to see bishops and priests leading a barefoot procession of crusaders around the

**right:** The siege of Jerusalem as depicted in the *Histoire* by Guillaume de Tyre (Archbishop William of Tyre). In the foreground on the right a trebuchet catapult can be seen. In the center, crusaders use scaling ladders, while the image of Christ looks on from high on the battlements.

On July 6 a crusader received a visitation from the late Bishop Adhemar, who urged the crusaders to "purge yourselves of your uncleanness, and let each one turn from his evil ways. Then, with bare feet, march around Jerusalem invoking God and you must also fast. If you do this, and then make a great attack on the city on the ninth day, it will be captured. If

walls of the city. The garrison's jeers were met by trumpet blasts and prayers. When the supplicants reached the Mount of Olives the bishops asked each man to forgive his fellow brothers. According to Raymond of Aguilers, "All were reconciled to each other, and with generous offerings we besought the mercy of God, that he should not now desert His people,

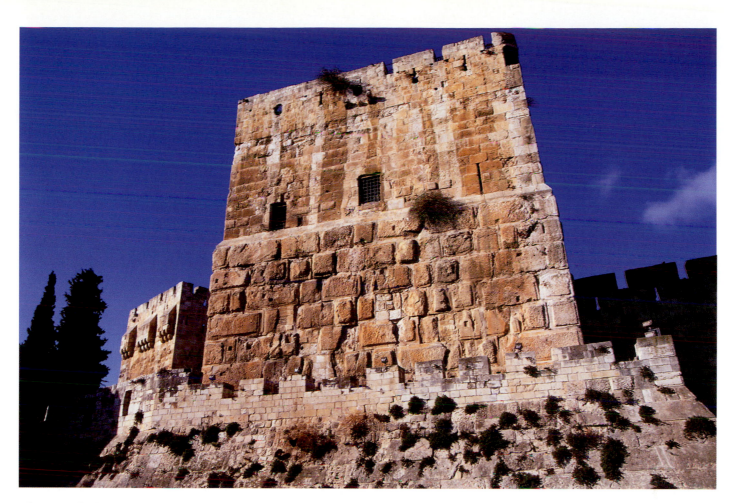

whom He had led so gloriously and miraculously to this goal." The crusaders had several more days to wait and used the time to complete their siege towers. Godfrey was to attack the northern wall and Raymond the southern wall.

During the following night of July 13/14, the siege engines were moved into place as either side hurled a barrage of missiles at the other. At dawn on July 15, the appointed moment came, and although the towers were badly damaged and burned, the structures held and had reached the city walls on two sides.

## A bloody victory

"When the hour approached… our knights began to fight bravely in one of the towers, namely the part with Duke Godfrey and his brother Count Eustace. One of our knights, named Lethold, clambered up the wall of the city, and no sooner had he ascended than the defenders fled from the walls and through the city." The crusaders had established a foothold on Jerusalem's northern wall.

Almost simultaneously Raymond of Toulouse and his men clambered onto the southern wall, forcing the defenders back toward the citadel known as the Tower of David. As Godfrey's men opened the Damascus Gate, Iftikhar took refuge in the citadel, where he parleyed for his life. Raymond took the payment and escorted the general and his garrison from the city. Other non-Christians were not so fortunate.

Muslims were cut down, irrespective of gender or age. Entering the al-Aqsa mosque, the crusaders slew everyone they encountered, including "a large number of Imams and Muslim scholars… who had left their homeland to live lives of pious seclusion in the Holy Place." The Jewish population took refuge in the city's principal synagogues, but the victorious Christians had little time for religious niceties. The synagogues were burned to the ground and those inside were immolated in the fires. The slaughter continued until only Christians remained alive in Jerusalem. Bishop Daimbert of Pisa wrote to the Pope, saying: "If you desire to know what was done with the enemy who were found there, know that in Solomon's Porch and in his Temple our men rode in the blood of Saracens up to the knees of their horses." As the *Gesta Francorum* recorded, "The army scattered throughout the city and took possession of the gold and silver… and the houses, filled with goods of all kinds." The crusaders had achieved the impossible, and perpetrated what was the worst massacre of the crusading era.

**above:** To weary crusader eyes, the formidable fortifications around Jerusalem would have appeared insurmountable. In fact, they were taken in only five weeks.

# Journey's End?

**The fall of Jerusalem and the bloodletting that followed was accompanied by a conflict between secular and spiritual interests. The Crusade was as much a pilgrimage as it was a campaign of conquest, and while the crusaders savored the spiritual and temporal delights of their prize, they also had to decide what to do with the city they had captured.**

One of the richest cities of the Middle East lay at the crusaders' feet and "our men went into the houses of the citizens and seized whatever they could. The first to enter the house, whatever his position or rank, had the right to plunder it, and this was acknowledged by all the Franks." Those whose minds dwelt on more spiritual matters visited the holy places, in completion of the armed pilgrimage they had begun so long ago.

A week after the priests had walked barefoot around the walls and suffered the taunts of the garrison, and on the evening of their amazing victory, the princes walked in solemn procession through the streets of the Holy City. Their final destination was the Church of the Holy Sepulcher, the most holy spot in the holiest of cities. Just by touching the slabs where mourners had anointed the body of Christ, the crusaders believed that the sanctity of the place would be transferred to themselves. There they heard a Mass and gave thanks to God for their victory, and to the end of their pilgrimage.

The chronicler Raymond of Aguilers wrote, "Now that the city was taken it was well worth all our previous labors and hardships to see the devotion of the pilgrims at the Holy Sepulcher. How they rejoiced and exulted and sang a new song to the Lord! A new day, new joy, new and perpetual gladness… drew forth from all new words and new music. This day, I say, will be famous in all future ages. This day, I say, marks the justification of all Christianity, the humiliation of paganism, and the renewal of our faith. This is the day that the Lord hath made, let us rejoice and be glad in it."

## Choosing a feudal leader

The majority of the crusaders were in no doubt why they had made their journey, and although they reaped a rich reward by their victory, their spiritual war far outweighed any temporal advantages the capture of Jerusalem had brought. In an intensely devout age, the most devout men in Christendom had achieved what they had set out to do. The only real question was, what were they to do next?

As the corpses were cleared from the streets, word was sent back to Europe via Constantinople, Antioch, and Edessa. Reactions were mixed. Alexius, the Byzantine emperor, was disappointed that the crusaders had branched out on their own, abandoning their vows to him. The Patriarch of Jerusalem, who had helped the crusaders before Antioch, found his fellow Orthodox priests barred from Jerusalem's holy places, which were now seen as the exclusive preserve of the Latin Church. For the Muslims who had lost one of their holiest places, it was unthinkable that these infidels should be allowed to retain their prize. Pope Urban, who had set the Crusade in motion, died before the news of Jerusalem's capture reached Rome.

While many crusaders headed home, others realized that their future lay in the Orient and that they would have to defend the territory they had captured. This meant establishing feudal control over the Holy Land. The leaders decided who would rule Jerusalem and act as feudal superior to his fellow crusaders. Their first choice was Raymond of Toulouse, who declared he was not prepared to wear a crown in the place where Christ wore his crown of thorns. The next obvious candidate was Godfrey of Bouillon, who declined the rank of king. Instead, he accepted the more diplomatic title of Advocate (defender) of the Holy Sepulcher. The feudal hierarchy had been established and the Crusader States had come into being. The main concern now was whether they would survive.

**above:** Godfrey of Bouillon could have been the first king of Jerusalem, but declined in favor of a more modest title. Here, he is depicted riding on horseback wearing the "instruments of Christ's passion."

**facing:** The Church of the Holy Sepulcher, Jerusalem, depicted in a French book of hours from the 14th century.

# Creation of a Crusader Kingdom

**The captors of Jerusalem, Edessa, and Antioch joined forces with their Armenian allies to create a crusader kingdom, an alliance of four Crusader States, stretching from Antioch to Jerusalem and beyond. First, they had to consolidate their tenuous hold on the Holy Land and repel Muslim armies that were gathering around them.**

The spiritual delight that accompanied the capture of Jerusalem failed to unite the leaders of the various crusading factions. Prince Bohemond of Antioch and Count Baldwin of Edessa were unlikely to agree to any unification under the feudal banner of Godfrey, the Advocate of the Holy Sepulcher. Raymond of Toulouse was campaigning along the Jordan Valley and Tancred was busy besieging Nablus within a month of Jerusalem's capture. Godfrey remained in his capital to consolidate control over the city.

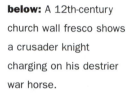

**below:** A 12th-century church wall fresco shows a crusader knight charging on his destrier war horse.

At the beginning of August 1099, word reached Godfrey that an Egyptian army was threatening to cut Jerusalem off from the coast. He summoned Raymond and Tancred and the crusader army marched out to meet the Muslims. Jerusalem was left in the hands of the clergy, whose spiritual defense was considered as effective as the power of the army.

The two armies met on the Plain of Ashod and the ensuing Battle of Ascalon was another demonstration of the crusaders' effectiveness. As the *Gesta Francorum* records, "our men entered into a beautiful valley near the coast and drew up their lines of battle... The pagans stood before us." The Frankish knights charged the enemy and "the Count of Normandy [Duke Robert], seeing the golden apple... that held the emir's standard, rushed straight to the bearer and gave him a mortal wound. The

Count of Flanders attacked from the other side, and Tancred charged straight into the middle of the enemy camp."

Egyptian commander Vizier al-Afdal and his army were caught completely unprepared by the ferocity of the crusaders' charge. The Egyptians waded out to sea to be rescued by their waiting fleet or sought refuge behind Ascalon's walls. The remainder, some 10,000 men, were cut down or drowned in the surf. The emir's standard was taken back in triumph and housed in the Church of the Holy Sepulcher. The fledgling crusader kingdom had been saved by a single cavalry charge.

## King of Jerusalem

The only remaining threat came from the north in the form of the Abbasid Caliph of Baghdad, al-Mustazhir. Refugees pleaded with him to attack the infidel but he lacked the military resources to do so. The Seljuk Turkish prince who ruled Baghdad was locked in a war with his brother, as were all the available troops. A counterattack to coincide with the Egyptian campaign should have had a high chance of success, since the handful of crusaders would be unable to meet two enemies in a pincer movement at the same time. At a time when one decisive blow might have prevented two centuries of Christian presence in the Holy Land, the Muslims of Syria were unable to counterattack. Due to Turkish inaction and political indifference to the fate of their co-religionists to the south, the opportunity was lost.

At this crucial moment a new papal representative, Bishop Daimbert, arrived to replace the late Bishop Adhemar. He was appointed to the patriarchy (archbishop) of Jerusalem, and in return for Tancred's political support, named him Prince Tancred of Galilee and confirmed Bohemond's position as Prince

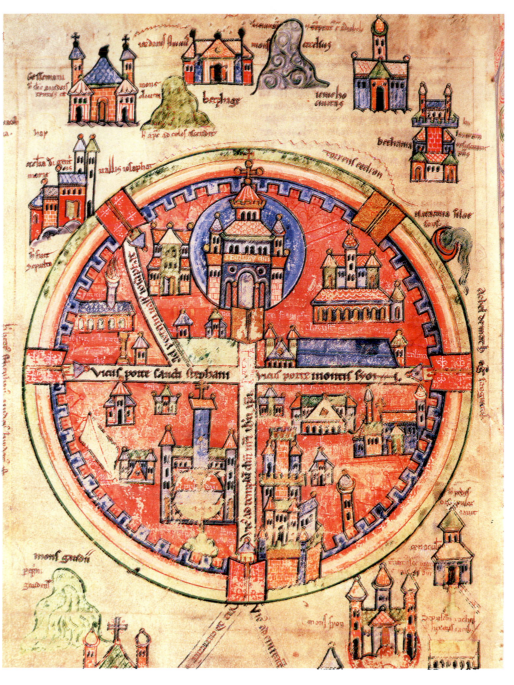

of Antioch. Godfrey considered this an affront but died before any serious division could take place. Godfrey's brother, Baldwin of Edessa, was prepared to march on Jerusalem and Bohemond was prepared to stop him. The bishop was playing two crusading princes against each other.

Fate intervened and Bohemond was captured by the Seljuk Turks, which left Baldwin free to seize power in Jerusalem. Unlike his brother, he had no compunction about being crowned. On Christmas Day 1100, Baldwin became the first Christian king of Jerusalem and uncontested leader of the Crusader States. A new kingdom had come into being.

**above:** Map of Jerusalem from Robert Monk's *Chronicle of the Crusades*, c.1099. The orientation has been turned through 90 degrees from the way a modern map would present it—in other words, North is positioned on the left. The Garden of Gethsemane and Mount of Olives are shown at the top.

# CHAPTER 4

# Outremer:

## Holy Kingdom

The [First] Crusade was completed. The Holy Land was liberated and the crusaders could go home. Instead, many stayed and created their own feudal domains in the Middle East. Surrounded by Muslim enemies, the Crusader States survived for almost two centuries, although this survival was often precarious. After 1100 crusaders protected Christian lands rather than holy sites. These lands were collectively known as Outremer, the lands over the sea. For many Christians, Outremer came to represent the rationale behind the crusading movement, the defense of a Christian state amid religious enemies.

The Kingdom of Jerusalem and its lesser companions, the Principality of Antioch, County of Edessa, and County of Tripoli, were created using the model of the feudal states of Europe but adapted to suit the requirements of the Holy Land. Godfrey of Bouillon was elected Advocate of the Holy Sepulcher, a suitable title for a lay defender of Church property. He died within a year to be succeeded by his brother, Baldwin Count of Edessa, who had no reservations about calling himself king of Jerusalem. When he was

crowned on Christmas Day, 1100, he became the *de facto* head of a feudal state, not a mere defender of the Church.

For much of the period, Outremer existed on the verge of extinction. During the 12th century Muslim opposition to the crusaders hardened and they faced near constant harassment, blockade, and invasion. With acute manpower shortages, the rulers of the Crusader States relied on a combination of fortifications, to defend their frontiers, and fresh waves of crusaders, who helped to defend Outremer. Although not a particularly rich land, Outremer developed into a thriving community, a link between East and West. Despite its collapse in 1187, Outremer survived for another century, and even after the fall of Acre in 1291 crusader outposts survived in the Aegean basin.

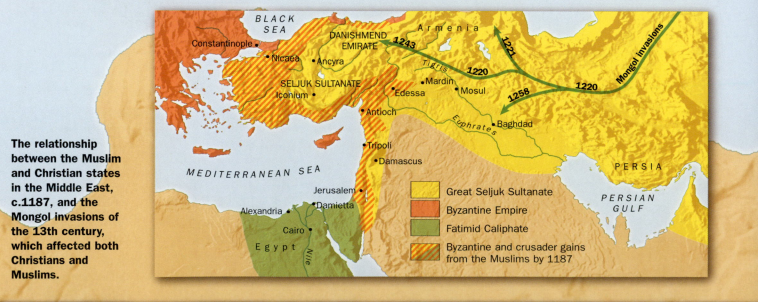

**The relationship between the Muslim and Christian states in the Middle East, c.1187, and the Mongol invasions of the 13th century, which affected both Christians and Muslims.**

Great Seljuk Sultanate

Byzantine Empire

Fatimid Caliphate

Byzantine and crusader gains from the Muslims by 1187

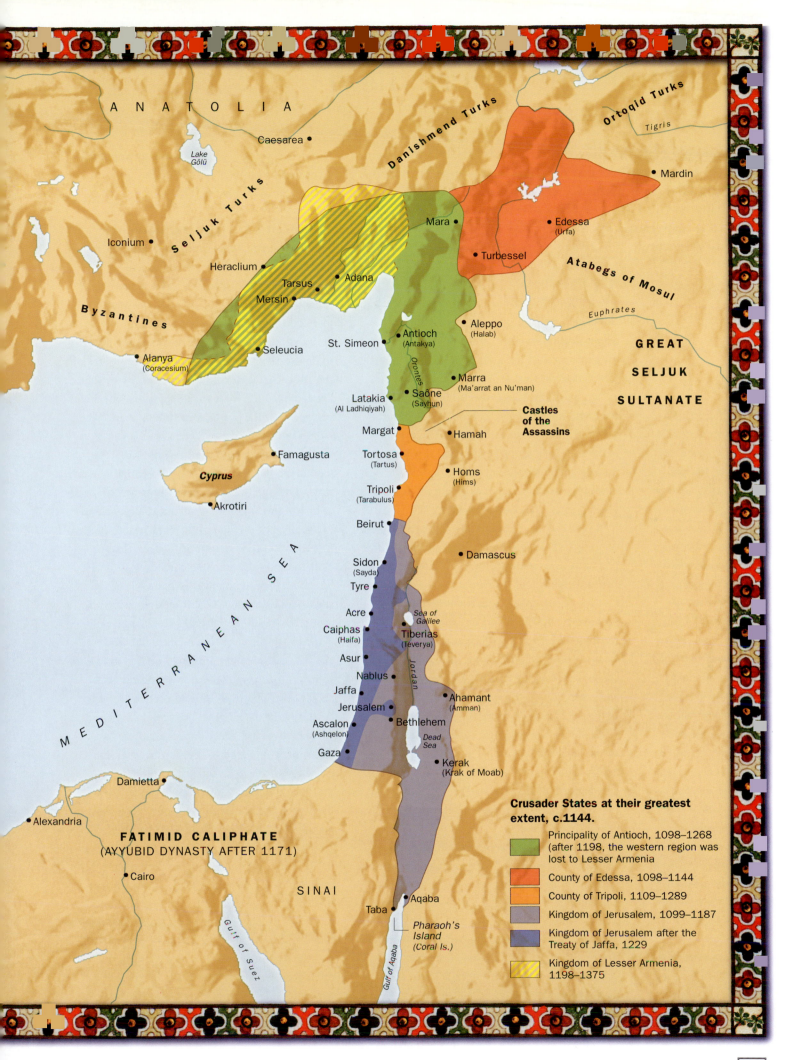

ANATOLIA

Caesarea

Lake
Gölü

Danishmend Turks

Ortoqid Turks

Tigris

• Mardin

Seljuk Turks

Iconium •

Heraclium •

Tarsus •

Mersin •

• Adana

Mara •

• Edessa
(Urfa)

• Turbessel

Atabegs of Mosul

Byzantines

Alanya •
(Coracesium)

• Seleucia

St. Simeon •

Antioch •
(Antakya)

• Aleppo
(Halab)

Euphrates

GREAT

SELJUK

Famagusta •

Cyprus

Akrotiri •

Latakia •
(Al Ladhiqiyah)

Margat •

Tortosa •
(Tartus)

Tripoli •
(Tarabulus)

Beirut •

Orontes

Saône •
(Sayhun)

• Marra
(Ma'arrat an Nu'man)

Castles
of the
Assassins

• Hamah

• Homs
(Hims)

SULTANATE

Sidon •
(Sayda)

Tyre •

Acre •

Caiphas •
(Haifa)

Asur •

Nablus •

Jaffa •

Jerusalem •

Ascalon •
(Ashqelon)

Gaza •

MEDITERRANEAN SEA

Sea of
Galilee

Tiberias •
(Teverya)

Jordan

Bethlehem •

Dead
Sea

• Damascus

• Ahamant
(Amman)

• Kerak
(Krak of Moab)

Damietta •

• Alexandria

FATIMID CALIPHATE
(AYYUBID DYNASTY AFTER 1171)

Cairo •

SINAI

Taba •

Gulf of Suez

Gulf of Aqaba

• Aqaba

Pharaoh's
Island
(Coral Is.)

**Crusader States at their greatest
extent, c.1144.**

Principality of Antioch, 1098–1268
(after 1198, the western region was
lost to Lesser Armenia

County of Edessa, 1098–1144

County of Tripoli, 1109–1289

Kingdom of Jerusalem, 1099–1187

Kingdom of Jerusalem after the
Treaty of Jaffa, 1229

Kingdom of Lesser Armenia,
1198–1375

# The Kingdom of Jerusalem

**On hearing of his brother Godfrey's death in Jerusalem, Baldwin had to politic and fight his way south to reach the Holy City and claim the crown Godfrey had wanted to belong to the Church. His coronation not only created a new kingdom, it also ushered in a new era in crusading history.**

**facing:** The severest problem for leaders of the First Crusade was manpower. The first battles had to be fought with the retinues who traveled to Byzantium and on into Asia. When the number of troops declined through death in battle, the crusaders were unable to easily replenish them. While fresh troops had a long, dangerous overland or sea journey to reach Outremer, the Muslims had an inexhaustible supply of eager warriors to draw from. This quite badly damaged fragment from an 11th-century manuscript shows an armed force preparing to meet a Muslim army. The commander on the left is the only one wearing a full suit of armor, probably reflecting the difficulty Outremer had in obtaining and replacing armor at such a distance from traditional supply sources.

When Baldwin I (r.1100–18) created the Kingdom of Jerusalem, his realm was threatened by Fatimid Egyptian (Saracen) armies from the south, who launched three invasions against the kingdom in just five years. The crusaders were helped by ships from the Italian maritime cities, who brought supplies, men, and a willingness to fight in return for a lucrative foothold in the Middle Eastern markets. While the Venetians had secured a trading agreement with Constantinople, rival maritime city-states such as Pisa and Genoa saw Outremer as a land of opportunity.

As the coastal cities fell into Christian hands, not only did the Muslims lose their bases, but they were also unable to stem the flow of reinforcements into the kingdom. Nevertheless, the lack of manpower was becoming a serious problem for Baldwin and one that would continue to plague his successors. A Second Crusade had been organized in Europe, consisting of all the knights and retainers who had taken vows but missed the start of the First Crusade. These reinforcements entered Anatolia in three separate columns, each defeated in turn by the local Turks, who were reinforced by large Seljuk armies sent from Baghdad and Aleppo. The handful of fresh crusaders who survived eventually found their way to Jerusalem and joined the defenders.

The Kingdom of Jerusalem and the other Crusader States in the Middle East were created through an unplanned consequence of events following the capture of the Holy City. The crusaders were also pilgrims and, having reached Jerusalem, they achieved the redemption of their sins that they desired. Divine Grace had, they believed, manifested itself in their favor and many wanted to remain in the land where God had blessed them. This developed into the notion that death in defense of the Holy Sepulcher would provide a virtual guarantee of ascension to Heaven and therefore the attainment of everlasting bliss.

## Creating feudal realms

In a devout age, when human life was short and brutal, religious considerations were of paramount importance. Men like Raymond of Toulouse or Godfrey of Bouillon originally planned to return home but after the "miraculous" capture of Jerusalem they decided to devote their remaining years to the service of the Holy Sepulcher. The Crusader States were created as much for a spiritual ideal as for any baronial lust for power, a fact often overlooked by modern historians.

In order to defend their newly-won territories, the crusaders had to organize their state. The only way they knew how was to impose a feudal structure over the Holy Land. Naturally, not all the crusaders shared the lofty spiritualism of Raymond or Godfrey. Prince Bohemond of Taranto considered himself the feudal and social superior of many of his fellow crusaders, and when he created his own realm around Antioch, he naturally made it a principality. Similarly his nephew Tancred claimed that his territorial acquisitions in Galilee formed a principality. Other crusading nobles such as the Count of Toulouse retained the term "county" for their feudal possessions.

There was a distinct danger that territorial divisions would lead to division between the crusading leaders, which would hinder the mutual defense of Outremer. Whether they liked it or not, the princes needed some form of overall control. When Baldwin I had himself crowned, he came to a title with roots set deep in the Bible. Previous kings of Jerusalem included Solomon and David—Baldwin had inherited a regal title with a spiritual weight unknown to European monarchs. The people of Israel had been ruled by a king of Jerusalem and the new king would remove any Jewish inference by adding the phrase "of the Latins" to the title. The Church approved the title but reminded Baldwin of his moral and spiritual obligations as a Christian monarch.

# Kings of Outremer in the 12th Century

**Throughout the 12th century, the kings of Jerusalem retained the pretence of ruling over all of Outremer. In reality, they had little influence over the northern Crusader States and the court was divided by factional fighting and dynastic squabbling.**

**facing:** An illumination of the early 14th century depicts a battle between Christian knights and Muslims. Many such illustrations accompanied popular books on the Crusades. The portrayal of the unarmored and turbaned Muslims is inaccurate, since they also wore body armor like the knights. Note that the many severed heads lying on the ground belong to the Muslims—a sure indication of the Christian origins of this illustration.

Even before the capture of Jerusalem, the crusaders were divided along national or regional lines. The Italian Normans followed Bohemond of Taranto, the southern Franks supported Raymond of Toulouse, and Godfrey of Bouillon's supporters came from Lorraine and Brabant. It was difficult for these men to appoint a king from among their peers, let alone someone from a different regional contingent.

Godfrey, and after him Baldwin I, had limited control over the other princes and consequently his influence outside the kingdom was often limited. The Kingdom of Jerusalem adopted the Frankish feudal hierarchy based on hereditary succession. The monarch's most immediate descendants succeeded him (or close relatives), but the Church stepped in to examine the claims of rivals if there was no obvious choice. It was the Church that then selected the heir.

The weakness of this system was apparent when succession went to infant kings governed by a regent. Relatives were ostracized, favorites raised, and inevitable conflict ensued, leading to a weakening of central authority. Surrounded by foes, this form of feudal government would prove fatal in Outremer. And so the courts of the Crusader States had more in common with the Byzantine Empire, where constantly changing alliances between the nobles kept the situation fluid.

Baldwin I's reign was marked by his consolidation of the coastal regions, which were still mostly in Muslim hands. He also repulsed several invasions by Fatimid Egyptians. When the childless Baldwin's death came during a raid into Egypt, the throne was claimed by his brother Eustace, Count of Boulogne, and his cousin Baldwin of Bourg, who had succeeded Baldwin as Count of Edessa. Eustace was in Europe so Baldwin secured the crown.

## The Baldwin dynasty

Baldwin II (r.1118–31) never trusted those who sided against him, and with good reason. When he was captured by Seljuk Turks (1123–4), rival nobles plotted to replace him with Charles, Count of Flanders. When he negotiated his own release, Baldwin secured his succession by marrying-off his eldest daughter Melisende to Fulk, Count of Anjou. Fulk duly succeeded Baldwin in 1131, but his favoritism for members of his entourage alienated the nobility of Outremer, including his wife.

When Fulk died in 1143, Melisende ruled as regent in the name of her young son, Baldwin III. Reluctant to relinquish her position of power, Melisende had to be forced from office by her son, who exiled her. Baldwin III died in 1163

and was succeeded by his younger brother, Almaric (also called Amaury, r.1163–73). Feuding in the dynasty weakened the influence of the crown in Outremer and none of these rulers was able to enforce their nominal overlordship on the rulers of Antioch, Tripoli, or Edessa.

Baldwin IV (r.1174–85)—one of the more accomplished rulers of Outremer—contracted leprosy and became unable to contain the undercurrent of dynastic scheming that was a constant byzantine feature of the Jerusalem court. Because he was also childless, his sister

Sibylla's infant son succeeded him. Baldwin V only survived for a year, after which his mother Sibylla—jointly with her husband, Guy of Lusignan—seized the throne in 1186. This move alienated Guy from the other princes, most especially Count Raymond of Tripoli, to whom the throne had been promised. The division would prove fatal during the disastrous campaign against Saladin in 1187. Guy of Lusignan became King Guy I of Jerusalem (r.1186–92), and is perhaps best known as the man who lost the Holy City to the Muslims.

**below:** The old city of Jerusalem silhouetted against the sunset.

# The First Princes of Antioch

**In 1098, Prince Bohemond of Taranto became the first Prince of Antioch. Much of the following century involved a struggle for survival, with the princes devoting as much energy to fighting off rivals and resisting the domination of Jerusalem as they did to their fight against the Muslim enemies who surrounded them.**

**below:** The Army Escorting Supplies, from a 14th-century manuscript. The securing of supply lines was to be the most formidable logistical problem faced by the crusaders. Even after securing Antioch, the principality faced seaborne attacks on crusader shipping from the Fatimid fleet. When food was available, there were too few men to protect the caravans.

Bohemond of Taranto had secured his principality by repudiating his crusaders' vows. Instead of driving Muslims from Jerusalem, he created his own feudal realm. Although his fellow Norman Italian knights supported him, his actions incurred the resentment of the other crusading princes.

On one of his several raids into the surrounding regions, Bohemond was captured by Turks in the summer of 1100 and his nephew Tancred became regent. When Bohemond was released in exchange for a substantial ransom three years later, he left Tancred in charge of the principality while he returned to Italy to raise reinforcements. There, he died and his three-year-old son succeeded him. As an infant, Bohemond II remained in Italy and Tancred

continued as regent until his death in 1112.

The regency then passed to Tancred's cousin, Roger of Salerno. He took power at a dangerous moment. Ilghazi, the Emir of Mardin, had recently also become Emir of Aleppo. A skilled military commander, Ilghazi joined forces with the Emir of Damascus to raise an army and invade the Principality of Antioch. King Baldwin II of Jerusalem raced to support Roger, but on June 28, 1119, 15 miles from Aleppo, the Seljuks surrounded the regent's crusaders.

It was a massacre. According to Muslim chronicler Ibn al-Qalanisi, "in less than an hour, the Franks were all lying dead." Christian sources suggest that only 20 crusaders escaped to return to Antioch. Among the dead was Roger of Salerno. To the remaining knights of Outremer, the battle became known as *Ager Sanguinus* (Field of Blood). This disaster highlighted the crusaders' acute manpower shortage. They could not afford to lose men. The Muslims had an unlimited supply of men eager to fight the infidels.

With its forces slaughtered, Antioch lay wide

open. The principality's merchants and clerics formed themselves into militias to guard the city, while King Baldwin assumed direct control. Only division within the Seljuk alliance prevented the Muslims from pouring in, and although Ilghazi was the hero of Aleppo, he preferred to celebrate his victory rather than exploit it. He died three years after the battle, allegedly from the effects of alcohol.

## Alliance with Byzantium

In October 1126, 15 years after his father's death, Bohemond II arrived in Antioch. Baldwin II welcomed the young prince, but required him to marry his daughter Alice. This secured a union between the kingdom and the principality, but four years later Bohemond II lay dead at the hands of the Turks, a present of his head made to the Seljuk caliph in Baghdad. The loss was indicative of the rising tide of Muslim opposition against the crusaders; Outremer needed to unite to counter the Seljuk and Fatimid threat. Instead, the crusaders became embroiled in another squabble over succession.

There was a new king in Jerusalem, and when Alice tried to claim her husband's realm, Fulk I (r.1131–43) proclaimed himself regent of Antioch in the name of Alice's daughter, Constance. In 1136, the young princess was married to Raymond of Poitiers, one of Fulk's supporters. Raymond I retained control of Antioch until he was killed in the Battle of Fons Muratus (1149) by the forces of Nur ed-Din, the fabled Seljuk commander. Once again, the king of Jerusalem—now Baldwin III—became regent of a principality that had lost its ruler and its only army.

Baldwin prevented a military collapse and ruled the realm in the name of Constance until she married again in 1153. Her new husband, Reynald of Châtillon-sur-Loing, ruled the principality for eight years, until his capture by a Turkish raiding party in 1161. Princess Constance held onto Antioch by allying herself with the Byzantines. Her daughter Maria was married to Emperor Manuel I Comnenus (r.1143–80), who became the titular regent of Antioch, although Constance retained her grip on the realm in the name of her son-in-law. All this intrigue took its toll, while the two military defeats sapped Antioch's ability to defend itself.

**Major castles of the Military Orders in Outremer in the 13th century**
- ■ Knights Hospitaler
- ■ Templar Knights
- ■ Teutonic Knights
- ■ other castles/strongholds

Krak des Chevaliers
Akkar
Tripoli
Beirut
Litani
Sidon
Megedel
Beaufort (Belfort)
Damascus
Tyre
Subelba
Manawat
Sumeriya
Chastiau dou Rei
Montfort
Juddin
Chastelet
Safed
Acre
Doc
Tiberias
Sea of Galilee
Caiphas (Haifa)
Cave de Suethe
'Atlit
Sephorie
Recordane
Belvoir
Jordan
Sabarim
Qaqun
Letaria
Seleth (Shiloh)
Jaffa (Tel Aviv-Yafo)
Rentie
Taiybe al-Bira
Beit Dejan
St. John
Huldre
Jerusalem
Ascalon
Bothme
Deirnachar
Deirelcobebe
Dead Sea
Semsem
Agelon
Gaza
Tel Jemmeh
En Boqeq
Sharuhen
Raqiq
Kerak (Krak of Moab)
Subeita
Wadi al Hasa
Eboda
Tannur
NEGEV DESERT
Wadi al 'Arabah
Petra
Timna
Pharaoh's Island (Coral Island)
MEDITERRANEAN SEA

**Key to plan of Beaufort**
1. Arab fortress built between 1190–1240
2. glacis
3. two-story, 12th-century donjon
4. inner bailey gate
5. gate to crusader fortress
6. southern plateau
7. east bailey built by Arabs
8. River Litani

**Plan of Beaufort (Belfort):** The original stronghold was captured in 1139 by King Fulk of Jerusalem. He constructed a considerable castle, its east side guarded by the sheer drop into the River Litani. Beaufort was held by the Lords of Sidon until its capture by the Muslims in 1190. It was recovered in 1240 and handed to the Templars in 1260. They added a vaulted hall and protective walls on a plateau to the south. Unfortunately, this made a perfect raised base for catapults of the Mamluk Emir Beibars, who beseiged and captured Beaufort in 1268.

# The Counties of Edessa and Tripoli

**The counts of Tripoli and Edessa created two thriving feudal states in the Holy Land. Although closely linked to the rest of Outremer, they were jealous guardians of their independence. Like the rest of the Crusader States, these small provinces existed in the shadow of Muslim neighbors.**

**above:** The Syrian plain lying below Tripoli, Lebanon—a landscape that countless armies have battled over for centuries past. For the crusaders, this land represented all the wealth and power they had been seeking since leaving Europe.

Edessa became the seat of the County of Edessa in 1098, when the Armenian city was seized by Baldwin of Boulogne (*see pages 66–7*). When he became the first king of Jerusalem two years later, he handed the province to his cousin, Baldwin of Le Bourg. Eighteen years later, Baldwin secured the throne in Jerusalem following the death of his brother. As King Baldwin II he handed Edessa to the Courtnays, a Frankish family from the Gâtinais region.

Joscelin I (r.1119–31), first Courtnay Count of Edessa, was succeeded by Joscelin II, who lost the city to Seljuk Turks in 1144. He made his new capital in Turbessel, a town roughly halfway between Edessa and Antioch. Five years later he was in a Turkish prison in Aleppo. What remained of his fiefdom became the responsibility of his wife, Beatrice, who had little option but to hand it over to the Byzantines in return for their protection from the Turks.

In 1148 the drama of the Second Crusade played itself out in front of Damascus, and with the failure of this crusading impetus any immediate chance to recapture Edessa was lost. Countess Beatrice and her children withdrew to the relative safety of the court in Jerusalem. Meanwhile, the Armenians in and around Edessa remained subjects of the Seljuk Turks.

## Dividing Tripoli

The story of the County of Tripoli is an entangled skein of internecine feuds and short-term rulers. In 1102, following his rejection of the offer of the crown in Jerusalem, Raymond of Toulouse adopted the new title Count of Tripoli. The port city was still in Muslim hands and although the count besieged it, Tripoli was still Muslim by the time of his death three years later. His widow and younger son, Alphonse, returned to Toulouse and the surviving leaders of the southern Frankish contingent elected their late leader's cousin as their new feudal commander. William Jordan, Count of Cerdagne, became Count of Tripoli only to have the position contested by Raymond's eldest son, Bertrand.

Asked to mediate, King Baldwin I was also attempting to resolve the claim of Bohemond's nephew, Tancred, to the County of Edessa. He came up with a complicated solution. This involved dividing Tripoli between William and Bertrand in return for Bertrand becoming the king's vassal. At the same time, in return for renouncing his claim to Edessa, Tancred became Count William's feudal overlord.

Tripoli fell in 1109 after a five-year siege, and William was killed shortly afterward in mysterious circumstances. Tancred was now forced to accept Bertrand's son, Pons, to become his vassal in replacement of William, but in reality it was Bertrand and Pons who ruled the entire county. In 1137, shortly after Bertand's death, Seljuks killed Pons, and Tripoli accepted Bertrand's brother Count Raymond II (r.1137–52), despite the claim by Raymond of Toulouse's youngest son, Alphonse, that he was the rightful heir.

When a terrorist sect of Muslims known as the Assassins murdered Raymond, Alphonse's 12-year-old son became Count Raymond III and ruled Tripoli until he was captured by Turks. He remained in captivity in Damascus from 1164 to 1172 and King Amalric of Jerusalem (r.1163–73) ruled the county as his regent. On his release, Raymond regained his position and ruled Tripoli until his defeat at the Battle of Hattin (1187).

Raymond III had proved to be a competent leader during the period when he acted as regent for the bed-ridden and dying leper king, Baldwin IV of Jerusalem. His period in captivity had given him a better understanding of the Muslims, whom he saw more as neighbors than enemies. Unjustly accused of treachery and blamed for the catastrophe of Hattin (*see pages 118–9*), Raymond was branded a traitor, forced from office, and died months later, a broken man. If King Guy of Jerusalem had listened to his advice at Hattin, Outremer might have survived the collapse of its frontiers after the battle.

**below:** A shaded walkway runs beside one of several ceremonial pools and mosques that surround the castle in the ancient Mesopotamian city of Edessa. The city was the seat of the Counts of Edessa, and was renamed Urfa in the 15th century.

# The Feudal Economy of Outremer

**The new Latin elite of the Holy Land had imported the Frankish feudal system that worked well in Europe. In Outremer, it was quickly perceived, something more flexible would be required to handle the mixed indigenous population while at the same time coping with the dire shortage of trained knights.**

**below:** Peasants working on vines, c.1160. In feudal Europe, knightly wealth relied on serfs working the land. In Outremer, there were few peasants (those that might have been used having been slaughtered in the Peasants' Crusade). Eventually, in a form of colonial feudalism, the indigenous population was drafted to tend olive groves and vineyards.

Outremer was created at a time when the feudal system was changing. Ties of dependence between various ranks within the feudal structure were becoming more flexible, and the growth of towns and commerce was changing the nature of Europe's early medieval economy. There were also variations in the implementation of feudalism between the north and south of Europe, and since the crusaders came from both regions, this difference became noticeable overseas.

The Kingdom of Jerusalem, Principality of Antioch, and counties of Tripoli and Edessa operated independently of each other, in a similar way to European kingdoms. But, unlike their European counterparts, in Outremer each had to rely much more on its neighbors for mutual defense against mutual enemies. Even the Church was divided between the patriarchal centers of Jerusalem and Antioch, so—in comparison to Europe—there was no effective spiritual system that spanned all the states.

Although the Kingdom of Jerusalem had no political grounds for claiming a feudal preeminence over the other states, the Counts of Edessa offered feudal homage. It was King Baldwin I who had presented the county to its ruling family when he became king. Although the first Counts of Tripoli offered homage to the king, part of the realm came under the political influence of the neighboring Principality of Antioch when Tancred became the feudal overlord for the northern section of the county. Through political maneuvering, a series of Kings of Jerusalem retained direct feudal suzerainty over the southern portion of the realm.

At first, the Princes of Antioch were fiercely independent and resented any interference from Jerusalem. This changed after several

...TAT · VINEAM · SEPEM · CIRCVDAT · FODIT

calamitous reverses on the battlefield where the Kings of Jerusalem had to intervene to prevent the principality from falling to the Muslims. After the battle of the Field of Blood (*see pages 86 & 97*), King Baldwin II exercized the right to control who succeeded to the princely seat. He ensured that the new princes would pay homage to him, substantiating his feudal pre-eminence over them. In return the king offered the protection afforded by his army.

## Distorting the system

In Outremer, the European pattern, where a leading noble held a tract of land as a fief of the king, was not usually followed. Instead, feudal bonds were imposed through oaths of fealty and homage, in return for mutual protection at critical times. In 1122 Count Pons of Tripoli revolted against the feudal overlordship of the king. The rebellion was crushed and the pre-eminence of King Baldwin II firmly re-established.

Further down the feudal ladder, lesser knights had little to gain in the defense of rival crusading kingdoms. Joint military ventures

were therefore only possible in times of grave crisis, when all of Outremer was threatened. In their stead, lesser nobles and knights were responsible for the direct administration of the feudal economy, through agricultural production within their fiefs and the gathering of taxes in the cities on behalf of their feudal overlords.

Experience showed that in order to reap the full economic benefits of their domains, crusading nobles would have to adapt their methods to suit the requirements of the Middle East. Non-Latin regional administrators appeared as the 12th century progressed, and particularly in the cities, Greek, Armenian, and even Arab administrators became common. While the Latin feudal elite maintained a stance of social superiority over the heterogeneous population, in time they became more of a military elite and left the administration of the Crusader States to clerics and professional non-Latin managers. This led to non-Latin influences in feudal administration. Without intending to, the princes gradually adapted the feudal system in Outremer to suit the Holy Land and its population.

**above:** Fishermen on a river bank, from a Mamluk manuscript of c.1350. One fishes with a net, while the other holds a water bag over his shoulder to carry the fresh fish to market. The Umayyad and Abbasid dynasties had promoted good agricultural practices throughout the Muslim world. The Seljuk Turks continued the work, even improving Anatolia's husbandry, ruined by years of Byzantine indifference. The crusades brought further ruination to Palestine. Eventually, the Crusader States adopted a more flexible approach that incorporated the best skills of local people.

# CHAPTER 5

# Jihad:
## The Islamic Response

At the start of the 12th century, the Muslim world was reeling from the effects of the crusaders' invasion of Syria, Palestine, and the fall of Jerusalem. When Jerusalem was captured the Muslim population was slaughtered without mercy. In 1109, the crusaders took Tripoli and destroyed the great Arabic library of Dar al-Ilm, one of the treasures of the Muslim world. Similar stories of massacre, eviction, and barbarism reached the remaining Islamic cities as tens of thousands of refugees fled from the Holy Land.

Viewed by the Muslim world as the successor to Mohammed, the Caliph of Baghdad came under increasing pressure to unite the Muslim factions in a *jihad* (holy war) in the name of Islam. The peaceable caliph had tried to follow a conciliatory path, as had the Seljuk Turkish sultan who was the main political power in the Muslim world. For the next two decades, while Muslim opposition to the Christians hardened, the pressure to launch a *jihad* intensified.

In response, a series of regional emirs took matters into their own hands. Under Ilghazi, Emir of Mardin, a Muslim army won a major victory over the Franks. The emir's nephew, Balak, and Imad ed-Din Zengi became the next true champions of Islam. Under the leadership of Zengi and the saintly Nur ed-Din, Muslim armies captured Edessa and defeated the Frankish

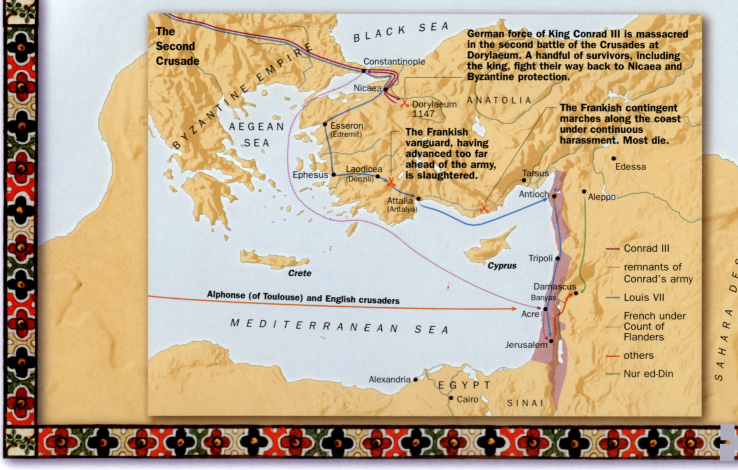

**The Second Crusade**

BLACK SEA

German force of King Conrad III is massacred in the second battle of the Crusades at Dorylaeum. A handful of survivors, including the king, fight their way back to Nicaea and Byzantine protection.

Constantinople

BYZANTINE EMPIRE

Nicaea

Dorylaeum 1147

ANATOLIA

Esseron (Edremit)

AEGEAN SEA

The Frankish vanguard, having advanced too far ahead of the army, is slaughtered.

The Frankish contingent marches along the coast under continuous harassment. Most die.

Ephesus

Laodicea (Denzili)

Tarsus

Edessa

Attalia (Antalya)

Antioch

Aleppo

Cyprus

Crete

Tripoli

Alphonse (of Toulouse) and English crusaders

Damascus

Banyas

Acre

MEDITERRANEAN SEA

Jerusalem

— Conrad III

∙∙∙∙ remnants of Conrad's army

— Louis VII

∙∙∙∙ French under Count of Flanders

— others

— Nur ed-Din

Alexandria

Cairo

EGYPT

SINAI

SAHARA DESERT

and Germanic crusaders of the Second Crusade.

For the first time Muslims began to unite in opposition to the crusaders of Outremer. Only the regional sect known as the Assassins had any dealings with the Franks as a new hard-line policy was adopted. There would be no more conciliation or co-habitation. From the mid-12th century onward, the Muslims fought a *jihad* that would end only when the last crusaders had been driven from their land.

Edessa
Aleppo
Antioch
Assassins
Tripoli
Beirut
Damascus
Acre
Jordan
Jerusalem
Ascalon
Dead Sea
MEDITERRANEAN SEA
Damietta
Pelusium
Tanis
Alexandria
EGYPT
Bilbeis
Cairo
NEGEV DESERT
SINAI
Gulf of Suez
Gulf of Aqaba
RED SEA
Day of Al-Babein 1167
Minya
Nile

**Key to crusader and Muslim campaigns in Syria and Egypt**

1. Imad ed-Din Zengi, Atabeg of Mosul campaigns to capture Aleppo, 1126–28.
2. 1128–34, Zengi campaigns against Antioch, attacks St. Symeon.
3. 1134–5, Zengi campaigns against the Assassins and King Fulk of Jerusalem.
4. Zengi marches on Edessa and besieges the city, taking it in 1144.
5. Zengi's son, Nur ed-Din marches to the successful relief of Damascus when Louis VII, Conrad III, and Baldwin III besiege the city, ending the Second Crusade.
6. King Almaric of Jerusalem's first invasion of Fatimid Egypt, 1163, only gets as far as Pelusium.
7. In response to deposed Fatimid vizir Shawar's call for aid, Nur ed-Din dispatches an army south.
8. The Turkish army refuses to leave Egypt. Shawar calls on King Almaric for help. The crusaders invade and catch up with the Turks at Bilbeis in 1164. The result is a stand-off and a treaty to leave Egypt alone.
9. Under Shirkuh's command, Nur ed-Din's army again marches south to invade Egypt. Met by Almaric, the two armies fight south along the Nile. Shirkuh turns back and becomes besieged in Alexandria.
10. Almaric's third invasion of Egypt. The king joins Shawar and fights the Zengid army in running battles down the Nile Valley, then pursues it to Alexandria in 1167.
11. In 1168, Almaric invades for the fourth time, takes Bilbeis and massacres the inhabitants.
12. Nur ed-Din's army marches south and joins forces with the Fatimid Egyptian army and forces Almaric to withdraw in 1169.
13. Crusader fleet invades by sea and takes Tanis late in 1168. The inhabitants are massacred.
14. Byzantine fleet joins Jerusalem in a joint attack on Damietta in October 1169.
15. Almaric's fifth invasion joins forces with the Byzantine fleet in October 1169 at Damietta. Despite having the land and sea aspects covered, the siege is unsuccessful.

# Jihad and Islamic Unity

**Many Muslims believed that a holy war was an archaic concept linked to the Arab conquests of the seventh century AD. However, in response to the Christian Crusade, there were Muslim leaders who felt it was time to resurrect the concept.**

The *jihad* is an extension of Islamic doctrine: by fighting the enemies of Islam, a warrior performs the will of Allah. In this medieval Islam and Christianity were similar— each faith offering spiritual blessings that outweighed any tribulations encountered by the soldier on earth. The first *jihad* was launched by the caliph, the successor of Mohammed. This resulted in the wave of Arab conquests which

Aleppo. He was a *ra'is* (equivalent to a mayor) and *qadi* (judge) and one of the most prominent men in the city. In the first decade of the Crusade, Aleppo found itself in the front line. At a time when the various Muslim states were divided and even at war, the crusaders were free to carve out a kingdom of "unbelievers" with little or no opposition. The result was large-scale disruption of the population, as thousands of survivors fled inland to Aleppo and Damascus.

A refugee from Marra recalled what happened when the crusaders captured the city in 1099: "I come from a town that Allah has condemned, my friend, to be destroyed. All the populations have died." Similar tales reached

carved out an Islamic empire in the sixth century AD and established the Muslim faith throughout North Africa, Egypt, the Middle East, Persia, and Central Asia.

By the start of the 12th century the concept of *jihad* was a 500-year-old relic of Islamic history. One of the first to take exception to this notion was Abu al-Fadl ibn al'Khashsab of

Aleppo from Jerusalem and Antioch, Tyre, and Tripoli. Ibn al'Khashsab became infuriated by the stories of crusader barbarity he heard from refugees. He was an Arab, rather than one of the ruling Seljuk Turkish nobility. While other Islamic peoples might hold the political reins in the Middle East, the Arabs regarded themselves as the guardians of Islamic beliefs and, more

The ruins of St. Symeon, **far left**, and the Great Mosque, **left**, summarize the city of Aleppo. The Christian church was built during the fifth century and dedicated to the hermit who squatted on top of a narrrow pillar to meditate. This region of Syria held onto its Christian beliefs even after the Arab invasions of the eighth century under the Umayyad dynasty, when the great Mosque at Aleppo was started. The First Crusade and its aftermath brought religious division to the old tolerance of the Middle East and ironically ensured the end of Christianity in the region—the opposite of Pope Urban's intentions.

particularly, Islamic will. Ibn al'Khashsab became the leading personality of a movement to force the Seljuk authorities to take military action against the crusaders. In 1111 he persuaded both the Caliph and the Sultan of Baghdad to gather an army to strike back.

## Division benefits the Franks

This was not the first military action taken by the Seljuks. A Turkish army under the command of Mawdud, Atabeg of Mosul, had already attacked Edessa, although not as part of a unified *jihad*. The local sultans and emirs remained wary of any holy war controlled by the religious and political authorities in Baghdad. In 1111, when Mawdud's army appeared at Aleppo, Emir Ridwan refused co-operation. In 1114, a second attempt at launching a *jihad* in Damascus ended in failure when the Emir of Damascus saw Mawdud as a threat to himself. Mawdud was assassinated and the emir then

signed a peace treaty with the crusaders in the following year.

Although the idea of a *jihad* was gaining popularity, the independent petty rulers of the Muslim world remained unconvinced of both the need for unity and the chances of military success. The upheaval caused by the crusaders' arrival was not universally felt across the vast and still largely unaffected Muslim world. To many, the Franks represented just another temporary reverse by an outside power. There was also reluctance to unleash a movement of religious fervor that the petty rulers might be unable to control.

Only when it became clear that the crusaders would only be defeated by concerted and long-term military action was the call for a *jihad* heeded. The Muslims needed a devout leader who could put aside regional suspicion and harness the *jihad* in a way that would benefit the entire Islamic world.

# The Emirs of Aleppo

**While the sultan and caliph in Baghdad tried to unite Islam in a holy war, the local Seljuk and Fatimid rulers of the Middle East attempted to defend their domains against the Frankish threat. It soon became clear that without a skilled military champion the Muslims would be unable to turn the tide.**

**below:** The citadel of Aleppo became one of the Muslims' strongest castles, dominating the city from its 160-foot steep-sided outcrop. Pictured are the stone glacis and massive gateway built by the Ayyubid Malik az'Zahir in 1203–4.

Although in theory the Seljuk Turks were united under the leadership of the Sultan of Baghdad, initial Muslim responses to the Frankish assault were not coherent. Years of power struggles had eroded unity and each regional emir was jealous of any threat to his authority. Strategically, the crusaders were strung out along a thin coastal strip, with inland enclaves to the north (Edessa) and south (Jerusalem). It followed that a co-ordinated attack on the weakest points in the Christian lines would cut the crusader enclave in two or more pieces.

Destruction of each would then be easier.

Fortunately for the crusaders, such a strategy required a degree of political unity and a skilled leader capable of holding a Muslim coalition together. In the first decade of the 12th century, neither was available. Only the growing call for a *jihad* seemed likely to provide the impetus to unite Islam.

In 1113 Emir Ridwan of Aleppo died and Ibn al'Khashsab forced the succession of the emir's teenage son, Alp Arslan. Unlike his father, who was willing to negotiate with the crusaders, Alp Arslan was an advocate of *jihad*. He was also a tyrant. After a year in which almost any potential opponent of the young emir was executed, Lulu, a court eunuch, took matters into his own hands and assassinated his master in 1114. After trying to retain power for three years, Lulu was himself murdered and the emirate was

plunged into a period of internecine turmoil.

Once again, Ibn al'Khashsab became the power broker. He selected Ilghazi, Emir of Mardin, to become Emir of Aleppo as well. Superficially, this was an unusual choice. Ilghazi was intemperate and had previously opposed the call for a *jihad*, but he was also one of the best military commanders in Syria. When, in 1118, Ilghazi joined forces with the Emir of Damascus, the Seljuk Turks presented the first serious unified opposition to the Franks.

## The raging dragon

In the summer of 1119, the combined Seljuk army marched on Antioch, ruled at the time by Roger of Salerno. The prince called on the support of King Baldwin II of Jerusalem. Baldwin, who had just come to the throne, was unready and anyway events moved too quickly. Roger was forced to meet Ilghazi's army northeast of Antioch, 15 miles from Aleppo, where the crusader force was outnumbered and outmatched. The Christian army was surrounded and massacred in the worst disaster inflicted on the Crusade since its arrival in the Holy Land. The battle became known as *Ager*

*Sanguinus* (Field of Blood, *see page 86*).

The entire military strength of Antioch had been destroyed in a single day and the principality lay wide open to Ilghazi. But disaster for the crusaders was averted because the emir was unable to keep his joint army united and in the field. Back in Aleppo he was feted as a hero of Islam, but he died before another joint invasion could be launched.

Around the same time a second Seljuk leader rose to prominence. Balak, Ilghazi's nephew, was seen as his military successor. In 1122 he captured Joscelin of Courtnay, cousin of King Baldwin II; a year later, Balak captured Baldwin himself. Balak, now nicknamed "the raging dragon," seized the Emirate of Aleppo for himself in 1124, then began a systematic reduction of Frankish fortresses.

It seemed the Muslim world had found their champion. But it was not to be. While laying siege to the northern Syrian town of Manbij an arrow struck Balak. His last words were: "That blow will be fatal for all the Muslims." Ironically, Manbij was a Muslim town that had rebelled against Seljuk authority. Islam still needed a champion to unite Muslims.

**above:** *The Massacre of the Monks of the Monastery of Saint Symeon by the Saracens.* This 16th-century illustration recalls an event that allegedly took place shortly after the Turkish general Zengi had captured Aleppo in 1128. While harrassing the Principality of Antioch, Zengi was said to have overrun the monastery, which is situated in the mountains between Antioch and the sea, close to the port of the same name. Still incensed at Christian acts of barbarism in Antioch and at other towns, the Turkish warriors put the monks to the sword.

# Assassins

**During the early 12th century, a sinister sect threatened to undermine the stability of the Seljuk Turkish realm through "contract" murder and potentially dangerous alliances with the Christian infidels.**

**below:** View of Alamut, near Khazvin, Iran and the landscape near the Caspian Sea where the Assassins had their center. The area below the mountain is known today as the Valley of the Assassins.

The Assassins were an extremist Shi'ite Muslim sect formed in response to Seljuk adoption of the Sunni branch of Islam. The schism between the Sunni and Shi'ite sects had come about following the death of Mohammed (*see page 16–7*). By the early 12th century, while the Fatimid dynasty in Egypt followed Shi'ite teachings, the Seljuk Turks remained defenders of Sunni belief.

The Assassins were Ismai'ilis, and opposed to the Seljuk-backed Abbasid Caliph of Baghdad. To these Shi'ites, wrapped in their mystic codes and sense of secret brotherhood, they were a religious order, fighting for the true interpretation of their faith. While many of these believers remained content with a theological opposition to the Sunni branch, others adopted a more militant stance. The term "Assassin" (*Hashishyun* in Arabic) was coined by the Franks and was probably based on the word hashish, as followers of the sect used the drug. The *hashishi*, or users of hashish, were thought to be men who combined drug-use with religious fervor to create an early form of suicide killer.

The Assassins were founded by Hasan as-Sabah, a Persian who fled to Egypt in 1071 when the Seljuks overran his homeland. He was supported by the Shi'ite Caliph of Cairo, who opposed the influence of the Sunni Caliph of Baghdad. The Caliph of Cairo encouraged

Hasan and his followers to infiltrate Seljuk Syria, while the resources of Fatimid Egypt were used to drive the Seljuks out of the holy places of Islam.

## Assassins create chaos

Hasan as-Sabah's followers established themselves throughout Syria, with a major stronghold at Quadmus, and began a series of assassinations designed to deprive the Seljuks of political leadership. The Assassins committed their acts in public places against the most influential enemies of their beliefs. Their first victim was Seljuk Vizier Nizam al-Mulk, followed by Sultan Malik Shah. Although these slayings plunged the Seljuk Empire into chaos, internal rivalry in Cairo prevented a Fatimid advance to take advantage of the situation.

The Assassins eventually split with their supporters in Cairo and Hasan continued the religious war on his own. Based in their stronghold of Alamut ("the eagle's nest") in the

mountainous region near the Caspian Sea, Hasan and his successors, each nicknamed Old Man of the Mountains, continued to destabilize the Seljuk Empire. They were even willing to side with the crusaders to further their religious ends.

In the mid-12th century, the sect was estimated to have up to 40,000 followers, making the Assassins a substantial power in the Middle East. In Syria, Assassin strongholds bordered the Principality of Antioch and County of Tripoli, from where they influenced the political development of the entire region. The emirs of Mosul, Aleppo, and Damascus were frequent targets, and their murder of Balak prevented an effective Muslim counterattack against the Franks. Victims who escaped assassination attempts included Edward I of England, and Saladin. The strength of the sect was broken in 1256, when the Mongols captured Alamut, and by the end of the 13th century the last isolated Assassin cells had been destroyed.

**above:** Today a Syrian village clings to the steep sides of the old castle of Assassins at Qadmus, a bare 18 miles from the Mediterranean coast. At the time between the First and Second Crusades, this indefinite region lay between the southern border of the Principality of Antioch and the northern border of the County of Tripoli. The Assassins maintained a wary but commercially fruitful relationship with their crusader neighbors.

# Fatimid Egypt: Defenders of Shi'ism

**When the crusaders advanced on Jerusalem, the Islamic world was divided by a religious war and this weakened them in the face of the onslaught. During the 12th century the Fatimid Egyptians launched a series of attacks aimed at reclaiming their territory. They even set aside religious differences with their Seljuk rivals to strengthen Muslim resistance to the Frankish invaders.**

**below:** A Fatimid illustration of two warriors on horseback fighting. Under the Fatimid dynasty, Egypt had enjoyed culture, wealth, and peace. But at the time of the crusades it was more characterized by civil wars brought about by poltical intrigues and power struggles.

The Fatimid movement began in modern Tunisia during the tenth century. It combined the Isma'ili version of Shi'ism with a ruling dynasty. Fatima was the daughter of Mohammed who married Ali, a cousin of the prophet. Following Ali's murder, Fatima and her children were regarded by the Shi'ites as the true Imams, or interpreters of the Koran. The movement upheld the right of these Fatimid descendants to rule the Islamic world rather than the Sunni Caliphs of Baghdad. In effect the Fatimids placed secular and religious leadership in the hands of one ruling dynasty. The Fatimids

conquered much of North Africa and, in AD 969, conquered Egypt and founded the new city of El Qâhira (Cairo), which became the administrative center of their empire.

The Fatimid caliphs and their controlling ministers (viziers or *wasirs*) pursued a policy of conquest throughout the 11th century. Fatimid troops—mostly recruited from among Arabs, Numidians, and Armenians—conquered Syria, and Fatimid control was exercized over Arabia and Azerbaijan. As early as 1030, the growth of the Turkish Empire of the Mahmud of Ghazni threatened the eastern borders of these Fatimid provinces, although Turkish campaigning in the Punjab delayed military expansion into the Middle East.

## Failure of Fatimid power

The high point of the Fatimid Caliphate came in 1059, when control of Baghdad was gained. From that point, the gains were lost and the

borders of the caliphate rolled back toward Egypt, although the Fatimids retained control of the coastal strip from Antioch south toward Ascalon. Part of the setback was a loss of revolutionary impetus. The breakaway Shi'ite Druze group in the early 11th century and the Assassins sect during the last decade of the century took over the messianic fervor from the *da'is*, Isma'ili preachers who spread the Shi'ite message throughout the Islamic world. Religious fervor in Cairo was replaced by complacency after the empire reached Baghdad. The onslaught by Sunni Seljuk Turks shook the Shi'ite state to its core and the Sunni caliph in Baghdad became spiritual leader of most of the Middle East. This was accelerated by hardening theological opposition to the Shi'ites and a consequent change in the religious alliances of much of the region's Arab population.

Following the onslaught of the crusade and the fall of Jerusalem, the Fatimid caliph called for a united front against the invaders. This meant setting aside religious differences and unifying Seljuk and Fatimid forces.

Although the Fatimids launched several attacks against the Kingdom of Jerusalem during the first decades of the 12th century, the assaults were unco-ordinated and the crusaders beat them back without difficulty. The military inferiority of the Egyptians was demonstrated in the battles of Ascalon (1099), Ramla (1101), Ramla-Jaffa (1102), and the Third Battle of Ramla (1105). Unable to reinforce their coastal enclave, the Fatimids lost control of the Palestinian coast.

After this string of defeats, the Fatimids seemed content to leave the fighting to the Seljuk Turks and any pretence at the establishment of a united Muslim front was abandoned. Despite the best intentions of the Fatimid caliphs, it was the Sunni Muslims in Syria who would be the real advocates of *jihad*.

By the 1160s, the Seljuks had to intervene in Egyptian affairs to help defend the Fatimid realm from invasion. In the battle known as the Day of Al-Babein (1167), the combined Muslim army won a strategic victory, forcing the crusaders to abandon their invasion. The Muslim general who played a leading part was a young Kurdish soldier called Salah al-Din. He became better known as Saladin, the commander who finally united Islam in a holy war against the crusaders.

**below:** Fatimid fresco of a seated man holding a cup.

# Syria and the Seljuk Turks

**During the mid-11th century, the nomadic Seljuk Turks migrated from the steppes and mountains beyond the Caspian Sea into the Middle East. Within two decades they controlled most of the Islamic world. Although the Seljuk Sultanate seemed a unified state, by the time the crusaders arrived, independent rulers and autonomous city governors had left the region divided and impotent.**

**below:** A Christian view of Arab horsemen. It is a popular view that only Christian knights were brightly caparisoned, but highly designed flags, banners, and shields had played a major role in Middle Eastern warfare since well before the Islamic era. The Muslims raised military visual forms to a high art.

The Seljuk Turks were one of the tribes collectively known as the Ghuzz (or Oghuz). These people had originated in Mongolia and migrated to a temporary homeland around the Aral Sea. From there, they moved on into Persia during the 1030s, entering the Empire of Mahmud of Ghazni, the most eastern state within the Islamic world. By 1040 this had developed into a full-scale annexation of the Ghaznevid Empire. The Seljuks then invaded the Buyid Emirate to the west. Their leader, Toghril, became the first Turkish sultan to rule in Baghdad in 1055. A decade later the

Seljuks had conquered Syria (then the emirates of Diyarerbekr, Mosul, and Aleppo). For the most part this was a peaceful invasion, since the Seljuks simply replaced the existing ruling elite while retaining the Arab administration to manage the economy.

By the time the Seljuks defeated the Byzantines at the Battle of Manzikert, they controlled a sprawling empire that stretched from the Indus River to the Mediterranean Sea. By the time the crusaders arrived, the Turks had added Anatolia and most of Arabia to their domains. As the *de facto* guardians of Islamic orthodox beliefs, the Seljuks' most serious threat came from their fellow Muslims in Egypt, the Shi'ites—until the establishment of the Crusader States created a deadlier enemy.

The Seljuk state was essentially run by a military aristocracy. In theory, the Sultan of Baghdad exercised power over the whole of the Great Seljuk Sultanate, but in reality his powers

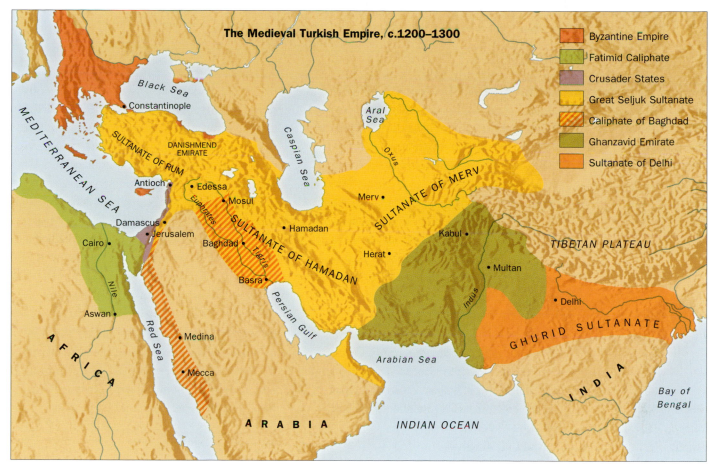

The Medieval Turkish Empire, c.1200–1300

Legend:
- Byzantine Empire
- Fatimid Caliphate
- Crusader States
- Great Seljuk Sultanate
- Caliphate of Baghdad
- Ghanzavid Emirate
- Sultanate of Delhi

were minimal. In this respect his position was similar to that of the monarchs of feudal Europe. In both cases regional potentates or nobles owed fealty to their superiors but ruled their territories with little regard to central authority. In no part of the Seljuk Sultanate was this more apparent than in Syria. It was the lack of central authority that made it so easy for the crusaders to invade the Holy Land and seize control.

## Divided and conquered

The problems facing the Seljuk sultans in the 12th century stemmed from the development of their role, from tribal leaders to rulers of a dynasty. Power tended to be shared with regional emirs and no sultan was able to establish himself in a position of autocratic authority over these local rulers. Their biggest ally was the Abbasid Caliph of Baghdad, whose status as the head of the Sunni branch of Islam was used by successive sultans to steer policy and discourage a complete devolution of power from Baghdad.

In Syria much of the coastline remained a Shi'ite enclave and most coastal cities remained in Fatimid hands until they were captured by the crusaders. The mountains of Syria and modern Lebanon were used as bases by

religious extremists such as the Druze and the Assassins. Seljuk emirs in cities such as Aleppo and Damascus were wary of any attempt the sultan made to extend his authority. This made Syria a patchwork of regional and religious diversity over which the establishment of an overall authority was extremely difficult.

Beyond Syria's petty states the Great Seljuk Sultanate was fragmenting into three virtually autonomous kingdoms: the Sultanate of Rum in Anatolia; the Sultanate of Hamadan, controlling the central portion of the Seljuk Empire; and the Sultanate of Merv, which included parts of Turkestan, Afghanistan, and Persia.

Without any central authority, a concerted counterattack against the crusaders in Syria seemed impossible. While the eastern sultanate was submerged by invasions of other Ghuzz tribes and the Sultanate of Rum struggled to retain control of central Anatolia, a new wave of Islamic conquerors fought for control of Syria and the Fertile Crescent (Mesopotamia). A new force was emerging in Syria that would achieve the political and military unity the Seljuks had been unable to provide. At last the Muslims would strike back.

# The Fall of Edessa

**Syria was in turmoil in the 1120s. Assassins had killed a series of promising leaders and little stood in the way of the crusaders if an attack was to be pressed. In Syria's darkest hour, a new defender of the faith emerged who would strike the first serious blow against Outremer.**

I n 1126, the Abbasid Caliph of Baghdad orchestrated a popular uprising designed to overthrow the Seljuk sultanate. He aimed to seize power, but the revolt was crushed by a Turkish general, Imad ed-Din Zengi. As a reward, the sultan granted Zengi the post of Atabeg of Mosul. Within two years he had seized control of Aleppo, as Emir Balak had since been assassinated (*see page 97*). Zengi spent the next few years consolidating his power base, defending it against Assassins, crusaders, and the entreaties of his mentor, the Seljuk sultan.

By 1135, Zengi was ready to take the field against the Franks and, after capturing several castles around Antioch, he moved south. Two years later he besieged King Fulk V of Jerusalem in Montferrand, a small castle near Tripoli. He knew the Byzantines had sent a punitive expedition south to help the king so Zengi bartered. He negotiated the payment of a ransom and for the keys to the castle in return for Fulk's freedom. It was a coup that electrified the Muslim world.

Zengi's plans to capture Damascus from elderly Unur, the Turkish governor, were thwarted when Unur allied himself with King Fulk. In return for the crusaders' help against Zengi, Unur offered a financial payment and the return of the crusader frontier fortress town and castle of Banyas, lost earlier to Zengi. Avoiding a

*right:* A Muslim army assaults a town, illumination from the *Byzantine Chronicles* written by John Skylitzes.

battle, Zengi withdrew and the Christian army recaptured Banyas. Zengi realized that if he was to expand his influence in Syria he would have to strike a blow against the crusaders, then subdue Damascus when the Franks were occupied elsewhere.

Zengi's opportunity came in 1144 when King Fulk died, leaving Baldwin III to succeed him. The power struggle in Jerusalem had caused a split between the rulers of the Principality of Antioch and County of Edessa. Joscelin II, Count of Edessa was left without allies and vulnerable. Zengi decided to strike. In late 1144, he captured a string of towns and fortified outposts to the east of Edessa, then laid siege to the city itself on November 28. The count was 30 miles to the east in Turbessel, having been lured away by a diversion created by Zengi.

## An ignominious end

The Muslims were determined to capture Edessa before reinforcements could arrive. The walls were mined while siege engines bombarded the city defenses. On December 26,

Zengi called on the defenders to surrender. The answer was a refusal. Zengi then had a section of the wall brought down by collapsing the mine, and stormed the city, which fell within

hours. In revenge for the barbaric treatment of Muslims in Antioch and Jerusalem, the Franks were massacred, although Zengi ordered that the lives of Armenian Christians be spared.

For a Muslim world used to division, failure,

and apathy, news that one of the four Crusader States had crumbled was a tonic. The adherents of *jihad* were encouraged to renew their call and it seemed as if Zengi was capable of leading the Islamic forces to victory. Instead, he was murdered in his bed by a servant, and the fall of Edessa led to the initiation of a Second Crusade rather than an Islamic *jihad*.

Zengi's realm was saved from collapse by his second son, Nur ed-Din (also: Mu'in ad-Din), who rode to Aleppo to ensure he retained control of the Zengid realm. The youth was a Sunni fundamentalist, earning him the title "the saint king," and his piety earned him the respect of the Arab populace. Unlike other Seljuk warlords, Nur ed-Din was an advocate of both Islamic unity and of *jihad*. When he banned Shi'ites from his domains, he ensured the support of the caliph and guaranteed that other Sunnis would flock to his standard if his realm was threatened. He would have need of their support in the years ahead.

# The Second Crusade

**When Pope Eugenius III heard about the loss of Edessa, he called for a Second Crusade to recapture the lost Crusader State. Encouraged by Bernard of Clairvaux, German, French, and English contingents descended on Outremer, spearheaded by King Louis VII of France.**

At first, Pope Eugenius III (p.1145–53) failed to elicit a popular response for the Second Crusade. Although King Louis VII of France (r.1137–80) was keen to participate, few others seemed willing to take up the Cross. This changed when Bernard, Abbot of Clairvaux, espoused the pope's cause.

On March 31, 1146 Bernard delivered a sermon in the French village of Vézelay that inspired a fresh wave of crusading fervor to sweep Europe. Like Pope Urban II before him, Bernard inspired the masses and people flocked to the Cross. They were offered the same chance of salvation and absolution that the participants of the First Crusade had been granted.

After spreading his message across France, Bernard toured Germany. The effect was the same. In his own words, "I spoke, and at once the crusaders have multiplied to infinity. Villages and towns are now deserted. You will scarcely find one man for every seven women." As before, the crusading message was accompanied by a wave of Jewish persecution.

The German crusaders set off for the Holy Land in May 1146, the French contingent shortly after. Led by King Conrad III (r.1137–52), the German crusaders included Frederick, the Duke of Swabia (soon to become Frederick Barbarossa) and Duke Welf VI, Lord of

Tuscany, the king's most bitter political rival. While this main German crusade was making its way through Hungary toward Constantinople, the "Wendish Crusade" saw an attack by the eastern German barons against the pagan Slavic tribes beyond the eastern frontier of the Holy Roman Empire. It was estimated that the German crusaders numbered up to 70,000 men, but the true figure was probably less than 10,000.

## Abandoned by their king

Pope Eugenius presented Louis VII with the oriflamme (the royal standard of France), and the French crusaders gathered under this holy standard. The papal banner came to represent French military pride for the next two centuries. The main French contingent traveled to Constantinople by the established land route, reaching the Byzantine capital in October 1148, a month later than the Germans. Other crusaders traveled by sea to the Holy Land. Among them was Alphonse, the son of Raymond of Toulouse, also a sizeable English contingent. The English knights, who interrupted the journey for a brief campaign against the Moors in Spain, arrived in Acre in late 1147.

Conrad had set out ahead of them. Having ignored Byzantine advice that the coastal route would avoid most Turkish harrassment, the German contingent intended to cross Anatolia diagonally. They did not get far. The Seljuks of Rum, who had spies in Constantinople, ambushed the crusaders near Dorylaeum. In this second Battle of Dorylaeum the king and a handful of his followers barely escaped with their lives, escaping to the Bosphorus. The emperor Manual I Comnenus shipped the survivors and Conrad to Acre, from where they made their way to Jerusalem.

Louis VII—wise for once in his reign— heeded sound advice and opted to march south through western Anatolia to Attalia (Antalya). From this Mediterranean port, the emperor had agreed to provide transports to ship the army to Antioch, avoiding the dangerous portion of the journey through Cilicia. However, on reaching Attalia, the crusaders found only a handful of the ships and a meager portion of the stores that were needed.

Impatient to be in the Holy land, Louis and

his court embarked what soldiers could be squeezed on board and took passage to Antioch, arriving with "the greatest magnificence." The remainder, under the Count of Flanders, set out east along the Anatolian coast from Attalia. Continuously harrassed by Turks, barely half survived the journey to Antioch, the rest succumbing to starvation or Turkish arrows.

In Antioch, Prince Raymond tried persuading Louis to launch an attack on Aleppo, Nur ed-Din's western stronghold, as a springboard to move on to recapture Edessa— the primary reason for the crusade. But the French monarch had other plans. Relations between the Prince of Antioch and the king broke down over the scandal that his queen, Eleanor of Aquitaine, was having an affair with Raymond. Without informing Raymond, Louis and the French contingent slipped away to join the rest of the crusaders in Acre. Edessa had been spared by the flirtations of a 26-year-old woman. The marriage was annulled in 1152 and within months Eleanor had married Henry of Anjou, father of Richard the Lionheart, shortly before he became Henry II of England.

**above:** Medieval illustration of a German knight. Conrad III lost most of his knights at the second battle of Dorylaeum and Germans remained thin on the ground until the Order of Teutonic Knights was recognized during the Third Crusade (*see page 147*).

**facing:** King Louis VII takes his vows before Pope Eugenius III and takes up the Cross. The lower panel shows the French army setting off for the Holy Land.

# On to Damascus

**As the participants in the Second Crusade gathered in Acre, Louis of France and Conrad of Germany decided what to do next. Encouraged by the king of Jerusalem, they decided to attack Damascus, 100 miles to the northeast. Unprepared and inexperienced, the crusaders placed their faith in God.**

The *parlement* held in Acre began on June 24, 1148. Louis VII and Conrad III were the conference's leading speakers but most leading nobles of their contingents joined in the debate, as did Queen Melisende of Jerusalem, her son, the young Baldwin III, and most of the principal nobles and clerics in the Kingdom of Jerusalem. Melisende was the principal suspect in the recent poisoning of Alphonse of Toulouse, who had been a rival of the Count of Tripoli, Melisende's brother-in-law.

Although Baldwin was beginning to assert himself, it was his mother who still ruled the kingdom. She was determined to capture Damascus, even though it made more sense strategically and diplomatically to attack Aleppo. Until then, Jerusalem had enjoyed cordial relations with Unur, the governor of Damascus and Outremer's only Muslim ally. Faced with the quagmire of Latin politics in Jerusalem, Louis and Conrad decided that Melisende was correct: Aleppo was an insufficiently prestigious objective.

Word of the impending assault on Damascus forced Unur to alter his alliances and make joint cause with his former Muslim enemy, the Emir of Aleppo, Nur ed-Din. Unur, who had fought against Nur ed-Din's father Zengi, offered his daughter's hand to Nur ed-Din to ensure that the Zengid army would

defend Damascus. Nur ed-Din had now secured what Zengi had always desired, Damascus as a power base for expanding Zengid rule south to Egypt and a center for attacking the infidel Christians in their coastal Crusader States.

## Under a gloomy forest

The army of the Second Crusade left Acre in July 1149, with Baldwin in command of the vanguard, Louis the center corps, and Conrad in command of the rear guard. The troops made their way to the shores of Lake Tiberius (the Sea of Galilee), which was to be their forward base. Then on to the much fought-over Banyas, from where it was planned to go north across the intervening highlands (Golan Heights) toward Damascus, approaching the city from the west. The idea was to take advantage of the abundant wells that lay along the route. This proved misguided because Unur had destroyed all the watering holes between Banyas and Damascus. Fortunately, in what was an otherwise badly planned expedition, the army was sufficiently well provisioned to make it to Damascus.

A plan of attack could only be drawn up when the crusaders reached Damascus on July 24. It became clear that the key to its defenses lay in the orchards that stretched for five miles around the western side, "like a dense gloomy forest." The orchards were surrounded and criss-crossed by walls, the outer ring pierced with defensive towers. By breaching the outer wall, the crusaders hoped to approach the city

under the cover of the trees.

A breach in the outer defenses, which were held by the local city militia, was successful, but as the crusaders continued toward the city more defenders appeared behind every subsequent wall. Muslim fanatics launched suicide attacks against the Christians but were unable to prevent the crusaders from cutting their way through to the main city walls. After a stalemate that lasted several days, Louis decided to switch his attack to the eastern walls, where there was no orchard to impede movement. As the crusaders marched out from the orchard, advance elements of Nur ed-Din's army made a sortie. The crusaders were left in the open, without adequate water and facing the strongest portion of the city defenses.

Ibn al-Qalanisi, an eyewitness, wrote an account of what happened next: "News reached the Franks… that the Muslims [Nur ed-Din's main force] were bearing down on them to attack them and wipe them out, and they felt defeat was certain. They consulted among themselves and decided that the only way to escape from the abyss that loomed ahead… was to take flight. At dawn on the following day they retreated in miserable confusion and disorder."

The Second Crusade had ended in disaster. The Muslims had been handed a victory that inspired them to further action against the Crusader States. Louis and Conrad returned home to Europe leaving Nur ed-Din to be hailed as Islam's new champion.

# CHAPTER 6

# Richard and Saladin:

## The Third Crusade

SCOTLAND

*NORTH SEA*

IRISH KINGDOMS

York

ENGLAND

London

Portsmouth

HOLY ROMAN EMPIRE

*Rhine*

Ratisbon

*Danube*

Buda Pes

Vézelay

FRANCE

Bordeaux

H U N

Venice

*Sava*

Belgrade

*A T L A N T I C   O C E A N*

LÉON

Marseilles

Genoa

*ADRIATIC SEA*

Pisa

CASTILE

ARAGON

*Corsica*

Rome

Lisbon

*Balearic Islands*

*Sardinia*

KINGDOM OF SICILY

Seville

Cordoba

A L M O H A D   E M I R A T E

Messina

*M E D I T E R R A N E A N   S E A*

*Sicily*

*Malta*

The Almohad dynasty inherited a vast empire from the previous Almoravid dynasty that stretched from Spain to the savannah kingdom of Ghana in the south. Ghana was a gold-producing region, which made the Almohads among the wealthiest of the Muslim emirates of the time.

**Europe in 1190 at the time of the Third Crusade**

- English and French Angevin Empire
- Holy Roman Empire
- Byzantine Empire
- Crusader States
- Ayyubid Emirate
- Almohad Caliphate
- gained by Richard I from Byzantium

**crusader routes**

- → English fleet
- → other Europeans
- ····▶ Richard I overland
- ····▶ Philip II overland
- → French fleet
- → Frederick I Barbarossa

After 1145, internal divisions and political intrigue plagued the Crusader States of Outremer. Although leaders such as Nur ed-Din in Syria ensured that Muslim military power was growing stronger, lack of unity within the Islamic world meant that no full-scale onslaughts were launched to take advantage of the crusaders' disputes.

By 1170, all this had changed. A minor Kurdish warrior increased his power and reputation to the extent whereby he was able to unite Egypt and Syria into one powerful Islamic state. Saladin became the new champion of Islam and began a campaign of re-conquest that demolished the divided patchwork of Outremer. For the first time, under a leader with acute strategic and tactical ability, Muslims had the power to strike back at the Christian invaders and drive the infidels into the sea.

The crusaders' disastrous defeat at the Battle of Hattin (1187) crippled their ability to defend themselves and Saladin exploited his victory to the hilt. Within a few years almost all of the crusader strongholds in the region had fallen to Muslim arms—even Jerusalem was once again a Muslim city. Saladin came close to wiping out the crusaders completely, but in the critical moment, a fresh wave of Europeans arrived to save the day.

A Third Crusade was proclaimed in Europe and its leading nobility took the call to arms to save the remnants of Christendom in the Holy Land. Frederick Barbarossa was the German emperor, while King Philip II of France and King Richard I of England were rivals for power in western Europe—and equally at odds in the Holy Land. While the crusading reinforcements were riven by internal disputes, Richard the Lionheart proved himself the one man capable of stopping Saladin's onslaught. The stage was set for a clash between the two great military titans of the age.

**Frederick Barbarossa is drowned while crossing the fast-flowing Calycadmus (Göskü) on June 10, 1190. The army refuses to elect Frederick of Swabia in his place, and the stragglers make their own way toward the Crusader States.**

**Cyprus is under the rule of a despot who has virtually broken away from the Byzantine Empire, which encourages King Richard I the Lionheart to invade en route for the Holy Land. Cyprus is to become an important staging post for food supply to the crusaders in Outremer, and eventually is joined with the Kingdom of Jerusalem.**

# The Rise of Saladin

**During the 1160s the focus of conflict shifted from Syria to Egypt. The weak Fatimid Caliphate invited attack, and soon crusaders and Turks fought for control of the richest land in the Middle East. Ultimately, neither gained control. Egypt's new Ayyubid dynasty was founded by a Kurd—Salah ed-Din Yusuf.**

Fatimid Egypt was nominally ruled by the Shi'ite caliph, both spiritual and secular ruler of his people. But in this almost Byzantine court, rife with administrators and bureaucrats, the real power was vested in the caliph's *wazir* (vizir or vizier). In a further echo of the Byzantine court, a near continuous struggle among the powerful for this influential position surfaced in an endless stream of intrigues, political back-stabbings (sometimes literally), and coups.

In 1163, Shawar, the recently ousted *wazir*, sought out Nur ed-Din in Damascus to elicit his support in regaining control of Cairo and Egypt. The Zengid ruler received Shawar in a kindly manner and offered him full support. Shawar would give Nur ed-Din something that was very important to him—the opportunity to extend Zengid influence. Under the command of his veteran general, Shirkuh, Nur ed-Din's army marched south to return Shawar to power. Shirkuh was a Kurd, not unusual in Nur ed-Din's army, which comprised men from every corner of the Great Seljuk Sultanate.

The campaign was successful in that Shawar was re-instated as *wazir* in May 1164 in Cairo. It seemed less satisfactory to Shawar, however, when he realized that he was only Nur ed-Din's pawn—the Seljuk army had no intention of leaving Egypt. Shawar now turned to the king of Jerusalem for help. Almaric (1163–73) was more than pleased to be invited to attack Shirkuh and help the Fatimids, for the new king also had his heart set on adding Egypt to his demesne. In the summer of 1164, he crossed the Negev and invaded Egypt, besieging Shirkuh's Turkish army inside Bilbeis, a town to the northeast of Cairo (*see map detail on page 93*). The vizir also gathered a force and joined his Christian ally.

The result was a stalemate, because Almaric was forced to withdraw in a hurry to march north in rescue of the Principality of Antioch, which had come under sustained attack from Nur ed-Din. The Zengid's plan was to relieve the pressure on Shirkuh, but thanks to crusader incompetence, things went much better. Before Almaric could get to Syria, Nur ed-Din had defeated the armies of Bohemond III of Antioch and Raymond III of Tripoli at Harim (Harenc). With both Christian princes in chains in Damascus, Almaric had little option but to make peace with the Seljuks and abandon his dreams of conquest, at least for the time being.

## Mutual withdrawal

In 1166, a second Turkish army of occupation commanded by Shirkuh headed south for Egypt. Almaric received a second invitation from Shawar and decided he had sufficient strength to match

The late 12th-century citadel at Cairo was built along similar lines to the one at Baghdad, although on a smaller scale. The construction was begun by Saladin and the citadel was completed by his son.

the Turks in another Egyptian expedition. By taking the shorter coastal route, Almaric arrived in Egypt at the same time as Shirkuh. While Almaric linked up with his Fatimid allies in Cairo, Shirkuh's army crossed the Nile and camped beneath the pyramids. This time he was accompanied by his nephew, a young Kurdish commander called Salah ed-Din.

When the Frankish-Fatimid army pursued him, Shirkuh marched south into upper Egypt, before turning to give battle. In the engagement, known as the Day of Al-Babein (1167), Salah ed-Din feigned flight and lured the crusaders into Shirkuh's ambush. It was a humiliation for the coalition but hardly a defeat. When Shirkuh moved north again toward Alexandria, the crusader and Egyptian armies followed closely. Shirkuh planned to use Alexandria, with its sea access, as a secure base for the conquest of Egypt. However, Almaric's fleet denied him the Mediterranean, and soon the Turkish army was beseiged in the city.

Shirkuh realized his position was difficult. He agreed to leave Cairo in Almaric's hands to give back to Shawar. At which point, both invading armies retired again, leaving Shawar in control in Egypt... but not for long.

In the following year, Almaric returned, intending to stay this time. To deny the stronghold of Bilbeis to any Muslim faction, he attacked the city and massacred its inhabitants. In alarm, Shawar again appealed to Damascus.

Two months after the Bilbeis massacre, Shirkuh landed an army in Egypt and marched on Cairo, but not to aid Shawar. With the support of the caliph, the Zengid general had Shawar put to death and claimed the post of *wazir* for himself. In this, Shirkuh was to be disappointed. He died shortly after in April 1169 and his nephew Salah ed-Din—Saladin— was appointed *wazir*. The 31-year-old Kurd was the master of Egypt.

# Outremer's Greatest Enemy

**With Saladin in Egypt and Nur ed-Din in Damascus, powerful opponents surrounded Outremer. For almost two decades after 1169, Saladin struggled to expand his power base and gain control of Syria. In achieving his goals, he became the first Muslim commander capable of destroying the Crusader States.**

**below:** The ruins of Qalat al-Gundi cover the top of Jebal Raha, in the Sinai. Saladin had the castle built to guard the route to Mecca for the protection of Muslim pilgrims from crusaders.

As the new *wazir* to Caliph al-Adid, Saladin looked to his own security in a court renowned for its intrigues. He was also a Sunni Muslim in an essentially Shi'ite realm. Although he brutally crushed a rebellion by the Fatimid palace "black guards," his religious tolerance and stable government gradually earned him the trust of the Egyptian populace. He did replace the Shi'ite judiciary with orthodox Muslims, but the Shi'ite population was allowed to practice their beliefs without undue persecution.

Outside the realm, there were still the crusaders. In the same year, a Frankish attack on the port of Damietta, supported from the sea by the Byzantine fleet, was effectively neutralized and the Christian forces withdrew. This campaign brought to an end King Almaric's dream of carving out a new Christian state in Egypt. In 1170, a series of earthquakes in Syria and Palestine suspended hostilities, but in December Saladin led an army out of the Sinai and attacked Gaza, massacring the city's Christian inhabitants.

This first operation was only a beginning. Before he could lead his army to further successes against the Franks, he had to deal with his Zengid superior in Damascus. Nur ed-Din's

orthodox beliefs led to continual demands that Saladin impose Sunni orthodoxy in Egypt, and destroy all traces of Fatimid religious beliefs. Saladin, fearing insurrection, was reluctant to do this in a region where the population was predominantly Shi'ite. However, he lacked the military or political power to defy Nur ed-Din. Then in 1171 Caliph al-Adid solved the problem for Saladin by dying.

In a stroke, Saladin extended the spiritual authority of the Sunni Caliph of Baghdad over Egypt, which he hoped would satisfy Nur ed-Din, but at the same time he continued to allow the Shi'ites to practice their own form of the Islamic faith. The Fatimid caliph's demise also made Saladin undisputed power in Egypt, which inevitably led to strained relations between himelf and his titular lord, Nur ed-Din. Saladin, who had to walk a political tightrope, halfheartedly campaigned in Transjordan, or *Oultrejordain* (now Jordan), on Nur ed-Din's behalf but avoided meeting him.

## Rising upstart

Over the next two years, Saladin's evasions drove Nur ed-Din to brand his former protege an "upstart." A war between Syria and Egypt seemed inevitable and plans were being formulated when fate took a hand. In the spring of 1174, Nur ed-Din died, leaving his realm to al-Salih, his ten-year-old son. Within months, in Jerusalem King Almaric also died, leaving the kingdom to his 13-year-old son Baldwin IV. Young Baldwin was a potentially gifted king, but he suffered from leprosy and the wasting disease made him an ineffective ruler. Saladin's luck continued to defy the odds.

The Atabeg of Aleppo declared himself regent for al-Salih, but the elite of Damascus realized that only Saladin could successfully unite Syria and protect the region from the crusaders. In October 1174 Saladin entered Damascus in a bloodless seizure of power and proclaimed himself the true successor to Nur ed-Din and regent to al-Salih. Now the leader of a *jihad*, the low-born Saladin had become the ruler of almost half of the Islamic world, and his territories effectively surrounded the crusaders of Outremer.

The Atabeg of Aleppo continued in his claim to be the true regent and claimed that Saladin was nothing more than an upstart. He was paid

little heed. Saladin's star was in the ascendant. He had brought effective military leadership and centralized government to both Syria and Egypt, and this he combined with a firm hand on the increasing wave of religious fervor. He was now the most dangerous opponent the crusaders had ever faced. Immediate action by the crusaders might have overwhelmed Saladin in the short period that it took him to unite the Muslim world, but the Christian princes were—as usual—embroiled in their own petty political games, which played straight into Saladin's hands.

**above:** Saladin holding a scimitar. Western medieval illustrators pictured Saladin in the manner of a European monarch, with a token turban wrapped around his crown.

# Division in Outremer

**While Saladin united the realms of Egypt and Syria, the crusading elite was embroiled in a dynastic power struggle as the sick Baldwin IV grew less able to govern. At a time when a united front against a powerful enemy was required, Outremer was tearing itself apart.**

Reynald of Châtillon built his castle of Kerak in Moab, Jordan. From this eyrie, he commanded one of the major pilgrimage routes from the Fertile Crescent and Syria to the Gulf of Aqaba and the coast or sea route along the Red Sea to Mecca. Châtillon became the most feared and loathed of the crusader nobles until his execution at Saladin's hands. Saladin also had the satisfaction of capturing Kerak in 1188.

According to his tutor, Archbishop William of Tyre, King Baldwin IV the Leper (r.1174–85) was a gifted teenager. If he had not been inflicted with leprosy, he might have been one of the best monarchs Outremer ever knew. Instead, his reign was an agonizing one in which his personal tragedy mirrored the national division. As his disability worsened, he was unable to prevent cliques and court intrigues from developing in his court in Jerusalem.

His father Almaric's first wife Agnes was left to guide her son through his first years on the throne. The king's sister, Sibylla, married in 1176 but her husband, William of Montferrat, died within three months, leaving her with a child to bear and raise. The young prince (who would become Baldwin V) needed a tutor and for this purpose Baldwin nominated his uncle, Count Raymond III of Tripoli. Raymond had just been freed from Damascus by Nur ed-Din after the payment of a large ransom raised by selling much of his land and title to the Knights Hospitalers.

The count was close to King Baldwin, but brought his own political influences to court with him. Despite the loss of much land, Raymond was still a powerful person. A marriage gave him lands of his own in Galilee and he retained close associations with the Hospitalers. He also despised Sibylla's new beau, the French nobleman Guy of Lusignan, another of Baldwin's close advisers.

By 1176, the king's health had deteriorated and he relied increasingly on Lusignan and Raymond to lead Outremer's armies into battle. Unfortunately, their mutual dislike of each other generated confusion and animosity within the army. William of Tyre described Lusignan as "unequal to the burden both in force and wisdom," but as the king grew weaker Lusignan's power increased, further heightening tension in the court. In 1180, Lusignan's marriage to Sibylla made him the center of a vicious intrigue.

## Sabotage from Châtillon

Another court faction centered around King Almaric's two queens. His first marriage, to Agnes de Courtnay, had been annulled, although Agnes' children, Baldwin (the leper) and Sibylla, remained successors to the throne. Almaric had then married the Byzantine princess Maria Comnena, who bore him a daughter, Isabella. Maria the Queen Mother had remarried, choosing Balian II of Ibelin, a follower of Raymond of Tripoli. Therefore an anti-Guy of Lusignan faction developed, which included Maria Comnena and the Knights Hospitalers.

Guy of Lusignan and Sibylla were supported by Agnes, the king's mother, the Knights Templars, and the former Prince of Antioch, Reynald of Châtillon. After his capture by Turks in 1161, Châtillon had spent 14 years in captivity, losing his principality during the incarceration. On his release in 1175, he gained the Seignory of Transjordan (Oultrejordain) through marriage, making him a powerful noble with a lust for revenge against Muslims. A combination of Châtillon's hatred and animosity within the court in Jerusalem would ultimately lead to a kingdom's collapse.

In 1180, Baldwin IV negotiated a peace treaty with Saladin, which included a guarantee of safe passage for the pilgrims who were flocking to the Holy Land. Châtillon, however, cared nothing for this peace, and his selfish obsession with killing Muslims sabotaged the fragile accord. In 1181, he attacked Muslim caravans bound for Mecca from his castle of Kerak in Oultrejordain. Two years later he led a naval expedition down the Gulf of Aqaba into the Red Sea, attacking Muslim ports and even threatening Mecca. Saladin was furious and executed any members of the raiding party his forces captured. He also decided that war was inevitable and prepared to launch a pre-emptive invasion of the Kingdom of Jerusalem.

At this crucial juncture, the non-confrontational policy pursued by Baldwin IV and Raymond came to an abrupt end in March 1185, when the 24-year-old king died of leprosy. From that point, war was inevitable.

# On the Horns of Hattin

**After the death of King Baldwin IV, Saladin and the crusaders were set on a course that could only end in a battle for supremacy of the Holy Land. King Guy of Jerusalem challenged Saladin at Hattin in 1187, a battle that ultimately led to the virtual collapse of Outremer.**

**right:** The Horns of Hattin, Galilee, scene of the worst defeat in the crusading era. The battle lasted all day and through the following morning, high up on level ground between the Horns and over the lower slopes, sometimes even ranging to the edges of Lake Tiberias (Sea of Galilee). The manuscript illumination paints a fanciful looking Galilee, with the city of Tiberias in the background at the edge of the lake and the Jordan snaking away to the horizon.

King Baldwin IV's death in 1185 prompted a power struggle. His sister Sibylla's son was crowned, becoming Baldwin V (r.1185–86), and Raymond III of Tripoli was named his regent. The count initiated a four-year truce with Saladin and it seemed that Outremer might enjoy a period of stability. This ended in August when the eight-year-old child-king died. There was a further struggle for the throne, from which the of faction of Agnes de Courtnay (King Almaric's first wife) emerged successful. They seized Jerusalem and crowned her daughter Sibylla. This meant that her husband Guy of Lusignan became King Guy I (1186–92). Worse still, Guy's

leading adviser was Reynald de Châtillon. Now completely free of Baldwin the Leper's peace edicts, he promptly attacked another Muslim caravan. Saladin considered the peace treaty broken and mobilized his Muslim army.

In the past decade Saladin's critics had accused him of being more willing to wage war against fellow Muslims than against the Franks. This was true to the extent that he had fought

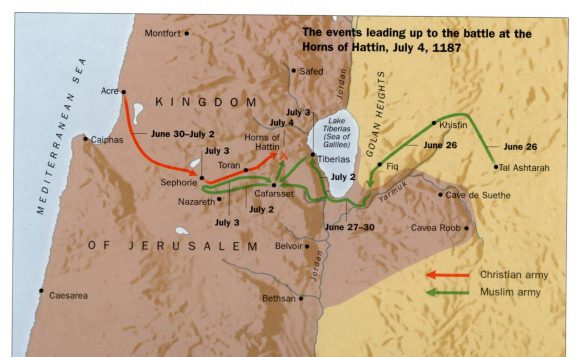

The events leading up to the battle at the Horns of Hattin, July 4, 1187

Christian army
Muslim army

several battles against the Emir of Aleppo, who had continued to use Nur ed-Din's heir, al-Salih, as a pawn in his attempts to set himself up as the rightful inheritor of Zengid Syria. Saladin had even survived two assassination attempts.

When the teenage al-Salih died in 1181, rumors circulated that Saladin had poisoned him, but these were never proven. With the Zengid prince in his grave, the emir sued for peace and there was a bloodless takeover of Aleppo in 1183. Syria was now united under Saladin and he could draw on its extensive military resources—by 1187 he had gathered about 30,000 troops, including Egyptian contingents and *jihad* volunteers. King Guy was aware of this military activity and called together his crusading army. His force was slightly smaller but included 2,000 knights, half of whom were members of the religious orders. A religious contingent led by the Bishop of Acre also accompanied the army, armed with a portion of the True Cross, the most sacred relic in Outremer.

## The trap springs

In late June 1187 Saladin invaded Galilee and besieged the city of Tiberias (modern Teverya), in the County of Tripoli. Count Raymond's wife Eschiva was trapped inside. By this time King Guy had gathered his army near Acre, where Raymond counseled caution. The king preferred to listen to Reynald of Châtillon. Châtillon was the kind of man who would suggest a course of action, however absurd, without counting the consequences, and in this case it was obvious that the chivalric course was to rescue the damsel. He also aimed to embarrass Raymond who, he was suggesting, was not man enough to care for his own wife. The king ordered the army to march on Tiberias, with Raymond in command of the rearguard.

On July 3, the crusaders were within ten miles of the city when they came under attack from Muslim skirmishers, who harassed the army for the rest of the day. Against Raymond's better judgment, Guy marched his troops across the arid Plain of Toran, then veered northward toward the springs near Hattin, a few miles west of Tiberias. Progress was slow, since the

crusaders were deprived of water, debilitated by heat, and subjected to constant attack. Exhausted, they camped in the mid-afternoon. At dawn on July 4, the crusaders renewed their attempt to reach water, but just below the mountainous outcrop known as the Horns of Hattin, Saladin sprang his trap. Smoke from Muslim fires disorientated the crusaders and the army began to lose its cohesion. The rearguard was cut off, and although Count Raymond escaped, most of his knights were cut down.

The Bishop of Acre was killed in the battle and the True Cross was taken up by the Bishop of Lydda. When he was captured by the enemy, the True Cross was lost. As numbers dwindled, the Franks made a last stand, but casualties, exhaustion, and thirst forced the handful of survivors to surrender. While King Guy and his leading nobles were taken prisoner, Saladin had Châtillon executed for what today would be dubbed "war crimes." With the only crusading army in Outremer decimated, the Crusader States lay at Saladin's feet. Hattin was Saladin's greatest victory and he was quick to exploit his success. His next target was Jerusalem, the greatest prize in the Holy Land.

**below:** The Loss of The True Cross. The artist who drew this medieval illumination appears to have merged two events: the battle of the Horns of Hattin, when the Cross was taken by Muslims, and the Christian siege of Acre in 1191 (*see page 123*), after which it was hoped that Saladin would return the Cross.

# Jerusalem Falls

**Following his victory at Hattin, Saladin found it relatively simple to subdue the rest of the Crusader States. Over the next two years, he conquered the entire country, with the exceptions of the cities of Tyre, Tripoli, and Antioch, and a few minor castles. Once again, the Muslim call to prayer was heard in Jerusalem.**

**facing:** Balian of Ibelin informs the people of Jerusalem that there is no hope of defeating the Muslims. In the lower panel, he meets Saladin outside the walls to sue for peaceful terms of surrender of the Holy City.

After the execution of Reynald of Châtillon, Saladin's next act was to hand over the members of the Christian religious Military Orders to his fundamentalist followers, who slew them. With his worst religious opponents dealt with, Saladin sent the others, including King Guy, back to Damascus as prisoners, while he advanced to occupy the virtually defenseless realm. Less than 3,000 crusaders escaped the battle and this small force was unable to stand against Saladin as he marched almost unopposed through Outremer.

On July 7, Saladin sent his lieutenant, Taqi al-Din, to seize Acre, the trading center of the Crusader States. He arrived on the next day, just as envoys came out to discuss peace terms. Resistance against the overwhelming numbers of the Muslim army would have been futile and invited a massacre. Saladin occupied the city and even offered feudal-style protection to the Frankish merchants and noblemen there. He freed the brother of the Byzantine emperor, who had been held prisoner in the city, and used him as an envoy to ensure peaceful relations with Byzantium. He wanted no interference to his dismemberment of Outremer.

Saladin advanced through southern Palestine, capturing the powerful fortress of Mirabel and the coastal cities before heading back north: Jaffa, Beirut, Caiphas (modern Haifa), Sidon, and the cities of Galilee all fell to the Muslims. Under Reginald of Sidon (and later Conrad of Montferrat) Tyre managed to hold on, as did the northern cities of Tripoli and Antioch. It is probable that they were saved by Saladin's desire to complete the conquest of the Kingdom of Jerusalem before dealing with the more northerly Crusader States. By August, apart from Gaza, the castles of Oultrejordain and a few minor defenses, only Jerusalem and Tyre remained in crusader hands in the southern portion of the Holy Land.

## In Muslim hands

On August 25, Saladin laid siege to Ascalon, and by September 5, the city was in his hands. Free now to march on Jerusalem itself, Saladin's army arrived outside the walls on September 20. Heracleus, Patriarch of Jerusalem, took charge of the city's defenses, supported by Balian of Ibelin, the new husband of Queen Maria Comnena. Queen Sibylla was also present, but both patriarch and garrison

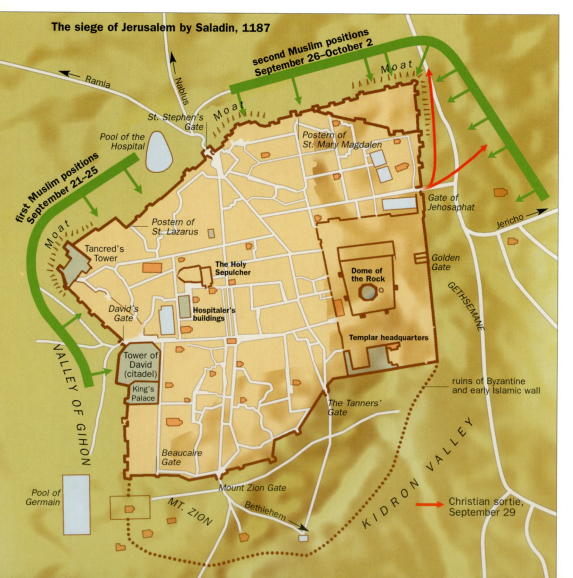

**The siege of Jerusalem by Saladin, 1187**

Ramla · Nablus · St. Stephen's Gate · Pool of the Hospital · *second Muslim positions September 26–October 2* · Moat · Moat · Postern of St. Mary Magdalen · *first Muslim positions September 21–25* · Moat · Postern of St. Lazarus · Tancred's Tower · The Holy Sepulcher · Gate of Jehosaphat · Jericho · David's Gate · Hospitaler's buildings · Dome of the Rock · Golden Gate · GETHSEMANE · Tower of David (citadel) · King's Palace · Templar headquarters · Beaucaire Gate · The Tanners' Gate · ruins of Byzantine and early Islamic wall · VALLEY OF GIHON · Pool of Germain · MT. ZION · Mount Zion Gate · Bethlehem · KIDRON VALLEY · Christian sortie, September 29

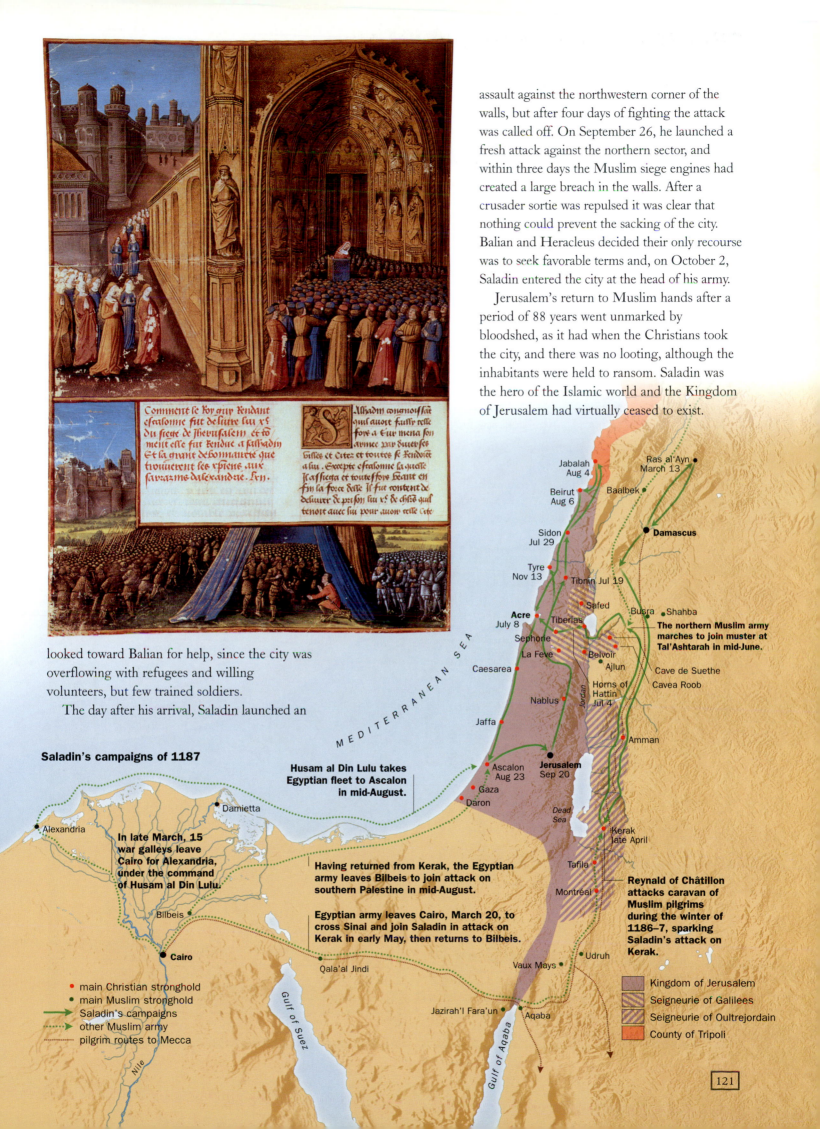

assault against the northwestern corner of the walls, but after four days of fighting the attack was called off. On September 26, he launched a fresh attack against the northern sector, and within three days the Muslim siege engines had created a large breach in the walls. After a crusader sortie was repulsed it was clear that nothing could prevent the sacking of the city. Balian and Heraclus decided their only recourse was to seek favorable terms and, on October 2, Saladin entered the city at the head of his army.

Jerusalem's return to Muslim hands after a period of 88 years went unmarked by bloodshed, as it had when the Christians took the city, and there was no looting, although the inhabitants were held to ransom. Saladin was the hero of the Islamic world and the Kingdom of Jerusalem had virtually ceased to exist.

looked toward Balian for help, since the city was overflowing with refugees and willing volunteers, but few trained soldiers.

The day after his arrival, Saladin launched an

## Saladin's campaigns of 1187

Husam al Din Lulu takes Egyptian fleet to Ascalon in mid-August.

In late March, 15 war galleys leave Cairo for Alexandria, under the command of Husam al Din Lulu.

Having returned from Kerak, the Egyptian army leaves Bilbeis to join attack on southern Palestine in mid-August.

Egyptian army leaves Cairo, March 20, to cross Sinai and join Saladin in attack on Kerak in early May, then returns to Bilbeis.

The northern Muslim army marches to join muster at Tal'Ashtarah in mid-June.

Reynald of Châtillon attacks caravan of Muslim pilgrims during the winter of 1186–7, sparking Saladin's attack on Kerak.

- ● main Christian stronghold
- ● main Muslim stronghold
- → Saladin's campaigns
- → other Muslim army
- ⋯ pilgrim routes to Mecca

Kingdom of Jerusalem
Seigneurie of Galilees
Seigneurie of Oultrejordain
County of Tripoli

MEDITERRANEAN SEA

Ras al'Ayn March 13
Jabalah Aug 4
Beirut Aug 6
Baalbek
Sidon Jul 29
Damascus
Tyre Nov 13
Tibnin Jul 19
Safed
Busra ● Shahba
Acre July 8
Tiberias
Sephorie
La Feve
Belvoir
Ajlun
Cave de Suethe
Cavea Roob
Caesarea
Horns of Hattin Jul 4
Nablus
Jordan
Amman
Jaffa
Ascalon Aug 23
Jerusalem Sep 20
Gaza
Daron
Dead Sea
Kerak late April
Damietta
Alexandria
Tafila
Montréal
Bilbeis
Cairo
Qala'al Jindi
Vaux Mays
Udruh
Jazirah'l Fara'un
Aqaba
Gulf of Suez
Gulf of Aqaba
Nile

# Richard the Lionheart

**The fall of Jerusalem sent shock waves through Christendom. Pope Gregory VIII (p.1187) proclaimed the Third Crusade, an appeal that was surprisingly popular among the European monarch. While Frederick Barbarossa led a German army toward the Holy Land, Richard I of England and Philip II of France led the contingents from western Europe.**

**below:** This detail from a medieval manuscript about the kings of England depicts Henry II on the left looking at his son Richard I. Despite the relatively crude rendering, the artist has caught the suppressed fury typical of the Angevin (Plantagenet) dynasty.

In England and France a tax called the "Saladin Tithe" was introduced to help fund the Third Crusade, but King Henry II of England (r.1154–89) was too embroiled in war with France to take up the cross. Instead, his eldest son Richard answered the call, but before he could leave, his father died and the prince became Richard I, King of England, Duke of Normandy, and Earl of Anjou (r.1189–99).

Richard's mother was Eleanor of Aquitaine (1122–1204), who had taken part in the Second Crusade with her first husband, King Louis VII of France. Following a scandal in Antioch (*see page 107*) and their divorce in 1152, she married Henry of Anjou Plantagenet, who became Henry II two years later. Born in 1157, Richard was their second son and, after the death of his elder brother Henry in 1183, he became heir to the Angevin Empire, his father's extensive domains in England and western France.

Despite his rebellious past, he remained his father's anointed successor. He was described as handsome and gracious, and was a renowned soldier. Immediately after his coronation he placed the kingdoms in the hands of his brother John and prepared to go on the Crusade. He was joined by Philip II Augustus of France (r.1180–1223). The two were friends (Richard spent hardly any time in England, preferring to reside in his French possessions), although they were both rivals for the control of the French Angevin lands. The friendship would soon sour.

In 1190, Richard and Philip met in Vézelay to assemble their national contingents and plan their journey. While Philip elected to move his troops by sea from Genoa, Richard preferred to rely on English ships, which were ordered to meet his army in Marseilles. Richard traveled on ahead through Italy and joined his army at Messina, Sicily, where he met again with Philip, whose fleet had already arrived *en route* from Genoa. Messina, however, was in uproar.

## Spurning a princess

King Tancred of Sicily had recently inherited the island from his illegitimate cousin and had imprisoned the former monarch's wife, Queen Joan. Joan was Richard's sister, so the king used the local hostility as an excuse to launch an attack on Tancred, after letting his men sack Messina. Joan was released and joined Richard's retinue. At this point his mother Eleanor arrived with Princess Berengaria of Navarre, her intended bride for Richard. This posed the king with a problem, since for political reasons he had allowed himself to become betrothed to Philip's sister Alice. However, Richard had evidence that proved Alice had been the mistress of his father Henry.

Philip reluctantly agreed to Richard's betrothal to Berengaria, but in reality the English king's rejection of his sister bit deep. A coolness came between them that in time would lead to outright hostility and influence the outcome of the Third Crusade. The winter season being over, Philip's fleet set sail for Acre on March 30, 1191. Because time was pressing, the marriage of Richard to Berengaria was put off until later. As the English fleet departed Messina on April 10, Berengaria was given her own ship, which also happened to carry Richard's war chest.

The fleet encountered severe storms in the eastern Mediterranean and several vessels were wrecked on the coast of Cyprus, including Berengaria's. The princess was rescued from the wreck as soon as the remainder of Richard's

fleet arrived on the scene, but not before much wreckage, including the war chest and the survivors of two further ships, had fallen into the hands of Isaac Comnenus, the island's Byzantine tyrant. The king demanded the return of his treasure and men, but was refused. He landed at Limassol and besieged the city, which soon fell. Comnenus fled a few miles into the mountainous interior. Richard soon followed, and a bloody battle ensued with the Byzantine household troops, during which the tyrant escaped. However, Comnenus left behind not only Richard's treasure but all of his own wealth as well, which the king seized.

Three days later, Guy of Lusignan sailed into Limassol with a small fleet. The King of

Jerusalem, who had been freed by Saladin, was now busy co-ordinating the defenses of the remaining crusading strongholds. Since 1189, he had laid siege to Acre but victory had proved elusive. Now he wanted Richard's powerful fleet to sail immediately with him to Acre where it would join with Philip's recently arrived army. Richard assented in return for Guy swearing fealty to him. The King of Jerusalem did so, and then helped Richard in a whirlwind invasion of Cyprus, during which Isaac Comnenus was captured. When he asked not to be chained in irons, Richard obliged by having silver fetters made.

Before he left Cyprus in May 1191, Richard married Berengaria of Navarre.

**above:** Ready to depart from England on the Third Crusade, a knight kneels before a monk to receive a crucifix in this 14th-century illumination.

# Frederick Barbarossa's Crusade

**By 1190, Frederick I Barbarossa (Redbeard) had ruled the Holy Roman Empire in Germany for almost four decades and was one of the most powerful and respected monarchs of his era. Despite his age and his past disputes with the papacy, Frederick decided to lead a German army to recapture Jerusalem.**

Frederick I Barbarossa (r.1152–90) set out from Ratisbon (Regensberg) in southern Germany for the Holy Land in May 1189. In a career marked by almost continual battle with the Church, it was an unexpected act of devotion for the 67-year-old emperor. Frederick was brought up amid rivalry between the two principal German houses of Hohenstauffen and

Lombardy in northern Italy brought him into conflict with the Pope, who feared any further erosion of papal supremacy. The bitter struggle lasted for 17 years from 1160, when Frederick was excommunicated by Pope Alexander III (p.1159–81). In response, the emperor elected a rival antipope. The two sides were publicly reconciled in 1177, but resentment lingered. Alexander probably assumed Frederick's crusading zeal was the result of guilt. In reality, Frederick saw the crusade as a means of bringing to heel the German nobility who— unlike their Frankish counterparts—had a healthy disregard for the principles of the feudal system. Under the banner of a religiously

**above:** German knights set off on the Third Crusade led by the Holy Roman Emperor Frederick I Barbarossa, from a 12th-century manuscript.

Welf. The son of a Hohenstauffen duke, his peers elected him Emperor in 1152 because he was considered the best candidate to bring an end to an era of warfare and rivalry.

Frederick spent most of his reign ensuring that Germany enjoyed a degree of political stability, while he struggled to improve the political power of his office. His conquest of

sanctioned common cause, he aimed to unite the nobles under his leadership.

The German crusading army numbered 15,000 men, including 3,000 knights. Frederick had managed to recruit the flower of the German nobility to the cause. Unlike the kings of England and France, the emperor elected to take the overland route through Hungary and

the Byzantine Empire. Envoys were sent ahead to ensure the army's safe passage. The king of Hungary obliged the Germans, but Byzantine Emperor Isaac II Angelus (r.1185–95) proved more fickle. He sent assurances to Frederick, promising guides and supplies, but blocked the mountain passes into his realm. Not to be outdone, Frederick forged an alliance with the rebel Serb princes and bypassed the Byzantines.

## Dwindling numbers

When the German crusaders arrived at Constantinople they found the city barred against them. Frederick immediately declared war against the Byzantine emperor. He defeated a Byzantine army in Thrace and campaigned in Macedonia before entering winter quarters in the Byzantine city of Adrianople. By this time the Byzantines had taken enough and made peace, agreeing to ferry the crusaders over to Asia Minor.

In March 1190, Frederick led his army east toward the Seljuk Turkish border. The Germans defeated the Turks in a battle near Philomelium, then captured the regional Turkish capital of Konya (formerly Iconium). The local sultan made peace and provided supplies to the near-starving crusaders, then hurried them on their way toward Cilicia.

The Germans crossed the Taurus mountains and entered the River Göksü (Calycadmus),

within easy reach of the Cilician capital of Tarsus, which was linked to Antioch by road. Then, on June 10, 1190, as the army crossed the river, Frederick drowned in the fast-flowing current. Half of his army had already perished on the long march. The emperor's son, Frederick of Swabia, tried to re-establish control of the army but old rivalries re-emerged and the survivors refused to elect him leader.

The survivors struggled on to Antioch, carrying Frederick's preserved body so that the emperor could fulfil his vow of reaching the Holy Land. When an epidemic swept the city, many Germans elected to return home by sea, while the few thousand who remained finally reached Acre in October, where they provided meager reinforcements for King Guy and his depleted army of Outremer. Saladin had been spared fighting a formidable foe. Outremer had to wait until Richard the Lionheart arrived to find its champion.

**left:** This gilded bronze reliquary, c.1160, containing the remains of St. John, was a gift from Frederick Barbarossa to the count of Cappenberg. It was found in Cappenberg church, Germany. It is regarded by scholars as the first independent portrait in Western art since Carolingian times, and can be considered a reasonably accurate depiction of the emperor. There was a (probably) silver knotted headband, now missing, which followed the convention of later ancient Roman emperor busts, emphasizing the legitimacy of the title Holy *Roman* Emperor.

**left:** An equestrian statue of Frederick Barbarossa stands in the Kaiserplatz of the Lower Saxony city of Goslar, Germany. Frederick was one of the most elderly of the crusading monarchs.

# King Richard in the Holy Land

**Richard the Lionheart arrived in Acre on June 8, 1191 and within weeks achieved what no other crusader had: he captured the city. From there, the road to Jerusalem led through Jaffa and, unlike Philip of France, the English king was keen to fulfil his crusader's vows.**

By the time the King of England's galley landed near Acre, King Guy of Jerusalem's small army had been besieging Acre for almost two years, the first stage of his campaign to reclaim some of the lands he had lost to Saladin. The chronicler Ambroise described Richard's arrival: "No pen can sufficiently describe the joy of the people on the night of the King's arrival." King Philip II of France had already arrived, and although his men strengthened the crusader's siege lines around the city, they had achieved little apart from commissioning the building of numerous siege engines. Richard's arrival invigorated the besiegers, and while the English king dealt with a Saracen relief army, Guy and Philip busied themselves by battering a breach in the city walls.

With the ships of Philip and Richard blocking any attempt at relief from the sea, Acre was beyond help. The leading citizens of Acre

negotiated a peace with Philip, before Richard returned. On July 11, Acre surrendered to the crusaders, while Richard lay prostrate with a temporary illness. Under the surrender terms, the city was to be spared in return for Saladin releasing 1,500 Christian prisoners of war, paying a huge ransom, and returning the True Cross taken at Hattin. Saladin only heard these terms after the city had surrendered.

It might be supposed that this first Christian success since the disaster of Hattin debacle would ignite the crusaders with a renewed fervor. What actually happened was that old divisions arose again and threatened to split Outremer anew. Guy of Lusignan held his claim to the throne by virtue of his marriage to Sybilla. Philip of France argued that Guy had forfeited his throne through the folly of Hattin and favored Conrad of Montferrat. Montferrat had fought bravely at Philip's side at Acre and moreover was married to Isabella.

Having received his fealty on Cyprus, Richard felt bound to support Guy—besides which, he was no longer saw eye to eye with Philip. The situation was exacerbated by the mercantile city-states of Genoa and Pisa. Guy enjoyed Genoese support, so this made their bitter rivals from Pisa align themselves with Montferrat. In the end, a suitable accord was arrived at: Guy was confirmed as King of Jerusalem but on his death the throne would pass to Conrad of Montferrat or any son he had by Isabella. In return for relinquishing the title at this point, Montferrat was given the fiefs of Beirut, Sidon, and Tyre.

## A brutal solution

Richard, always more a man of action than talk, tired of the Christian-Muslim diplomatic discussions. Saladin was temporizing over the demands made of him while awaiting reinforcements, and Richard wanted to move on, toward Jerusalem. He had set Saladin a time limit, and now it had passed. On the morning of August 20, he had 3,000 of Acre's leading citizens led out to a place in full sight of the encamped Muslim army, where they were executed. After this appalling act, it was clear that there would be no further negotiation with Saladin. Although the act horrified his critics, it had its desired effect and left Richard free to fight Saladin.

King Philip, who suffered frequent bouts of illness, decided to return to France. An even more pressing reason might have been the death of the crusader Philip of Flanders, whose European lands the king coveted. The remaining 10,000 French crusaders were placed under the command of Hugh, Duke of Burgundy, while King Richard remained in command of all three foreign contingents.

Dismayed by the squabble over who should have the throne of Jerusalem, Richard decided to continue unaided by local allies. He left Acre in 1191, four days after the hostage massacre. The vanguard consisted of knights of the military orders, newly shipped out from Europe. Saladin expected Richard to march on Egypt so he ordered the fortifications of Jaffa and Ascalon to be dismantled, to deny Richard any bases.

Saladin gathered another powerful army and attacked Richard's army at Arsuf on September 7. Saladin commanded about 80,000 men and Richard about a third of that. This would have been a serious problem for a lesser commander, but Richard held his men together, despite the hail of Muslim arrows. When the moment was right, he smashed Saladin's army with an all-out cavalry charge. The Islamic army fled the field, leaving 7,000 dead behind them. Richard continued his march to Jaffa unopposed.

**above:** The Conquest of Acre and the Return in France of Philip II, from a manuscript titled *Speculum Majus*, shows the French king receiving a hero's welcome combined with a scene of crusaders scaling the walls of Acre.

**facing:** Massacre at Acre, from *Histoire d'Outremer*. Failing to wring a deal out of Saladin for the return of the True Cross taken at Hattin, King Richard had 3,000 Muslim hostages from Acre executed. In the illumination, the massacre is seen taking place in Acre. In fact the site was on the hill of Ayyadieh, some miles from the city, in full view of Saladin's encamped army.

# Peace with Saladin

**After a rebuff before Jerusalem, King Richard opened negotiations with Saladin, while trying to retain control of his allies. Richard the warrior proved a match for the political skills of Saladin and the lords of Outremer.**

King Richard followed his victory at Arsuf with a drive on Jerusalem. The army left Jaffa in late October, but Saladin had fortified the mountain passes between Beit Nuba and the Holy City and Richard lacked the men to risk a frontal assault. It is unclear whether the French contingent refused to continue or whether the lords of Outremer refused to attack, but the effect was that by the end of January 1192 Richard and his army were back in Jaffa.

Saladin sent his brother al-Adil to open negotiations with Richard, who was busy planning an alternative campaign against Egypt and supervizing the rebuilding of Jaffa and Ascalon. At the same time, Saladin began negotiating with Conrad of Montferrat. The negotiations with Richard stalled over three issues: Jerusalem; the return of the True Cross; and territory. Saladin refused to give up Jerusalem and would only trade the Cross for a tangible reward. Richard tried to break the impasse by offering Saladin the hand of his sister Joan, creating a joint crusading and Muslim kingdom in Jerusalem. The offer came to nothing and a bizarre opportunity for peace was lost.

In June 1192, Richard tried one last time to capture Jerusalem, but the Duke of Burgundy was planning his own military venture and refused to co-operate. The campaign was abandoned. Richard clearly wanted to return home, but his army was too small to capture Jerusalem without help from Outremer. It was also clear the local crusaders would be unable to hold both Jerusalem and the coastal cities without outside help.

## A truce is agreed

Richard's decision to abandon Jerusalem was a practical solution to the impasse. As Richard retreated, Saladin launched an attack on Jaffa, entering the town before Richard arrived at the head of a small army on August 5. Saladin turned to face Richard, who held his troops in a tight defensive formation that Saladin's light cavalry were unable to break. Saladin retreated, giving Richard his second great military victory in Palestine. Saladin offered no further military challenge to Richard and instead relied on his diplomacy skills.

The troublesome French contingent occupied Acre while the English held Ascalon, the new southern limit of the Crusader States. As early as April 1192, Richard had called a meeting of all the leading Christian nobles in the Holy Land to discuss future plans, while al-Adil returned to renew peace. King Guy was a spent force and was removed from power, although in consolation he gained Cyprus, which lay in Richard's gift.

This now left Conrad of Montferrat free to take the crown and he was duly declared the new King of Jerusalem. Unfortunately his path to power had led to discord among the merchants. His alliance with Genoa meant that Pisa was now to be ostracized from the ports of Outremer. When Conrad was assassinated just before his coronation, his successor, Henry of Champagne, blamed the Pisans. In all probability, Henry hired the assassins himself. For the moment, the murder ended factional fighting, and for once the nobles of Outremer could concentrate on the Muslim threat, just in time for Richard to vanquish Saladin's Muslim army in battle.

Following the Battle of Jaffa (1192), Richard became the arbiter of peace in the Holy Land. Both he and Saladin fell ill and exchanged gifts of medicine and fruit. This led to the re-opening of peace talks. On September 2, 1192, a three-year truce was signed. Although the crusaders were forced to abandon Ascalon and the Muslims held Jerusalem, their hold over the coastal strip from Tyre to Jaffa was recognized, as was their retention of the hinterland of Tripoli and Antioch.

The peace concluded, Richard sailed for England on October 9. The Third Crusade was over and, following the death of Saladin in March 1193, a period of relative peace descended over Outremer.

*facing:* "Men of the Crusades and their Enemies in Captivity," illustration from a 14th-century French manuscript. By the time Richard I was ready to return home, the English king had brought Saladin to a standstill. Nevertheless, regaining Jerusalem for the Christian cause appeared to be as far out of reach as it was when he had arrived in Outremer.

# CHAPTER 7

# The Sword and the Scimitar:

# Crusading Warfare

The Crusades brought two very different military systems into conflict. The first crusader armies were built along principles developed in feudal Europe, although they had to be adapted to suit the nature of the region. For the Muslims, both the Turks and the Egyptians tended to field larger armies. Although these forces contained contingents of heavy cavalry roughly equivalent to the European knights, the bulk of the Eastern armies were light troops, trained to skirmish rather than attack their foes in pitched battle.

The nature of crusading warfare changed over time, as the Franks gradually adopted some of the tactics and stratagems used by the Muslims. This was particularly true of the crusading armies that were raised in Outremer. By contrast, successive waves of crusaders from Europe were fired by religious zeal but unused to Eastern fighting methods. Faced with a foe whose army was designed to harry and skirmish, the crusaders had to reinvent their traditional feudal doctrines of war.

Two additional factors dominated crusading warfare. The first was religion. Both the Muslims and the crusaders occasionally rallied support for their cause by declaring a holy war or *jihad*, although the appeal diminished with time. The high point of the crusades as a form of religious war came during the heyday of Saladin, as the Muslim leader could draw on thousands of volunteers, willing to give their lives in the name of their Islamic faith. For their part, although religious fervor played a significant role in any crusading army, the brother knights of the Military Orders were particularly zealous.

The second factor was the use of many fortifications. To offset their lack of numbers, the crusaders relied on fortifications to guard the borders of their states. Cities were also fortified; many key events took place when major cities such as Antioch, Acre, and Jerusalem were besieged and captured. East and West learned a lot from each other, adopting and adapting what they considered to be the best tactics, weapons, and architecture from both cultures.

SELJUK SULTANATE OF RUM

ANATOLIA

Baku •

• Konya
(Iconium)

LESSER ARMENIA

• Tabriz

Lake
Van

• Mardin

Lake
Urmia

• Alanya

• Mara

• Edessa

• Tarsus

• Seleucia

Antioch •

• Aleppo

Mosul •

• Irbil

Latakia •

Cyprus

• Marra

• Kirkuk

• Limassol

• Hama

Tigris

• Homs

Euphrates

Tripoli •

• Palmyra

Beirut •

Sidon •

Tyre •

• Damasucs

• Baghdad

Acre •

Caiphas •

✕ ⟶ **Battle of Hattin 1187**
victory for Saladin

Jaffa •

✕ ⟶ **Battle of Arsuf 1191**
victory for Richard the Lionheart

✕ • Jerusalem

Gaza •

⟶ **Battle of Jaffa 1192**
victory for Richard the Lionheart

The Abbasid Caliphate
of Baghdad retained titular
sovereignty of the Islamic
states, including the hinterland
of Arabia, particularly after
Saladin came to power in 1169
and removed the institution of the
Caliph of Cairo. However, the real
power lay in secular Muslim hands, and
the Caliphate of Baghdad fell in 1258 when
Mongols overran the entire region.

• Basra

• Aqaba

PERSIAN
GULF

R E D   S E A

Aswan

• Medina

**Saladin's Empire, 1169–92**

Byzantine Empire

Seljuk Turks

Abbasid Caliphate

Saladin's Ayyubid Emirate, 1174

Muslim territory gained by Ayyubid Emirate after 1174

Kingdom of Jerusalem lost to Saladin after Battle of Hattin, 1187

Crusader States after 1187

# Crusading Armies

**The crusading army that faced the Turks at the end of the 11th century was organized in the style of feudal Europe. Following the establishment of the Crusader States after the capture of Jerusalem, this feudal array was adapted to better suit the style of warfare and economic necessities of the Middle East.**

Heavily armored, mounted knights formed the core of any medieval European army. Although the main constituent was infantry, everything centered on knights—the army's shock troops. The Frankish knights rode massive war horses called *destriers* and, locked tightly together in formation, the sheer brutal force of a single cavalry charge could prove decisive in battle.

Under the feudal system, a knight usually owned land and at least one castle as a gift from his feudal superior to whom in return he supplied a quota of fighting men, including himself (*see also pages 32–33*). However, the term "knight" also described the mounted soldiers of a knight's feudal retinue. The quality and extent of their armor reflected their status within the retinue (although a lesser knight might receive a reward for good service from his lord, he was often expected to improve the quality of his armament through defeating a better-equipped enemy in battle). In 1097, the army of the First Crusade was composed of the feudal retinues of a number of European nobles. For the lesser knights of these retinues, the promise of gaining land and greater status was a prime driving force.

After the formation of the Crusader States following the capture of Jerusalem, it was clear that Outremer did not have sufficient land for the princes to grant to their followers. This limited the number of knights available to muster in an army. To compensate, money fiefs were introduced. Under this system, a deserving knight was granted the revenues from a city or a number of villages, in return for an agreed quota of troops. As a result, it was quite common in Outremer to find many knights living in property they owned in towns, rather than in castles, as would be the case in Europe. The third form of knightly service was provided by the three major military orders, the Knights Templar and Hospitaler, and the Teutonic Knights (*see pages 146–7*).

The lowest social class of a knight's retinue were the peasants paying their dues through armed service. Too poorly trained to be useful in battle, they acted as servants to their betters. In

**from left to right:** A knight, sergeant, foot soldier. and *turcopole* archer. In the 13th century, knights began to wear better protection. Sergeants had inferior armor, whether mounted or on foot, although still much better protection than the non-professional infantryman.

Europe, peasant militias provided the bulk of infantry, but they were also poorly trained. The Crusades needed a better trained resource, and so paid professional soldiers instead. In Outremer, these mercenaries were financed by urban centers or by the Church at first, but in the later crusades, their services became more essential and the Kingdom of Jerusalem had to levy a tax to pay for troops. Mercenaries were drawn from all over Europe. Bretons, Flemings, and Aragonese Spanish (or Catalans) were well known in crusading armies. After his trip through Italy *en route* for Acre, King Richard I employed a contingent of mercenary Italian crossbowmen on the Third Crusade.

## Numbers tell

Feudal militias were called up in emergencies. These included Christian Arabs or Armenians (allies to the crusaders in any case) where appropriate. Muslim captives prepared to convert to Christianity, called *turcopoles*, were also used to counter enemy light cavalry. *Turcopoles* gave crusading armies a match to the Muslim's light cavalry or horse archers.

During the First Crusade, the army was led by a coalition of nobles, each with their own retinue of knights, infantry, and camp followers. By the 12th century, the leaders of the Crusader States had created their own feudal hierarchy, under the nominal suzerainty of the king of Jerusalem.

In theory, the king led the army, but usually command decisions were made after consultations with the other princes and senior knights. Getting agreement was sometimes difficult, owing to the king's weak position in relation to his powerful vassal princes. Since Antioch and Tripoli were not a part of the kingdom, the king could only request, not insist on, their help. At crucial times, therefore, under a weak sovereign, the numbers mustered were often small.

Contemporary numbers given for those who went on the Crusades must have been exaggerated. The army that faced the Turks at Nicaea in 1097 probably numbered around 30,000 men, of whom approximately 4,000 were knights and mounted retainers. Raymond of Toulouse (and later Tripoli) had the largest army, with about 1,200 cavalry and 8,500 infantry. After appalling losses in Asia Minor and Antioch, the army that besieged Jerusalem two years later had dwindled to about 12,000 men, of which only 1,500 were knights.

In 1115, the army consisted of less than 6,000 men, including 1,000 knights. These troops were augmented by 5,000 *turcopoles*. The largest force ever gathered participated in the Hattin campaign and comprised 20-25,000 men. Compared to the armies of their Muslim opponents, these numbers were paltry, and Outremer would have fallen if there had not been regular reinforcements from Europe.

# Frankish Warfare

**For the Franks, crusading warfare centered on the defense of their conquests. As in feudal Europe, this meant relying on castles and fortifications. In the field, armies were used defensively in strategic terms, while on the battlefield the crusaders relied on the offensive power of their knights.**

Geography and available manpower dictated crusader strategy after the capture of Jerusalem in 1099. The evolving Crusader States were surrounded by far more numerous enemies, and the best possible use of their limited resources lay in building and holding a string of fortresses, fortifying cities, or strengthening existing city walls. When invasion threatened, a mobile field army was mustered to augment this static defensive line. Its purpose was more the protection of important strongholds from siege and vital agricultural land from raiding than to repel the invader.

Since the fall of the Roman Empire, medieval European armies mostly lived off the land. In Outremer, longer campaigns and arid landscape forced the crusaders to learn the art of logistical supply; either that or die—there simply was not sufficient to live off. In fact more men died of starvation and thirst in the First and Second Crusades than from any other single cause.

The crusaders constructed a network of roads and points throughout the Holy Land to provide relatively secure lines of communication. By contrast, the Muslims had

difficulty maintaining contact with their armies at the end of such extended supply lines. Nevertheless, in one vital aspect—the knights, their expensive destriers, and the infantry—the crusaders faced an even longer line of supply from Europe. Stripping castles and cities of their garrison troops was the only way in which a field army could be mobilized.

By the same token, the loss of an army in the field had unthinkable consequences, with virtually undefended strongholds awaiting investment by the victorious enemy. The Franks were fortunate after the First Crusade that the Muslim victors were slow to take advantage of the situation on the several occasions when this happened. That all changed with Saladin. In 1187, after his victory at Hattin, Saladin, as we have seen, capitalized on his conquest with efficient ruthlessness. Even when the Christians were victorious, all they gained was a temporary respite from an enemy who was able to bring fresh troops into the region quickly. This made diplomacy or the tactics of fast maneuver preferable to risking all in battle.

## The waiting game

Despite their Muslim foes holding a deal of the cards, the crusaders enjoyed one advantage in being so far from home—the Christian princes' men were virtually committed to being in the Holy Land, partly by vow but mostly by geography. For the Muslims it was different. Because Muslim armies were larger, they were tougher to hold together (see pages 136–7). Before long, the crusaders realized that a policy of temporizing eventually reduced the Muslim threat as the army gradually dispersed.

When battle became inevitable, the Franks still had some military advantages, and their battlefield tactics reflected this. Turkish tactics were to make lightning-fast hit-and-run missile attacks, so emphasis was placed on disciplined crusader formations. Until the time was ripe to launch a decisive heavy cavalry charge, the mounted knights were kept screened behind ranks of infantry armed with a mix of spears and crossbows. Their primary task was to protect the knight's valuable horses, while enduring a hail of arrows. The knights' heavy armor meant that the lightweight Turkish arrows held little danger, but foot soldiers often suffered serious injury. Their secondary task was to try to bring down the enemy horsemen, often by shooting at the horses. Brought down in close proximity to the line of infantry, the unhorsed Muslim cavalryman was an easy victim.

It was crucial for commanders to time the moment of a charge. Mounted Frankish knights were said to be capable of a charge that could "make a hole through the walls of Babylon." The Muslims had nothing capable of stopping the onslaught—when charged, their men rarely stood to fight. Muslim commanders tried to avoid situations where they faced a charge, while a good crusading commander, like King Richard I, was able to maneuver his opponents into a position where they were unable to avoid a mounted charge (see page 145).

Frankish warfare, then, was a matter of stalwart defense, followed by the launch of a crushing attack, where timing and surprise were critical.

There are many superb examples of crusader castles throughout Palestine, Jordan, and Syria, but few exemplify the crusaders' defensive strategy as well as Shobak, a few miles south of Tafila in what was Oultrejordain. Sitting stolidly on top of an eliptical hill, the castle has two concentric curtain walls. Its battlements were equipped with catapults capable of hurling large boulders down on top of any attackers foolhardy enough to assault the steep hill. In keeping with many crusader strongholds, it acted more like a town than any European equivalent, containing two churches, extensive domestic quarters, prisons, and a Judgment Hall. Its strategic position put it astride the main caravan routes from Damascus in the north to Cairo (via the Sinai) and Mecca in Arabia.

# Muslim Armies

**The Islamic armies that fought the crusaders for control of the Holy Land were drawn from a vast area, encompassing much of the Middle East and Central Asia. The Seljuk Turks, Fatimid Egyptians, and mamluks all contributed different elements to the Muslim force that would drive the crusaders from Outremer.**

**below:** This engraving based on a window at the Abbey of St. Denis, France, depicts a battle between Christian knights and the Fatimid cavalry at Ascalon in 1099. The crusaders' victory left the region around Jerusalem in their hands.

At the end of the 11th century, the Seljuk Turkish Empire ruled by Sultan Alp Arslan stretched from modern Turkey to Afghanistan, and from the Caucusus Mountains to the Persian Gulf. Although once united, by the time the crusaders arrived in 1097, the sultan retained only nominal control over much of this territory of numerous virtually independent smaller states.

The typical Seljuk army consisted of a core of professional soldiers, backed by militia or volunteers of various ethnic origins, including Turks, Arabs, Persians, and Kurds. The professionals were either *ghulams* (Turkish heavy cavalry), former slaves who provided swarms of bow-armed cavalry, or heavier horsemen, usually contingents from an emir's personal bodyguard, called *askars*.

Infantry made up the main body of the army and were armed either with bows or spears. These included religiously motivated *mutatawi'ah* volunteers. There was an element of feudalism in the Seljuk military structure. The sultan made grants to deserving men, who became emirs. As in Europe, the emir was required to pay an annual tribute and also supply the sultan with fighting men when called upon.

Fatimid Egypt's great wealth meant the *wazir* could field enormous armies, which placed a greater reliance of regulars. Permanent regiments were organized in the manner of the earlier Abbasid caliphate. Egyptian armies had used regular *ghulam* troops from the mid-ninth century, including white-skinned Turkish slaves known as *mamluks* (from a Turkish word meaning "owned"). These, too, were organized in a feudal manner but formed a standing army. The royal *mamluks* formed a central core, while the remainder owed their allegiance to leading Egyptian nobles.

Unlike their Christian foe, cavalry made up the larger part of the troops. Cavalry units came either as heavy units equipped with armor, bow, or spear, or else more lightly equipped horse archers or light cavalrymen. In addition, light cavalry or horse archers were recruited from Syria, Arabia, or Turkey. Most of these were *ghulam* units, although mercenaries and militia were also employed. Infantry regiments consisted of African *ghulams* recruited from what would now be the Sudan or Ethiopia, as well as Armenians and Persians.

left to right: Syrian emir 12th–13th centuries, mamluk warrior, Turcoman auxiliary, and mamluk askar. Syrian emirs favored knee-length mail hauberks covered by rich fabrics. Initially, the Franks failed to recognize the garments as armor and referred to the Muslims as being unarmored. The Turcoman carries an ax that was often preferred instead of a sword in close combat. Askars carried a javelin for use as a shock weapon and also carried a bow and a sword, or small ax or mace.

# Mobile supplies

The Muslim army commanded by Saladin (1137–93), founder of the Ayyubid dynasty, was largely a Turkish one, backed by an elite force of Egyptian *mamluk* horsemen. A stranger to Egypt, Saladin was forced to crush a revolt among the Sudanese guards when he came to power. These he replaced by 3,000 troops from Shirkuh's army who were loyal to him, of which 1,000 were Kurdish men from among his own family's retainers.

Unlike his predecessors, Saladin encouraged rigorous training, particularly in archery and cavalry tactics. He reduced the Muslim reliance on non-professional troops and increased the pool from which *ghulam* troops could be drawn. Later Seljuk armies relied on *ghulams* from Europe and Asia Minor, as well as traditional Persian and Syrian sources. In 1169, the Fatimid Egyptian army commanded by Saladin consisted of approximately 80,000 men, of which half were cavalry. His cavalry force included African *ghulams* and *mamluks*, supported by Arab (Bedouin, not always very trustworthy, but good scouts) and Turcoman light horsemen.

Saladin also developed logistical concepts designed to let his armies operate further afield and remain on campaign for longer periods. These were the *atlab al-mira* (supply train) and the *suq al-'askar* (a form of traveling market), both of which accompanied the army on campaign. This logistical support was one of the most pronounced differences between crusader and Muslim armies. While the former were able to support themselves within Outremer, attacking Muslim armies had to carry everything with them. The disadvantage encouraged rapid improvements until a Muslim general could draw on an extensive network of administrative, financial, and logistical support.

With the crusaders hiding behind the walls of their castles, Muslim strategy altered to become more based on siege warfare. It was not an aspect for which the Turks or Fatimids had been noted previously, and most generals preferred to lure their enemy into a field battle, as Saladin managed at Hattin. Here, he commanded approximately 12,000 Egyptian and Turkish cavalry, supported by a similar number of *mutatawi'ah* volunteers and auxiliary infantry (mainly archers). His armies were consistently larger, better supplied, and more mobile than the crusading forces he faced.

# The Muslim Art of War

**If the crusaders were defensive, Muslim strategy centered around seeking out their enemy's field army and destroying it as quickly as possible. In battle, Muslim commanders relied on their numerical superiority in cavalry and missile fire to wear down the crusaders, before encircling and destroying them.**

**below:** In close combat during the early crusades, Frankish knights deemed themselves invulnerable to the light arrows and puny mounts of the Seljuk Turks. However, once a knight became isolated, his horse was vulnerable to mass arrow attack. If the mount fell, the knight's heavy armor became a liability. Unable to move freely, the unmounted Frank was easily dispatched by the more numerous Turks.

The crusader policy of relying on fortified cities and castles supported by a small but heavily armored field army (or armies) dictated Muslim strategy. Simply, they had to bring the crusaders to battle as often as possible—the advantage of numbers was then on their side. In the beginning, the Franks were canny, and avoided as many open confrontations as possible, having seen the disastrous outcome of battles like *Ager Sanguinus*.

It was, therefore, an unfortunate confluence for the crusaders that brought Saladin up against them at the same moment their leaders were under the influence of men like Reynald of Châtillon—long in feudal chivalry and grace but selfish, headstrong, and lacking in military shrewdness. With the Christian fortresses emptied of men to support the army, and by enticing the crusaders to battle and then destroying the army at Hattin, Saladin had the Crusader States at his mercy in only one action. Before Saladin, skilled Muslim generals, frustrated by the crusaders' delaying and avoiding tactics, tried to force the crusaders out from behind their ramparts and onto the battlefield through two primary tactics: raiding Outremer's agricultural heartland, and besieging some of its most important cities or fortresses.

Muslim forces operated continuously in the north (Syria) and south (Egypt and the eastern edges of *Oultrejordain*). Due to the extended lines of communication along the length of Outremer, it was unusual for generals in these different sectors to co-ordinate their strategy. Independent military action meant that objectives were frequently limited and an attack on the Principality of Antioch, for example, would go unsupported by Muslim troops in Damascus. Outstanding generals like Nur ed-Din and Saladin needed to possess the skills of trained diplomats, as much as military genius, to encourage regional groups to join up and then

to hold the force together while it was in the field. Volunteers were prone to dispersing to return home to their fields, or when winter brought harsh campaigning conditions.

## Bristling with arrows

Muslim armies had no heavily armored knights to act like war machines. Instead, they relied on—often overwhelming—superiority in numbers of light cavalry. These troops, armed with bows and sometimes light spears, harassed Frankish units from a distance, relying on their archery to whittle down enemy numbers before joining in closer combat. Large units of light cavalry could cut off contingents from their supplies or ride down stragglers. Once battle commenced, large squadrons of cavalry skirmished with their opponents, avoiding close combat but trying to pierce the infantry screens that protected the knights, hoping to sting the Frankish cavalry into a premature attack. The tactic frequently worked on individual Franks, who broke ranks to fight for their honor. They were quickly dispatched by the waiting Muslims.

In a dry land, having enough water was always a serious problem for both sides, but the lighter equipped Muslim forces and their mounts wore better. For the Christian foreigners, unused to the heat, men and mounts soon wearied. Since the Muslims found it difficult to withstand a charge of mounted knights, they preferred to lure the Franks away from their infantry screens. Once a knight's horse was blown, the knight's hefty armor became a liability. Trapped inside, the metal armor acted like an oven. Soon enough, lightly darting Muslim cavalry would finish him off.

Horse archers were divided into groups, each alternating in the fire line with tight discipline. After loosing their arrows, a group immediately retreated, allowing the next group forward to fire, before restringing and wheeling to take over in the front line again. This tactic created a continual hail of arrows. Crusaders recalled how the arrows from Muslim horse archers fell "as though rain was falling from the sky." The Muslim chronicler Ibn al-Qalanisi wrote that after *Ager Sanguinus* (1119) he saw "dead horses bristling like hedgehogs with the arrows sticking from them."

Although the arrows were light, sheer numbers meant that they were likely to find some unprotected spot in an opponent's defenses. Even more commonly, the archers fired first at the knights' horses. In many cases, a dismounted knight was worse than useless, and certainly far more vulnerable. And the huge *destrier* war horses had to be imported all the way from Europe, further hampering the crusaders.

**above:** This vivid medieval church fresco shows a crusader knight charging with a spear after a Turkish horse archer. The artist has shown the horses as being of similar size, although the Christian knight's *destrier* would have been several hands taller. The archer is accurately shown guiding his mount only with his knees, leaving both hands free to fire over his shoulder.

# The Byzantine Army

**By 1097, when contingents of the First Crusade arrived at Constantinople, Byzantium had been "crusading" against Islam since the eighth century. Although the defeat of the Byzantines by Seljuk Turks at Manzikert left the empire weakened, the Byzantine army still had an extensive role to play.**

The Byzantine army had declined by 1097. What had once been a powerful standing army organized along recognizably ancient Roman legionary lines, was now largely composed of mercenaries. At the height of its power in the sixth century AD at the conclusion of Justinian's expansionist reign, the Byzantine army was the most powerful military force in the Mediterranean. Justinian's general, Belisarius, had even reconquered Italy from the Ostrogoths. Byzantine warships ensured the stability of the sprawling empire. That all ended at Manzikert (1071), and what little military force survived the Seljuk invasion was destroyed in a power struggle that lasted a decade. When Alexius Comnenus seized the throne in 1081, he tried to rebuild his country's defenses.

The Byzantines had relied on Anatolia for much of their revenue and military manpower. With this resource lost to the Turks, Alexius was forced to rely on foreign troops to augment his army. Because the men were regulars, under strict discipline and training, it was still a formidable force of some 20,000. This was divided into heavy cavalry, light cavalry, light infantry, and the Imperial Guard. The standing army no longer operated throughout the empire as had once been the case. Each *theme* (province) was expected to look after itself, and conscript its own *thema* (militia).

Even at the provincial level, the vestiges of ancient Roman military organization were visible in the numerical division of a *thema* in order to provide a chain of command and the discipline required in a well-run army. At the base level, a *numerus* (equivalent to a modern company) numbered 300–400 men, itself split into several platoons. Between five and eight *numeri* made up a *turma*, and each *thema* consisted of between two and three *turmae*. It was Byzantine policy to vary the numbers of the component parts to make it harder for an enemy to calculate a *thema*'s

exact strength. Although the *thema*'s task was to provide defense for its own *theme*, the province was also expected to reinforce the standing army.

In 1097, the total strength of the Byzantine army has been calculated at about 70,000 men. This figure does not take into account the large number of support units, which consisted of supply and siege train personnel, drovers, and pack animal handlers, medical corps and a highly skilled engineer corps. The latter found itself often thrown together with the crusaders, especially in the early years, when the "Western Barbarians" had neither the materials nor the skills of the Byzantines in siege warfare.

The mercenary composition of the Byzantine army included Turks, Russians, Norsemen, Anglo-Saxons, Danes, Franks, and Normans. The Turks were the light cavalry, the Franks and Normans for heavy cavalry. For obvious reasons, neither was used in any Holy Land campaigns, although Turks were used to escort crusaders across some stretches of Anatolia. The elite force was the Varangian Guard, composed of Vikings, or Norsemen.

Vikings had served in the Byzantine army and navy since the mid-ninth century, and by 1097, Varangians were the best paid of all Byzantium's soldiers. Norsemen from all over Russia and Scandinavia came to Constantinople to join the Guard, which was so popular, they had to pay a membership fee to get in. Because of their renowned loyalty, Byzantine emperors felt secure under Varangian protection—a comfort in a court of volatile intrigue. The Varangians accompanied John II Comnenus to Antioch in 1137 when the emperor decided it was time to force the prince of Antioch to pay homage and desist in his depradations of Lesser Armenia, a territory that should have been returned to Byzantium. The Varangians also fought against crusaders in the 1204 sack of Constantinople.

Scholars of language have pointed out that the word Varangian may have come to have a wider meaning by the time of the Crusades. Since it is derived from the word Viking, which essentially means "to go traveling," it was probably applied to any foreigner in the service of the emperor, or even more widely to any foreign merchant or pilgrim passing through.

The Byzantine army combined forces with the Franks in an assault on the emir of Shayzar

in 1138, and were successful. In 1142 and again in 1157, the Byzantine army advanced on Antioch, but on the last occasion, with the prince—Reynald of Châtillon—suitably disposed to paying homage to Manuel Comnenus in order to get rid of the annoying emperor, the Franks and Byzantines again combined for the 1158–9 campaigns. This army, much despised by the crusaders, was to keep the Byzantine Empire alive for another 400 years, long after the crusaders had all gone home.

# Byzantines versus Crusaders

**Although the two religious leaders of Christianity decreed a crusade to recover the holy places of Christendom from the infidel Muslims, it was hardly a match made in heaven. For the Byzantine emperor it was an extended period of playing host to unruly guests.**

**facing:** In the 12th and 13th centuries, Arab scholars were already producing maps of considerable accuracy. To the medieval Christian mind, however, any *Mapa Mundi*, or map of the world, had to show Jerusalem at its center (with Bethlehem just below), emphasizing the degree to which the Holy City was identified as being the center of the universe. It is no coincidence that a number of world maps like the one pictured here were published during the crusading era, almost as though the religiously motivated map-makers were showing the believer a dart board with the message, "there, that's where the crusaders are aiming."

Constantinople in the 11th century was almost certainly the most glorious city any crusader prince would have seen. The city was also the keeper of the largest collection of relics anywhere. These included a large piece of the True Cross, Christ's shroud, the Nails, and the Holy Lance. To western Christian eyes, these treasures could only have induced a deep-seated envy and a determination to find equally powerful relics in the Holy Land.

The emperor who effectively owned all this was revered as almost divine, an incarnation of Christ. However, the emperor's absolute power was severely limted by the typically Byzantine administration, which numbered into the thousands—clerks, spies, eunuchs, chamberlains, military advisers, and so on. Corruption was endemic. The civil service was a self-seeking means to riches. Alexius Comnenus had seized power after successes as a general and had no time for peculators. Tough-speaking, unaffected, army man in manner, this was the emperor who had to deal with the unrefined barbarian Franks who were about to descend on his capital.

Most, he had never met. One, he knew all too well. For years, Alexius had faced Bohemond of Taranto, whose greedy eyes ever lay on the Byzantine Adriatic coast opposite the Kingdom of Sicily, and Byzantine Greece after it. The two had faced each other in battle on several occasions. It was a typical act of Bohemond to agree to swear the oath of allegiance to the emperor in return for being appointed Viceroy of Asia. Alexius declined the honor, but did give his old enemy a vast amount of treasure to help him on his way. Anything to get the crusaders over the Bosphorus and away from Constantinople.

This instance illustrates the relationship that would develop between the two Christian factions: the Byzantines would give, the crusaders would take, but Byzantium could only be pushed so far. In many instances, the military help was unstinting, for instance at Nicaea in the First Crusade. Faced with assaulting or collapsing the great Byzantine-built walls of the city, the count of Toulouse called on Alexius for help. The crusaders had surrounded three sides, but the fourth faced onto a lake, across which came all the city's supplies. The Byzantines assembled a fleet of ships and then transported them over the intervening mountains on carts. This super-human effort paid off. The Turks surrendered when they saw the lake filled with the enemy fleet.

Byzantium's relationship with the Principality of Antioch was always sour, and emperors attacked Antioch on three occasions. By contrast, relations with the Kingdom of Jerusalem were warmer, aided by the fact that the kingdom did not adjoin disputed territories with the Byzantine Empire as did Antioch. Indeed, in 1157, Manuel Comnenus agreed to the marriage of his brother's daughter, Theodora, to King Baldwin III. There was, of course, a political reason. Baldwin was able to call on the emperor for greater use of the Byzantine army against the Turks, and Manuel was free to attack Antioch without Baldwin's interference. Manuel was settling a score against the prince of Antioch, Reynald of Châtillon, who had earlier raided Byzantine Cyprus for booty.

Eventually, Châtillon knelt (seething) before his emperor. Baldwin arrived days later, and the two monarchs became good friends. On one occasion, after Baldwin had taken a fall from his horse that broke an arm, Manuel personally set it for him—the emperor prided himself on his medical skills. The friendship welded bonds between Byzantium and the Holy Land, and Baldwin was confident of an immediate advance on Aleppo. But Manuel had no intention of engaging the Turks in battle and his visit was just a show of Byzantine strength aimed at both Christians and Turks. He signed a treaty with Nur ed-Din before rushing home to deal with another palace plot.

This to and fro of crusader-Byzantine relations continued throughout the First, Second, and

Third Crusades—King Richard the Lionheart even copied Châtillon in invading Cyprus, except that Richard kept the island for his own. In 1204, however, the discord was to end with a vicious finality when the leaders of the Fourth Crusade decided that quicker and easier spoils were available by attacking Constaninople rather than Cairo, Aleppo, or Edessa.

# The Battle of Arsuf, 1191

**As a case study in warfare, the Battle of Arsuf, between the armies of Saladin and King Richard the Lionheart, displays all of the typical components of a crusading battle. It also demonstrates the strengths and weaknesses of both sides and the way skilled commanders could play on these to achieve victory.**

Following the siege of Acre, Richard led his army south through Caesarea to Jaffa, conquering a series of coastal towns and cities on behalf of the king of Jerusalem. A strict commander, he ensured that the army kept tight, easily controlled formations. The Muslim historian Baha' ad-Din described seeing the Frankish troops "packed together like a wall." Richard paid close attention to the order of march, posting the military orders to the vanguard and the rearguard. He kept the sea on his right side, so if Saladin attacked there would be one secure flank.

Accounts differ, but it is probable that Richard had 10–20,000 men, including about 4,000 knights and 2,000 *turcopoles*. The remainder of his army were foot soldiers organized into units of a thousand men or less, with one rank of crossbowmen attached to a unit of spearmen, to provide covering fire.

They progressed at a leisurely pace, marching only four miles during the morning. At noon, the army halted and pitched camp. Some 15 miles north of Jaffa, the crusaders passed the small village of Arsuf, where the Forest of Arsuf lay within three miles of the sea. Saladin's army lay in wait in the forest and attacked as soon as Richard's men passed the village.

The exact composition of Saladin's army is unknown, but the chronicler Ambroise mentioned that it contained Bedouin and Sudanese infantry, Syrian and Turcoman light cavalry, and heavy cavalry of *mamluks* and *askars*, and Saladin's personal guards. Of the total strength of 50–80,000 men, it most probably contained 40,000 cavalry, including at least 25,000 horse archers. In any event, he outnumbered the crusaders three to one.

## Goaded into a trap

Richard's army was organized into 12 divisions, grouped into five *battles* (battalions). The knights marched on the seaward side of the column, protected by a line of infantry on the landward side. Richard's baggage wagons and supply carts, guarded by infantry spearmen, traveled between the cavalrymen and the sea. The Knights Templar formed the vanguard, or

front *battle*, and the Knights Hospitaler were at the rear of the column. It was written that the knights were drawn so close together that "an apple could not be thrown to the ground without touching the men or the horses."

Some of Saladin's light troops had been harassing the column for a week; Richard had ignored them. This time he realized he was under a full-scale attack, so he turned his army inland and the line of march became the line of battle facing the enemy, with the infantry screening the knights.

Saladin's main thrust was against the *battle* of the Hospitalers, aimed to draw them out from their tight formation. Provoked beyond endurance and acting against Richard's instructions, they eventually charged the Muslims in front of them,

falling into Saladin's ambush. Richard's reaction caught the Muslim commander by surprise: Richard ordered an immediate full-scale charge by his knights, before the rest of the Muslim army could get out of reach.

Saladin threw in his reserves against the Hospitalers and the English knights surrounding Richard's standard, but a prompt attack by Richard's reserve drove the Muslim cavalry from the field. The knights halted their pursuit at the edge of the forest and rejoined their march formations. While Richard's army lost less than 700 men, Saladin lost over ten times as many. He learned not to underestimate the power of Frankish cavalry and the tactical abilities of a medieval commander who knew exactly how to use them.

**above:** Mounted knights break out from behind the screening infantry to charge Turkish light cavalrymen, from a 15th-century manuscript depicting the taking of Antioch.

**facing:** Sword raised on high, Richard the Lionheart stands guard outside the Palace of Westminster, London.

# Military Orders: The Knights of Christ

**The most important steady source of military reinforcements to Outremer came from the military orders. Answerable only to the pope, they remained a law unto themselves and became a powerful semi-independent military society in the Holy Land. They also became the Muslims' most implacable foes.**

**facing:** The refectory of the Knights Hospitaler inside St. John's Church, Acre. The austerity of the bare walls and ceiling seen today would have been well appointed with hangings and other comforts.

**below:** Detail from the 12th-century wall-painting at Cressac, France showing a Knight Templar on horseback. The pope granted the Templars permission to wear the white, hooded mantle of the Cistercian monks in 1145. The red cross worn on the left breast and displayed on the shield only came in use with the Second Crusade.

The principal military orders, the Order of the Temple (Templars) and the Order of St. John's Hospital (Hospitalers) began as organizations dedicated to assisting pilgrims and tending the sick. These and other orders, notably that of the Teutonic Knights, operated at first more like monasteries, their members even referring to each other as "brother." They transformed religiously motivated volunteers into military orders, whose brethren became the mainstay of Outremer's defenses.

While retaining their independence from the king and other princes in Outremer, they were presented with frequent donations of land and fortifications during the 12th century, as well as special financial and legal privileges. In 1244 the Hospitalers held 29 castles in the Holy Land; the Templars maintained similar holdings. These inducements were necessary for Outremer, because the realm would have been unable to survive without the Orders and their military muscle. Both Orders—and scores of smaller organizations—also held extensive estates in Europe, donated by grateful benefactors. This ensured the Orders were financially as well as politically independent.

The Order of the Temple was founded in 1115 to protect pilgrims traveling within the Holy Land by two knights who shared a horse as a symbol of their poverty. Their image became the Order's symbol. Originally known as The Poor Knights, their first headquarters in the Temple of Solomon, Jerusalem, provided the Order's name. The Templars mirrored the strict personal rules adopted by monks of the Cistercian Order, avowing chastity, poverty, and obedience.

Ironically, in the face of this asceticism, the Templars rapidly became money brokers across Europe and Outremer. Their role as bankers evolved through the common recognition of the Order's scrupulous honesty. Above all, their strict discipline, courage, and Christian fanaticism made the Templars a highly respected weapon in the crusading arsenal.

## Decimated at Hattin

At the Battle of Hattin, the Order was all but destroyed, and many of their castles fell in the months following the disaster. The Order survived into the 14th century and held extensive lands in Europe. Jealousy from all quarters, secular and ecclesiastical, led to bogus charges of heresy and homosexuality, and the Order was denounced by Pope Clement V in 1307. The Templars were rounded up, imprisoned, tortured, and their lands and treasures confiscated.

The Hospitalers were named after a hospital for pilgrims in Jerusalem before the First Crusade. Following the capture of the city by crusaders, the hospital became a Benedictine institution, and in 1113 it was granted papal protection and became the Order of the Hospital of St. John. By 1120 the Order had expanded, running several hospitals throughout Outremer.

While the nursing element of the Hospitalers remained important, the organization gradually adopted a more military aspect. In 1136 it was given the fortress of Gibelin (Jabalah) and its military aspect increased steadily during the 12th century. By 1160 at the latest, the term Knights of St. John had fallen into disuse and

members of the Order were known as the Knights Hospitaler. After Hattin they became recognized as a fully-fledged military order and by 1206, while still operating hospitals, the military organization of brother knights had become an independent military formation.

Although the military orders had re-established themselves in the Holy Land by the time of the Third Crusade, all were in decline and their fortunes never fully recovered from the catastrophic losses at Hattin, where almost every brother knight in Outremer was killed. Following the fall of Acre in 1291, the Hospitalers established a new base in Cyprus, then Rhodes, transforming themselves into a naval power that would rule Malta until 1798.

The third order was the Teutonic Knights, founded during the siege of Acre in 1189–90 as a hospital for German crusaders. It was recognized by the pope in 1191, and became a military order seven years later. The Teutonic Knights were concentrated in the north of Outremer, but suffered a severe defeat in 1210, and the reduced Order re-established itself at Acre. The Order held a number of significant castles, but remained under the shadow of the Templars and Hospitalers. However, when sent to northern Europe to subdue and Christianize the pagan tribes of Prussia, the Order came into its own through ruthless, fanatic conquest.

**left to right:** Knights of the military orders— Templar, Hospitaler, and Teutonic.

# Crusading Castles: Bastions of Faith

**The crusaders built castles throughout Outremer to defend their newly-won possessions. Rather than imitating styles of European castle, many of these fortifications were based on Byzantine designs. Castles played a vital part in the realm's defense throughout the crusading period.**

**facing right:** This reconstruction of Belvoir, in Galilee, shows the castle's concentric plan and wide Byzantine-style battlements. The knights' private quarters are in the inner area.

**right:** Krak des Chevaliers from the southwest corner above Baibars' Tower (16 on the plan opposite). The nearest tower in the picture is the Warden's Tower (20 on the plan). This is the side attacked by Mamluk Emir Baibars in 1271, when the mighty crusader castle fell into Muslim hands. The large corner tower and square tower on the outer walls were built later by Muslims.

In feudal Europe, castles were not only strongholds, but also seats of power and the place where the king's justice was dispensed. The Kingdom of Jerusalem was to be little different. Over the 80 years following the crusaders' capture of Jerusalem, 64 castles were built, from the northernmost at Beirut to the Île de Graye in the Gulf of Aqaba. Further north, similar castles were constructed to defend the County of Tripoli, Principality of Antioch, and County of Edessa. The crusaders adapted their fortifications to suit the terrain on which they were built, and freely imitated Byzantine and even Muslim designs they encountered during their campaigns.

Both lords and engineers had been deeply impressed by Constantinople's defenses, the most extensive city fortifications they had ever seen. The crusaders decided to emulate this form of staged defensive line. The main "Wall of Constantine" was buttressed by a series of massive towers, while an inner wall with more towers provided a second line of defense. These two walls were further protected by a lower

outer wall to deter attack by siege engines. And around these three lines ran a deep moat filled with underwater stakes. Constantinople was considered impregnable. The Byzantine capital would eventually fall to crusaders in 1204, but not because of failure of the walls: the crusaders would bypass the defenses and land on the lightly protected seaward side of the city.

The best of the crusader castles were built on these Byzantine principles: massive inner walls protected by large round towers, surrounded by a lower outer wall with its own set of towers, and the whole structure surrounded by a dry moat where applicable. Defenders could fire over the top of the outer wall, providing supporting fire for soldiers positioned there.

## Manning castle and field

Due to the shortage of local wood, castles in the Crusader States lacked the numerous internal floors of European keeps and so had to be built as lower structures. The crusaders also adopted

**above:** The castle on Coral (or Pharaoh's) Island in the Gulf of Aqaba near Elat, Israel, was the most southerly of crusader fortifications. Straddling the main route from Cairo to Mecca, it was a serious danger to Muslim pilgrims.

garrisons, augmented in times of war by mobile field armies, guarded the Crusader States. The biggest problem was lack of manpower. Most castles required a substantial garrison, so when men were in short supply the kings of Jerusalem called on the military orders (*see previous two pages*) to help defend key sites. Personnel shortages meant denuding garrisons to raise field armies. In turn, a defeat on the battlefield left castles virtually unmanned and defenseless. After the Battle of Hattin (1187) most of the undermanned castles fell to Saladin, a blow from which the crusaders were unable to recover until the advent of the Third Crusade.

the Byzantine feature of wide battlements that allowed defensive artillery to be moved along the walls. Muslim fortifications were similar to those of the Byzantines, and cities such as Cairo, Aleppo, and Damascus boasted defenses that dwarfed those built by the crusaders to protect their principal cities, such as Tripoli, Antioch, and Acre. All groups in the Middle East freely copied construction techniques from each other.

The most impressive crusader castle in the Holy Land is Krak des Chevaliers. It was held by the Knights Hospitaler from 1142 to 1271, before it finally fell to a Muslim army. A similar design was used in the construction of castles at Beaufort (Belfort), Latrun, and Safed. The crusaders also made use of natural defenses, such as the fortification of a spur of land extending into the sea at Atlit, or a river junction at Saône (Sahyun). Defenses might also incorporate natural rocky escarpments, such as at the castle of Kerak des Moabites.

Crusader strategy inevitably centered around its castles and defending them against sieges (*see following two pages*). A network of castles and

**Plan of Krak des Chevaliers**

1. outer gate
2. tower protecting inner gate
3. gate to inner keep
4. Mamluk tower
5. warehouse
6. hall/refectory
7. warehouse for olive oil
8. warehouse with oil press
9. entrance ramp
10. tower above entrance
11. Turkish bath (*haman*)
12. tower with postern gate
13. water-filled moat
14. Baybars' Tower (long, vaulted chamber)
15. Mamluk tower, c.1285
16. tower reconstructed by Mamluk Emir Baibars, 1271
17. entrance stairs to outer ward
18. machicolated outer wall
19. residential tower
20. warden's tower
21. glacis
22. long, vaulted chamber
23. chapter house and cloister
24. inner courtyard
25. long, vaulted chamber
26. small courtyard
27. northwest tower (also called Tower of the King's Daughter
28. chapel (later a mosque)
29. rock-cut second entrance between two towers

# Sieges and Siegecraft

**Warfare in the Holy Land was dominated by fortifications, and campaigns revolved around the capture of key castles and walled cities. Both crusaders and Muslims became adept at siegecraft, the scientific investment and slighting of fortresses.**

**right:** This 14th-century manuscript illumination shows a castle (Chinon) under siege. It includes an unusually accurate depiction of a counterweight trebuchet, with a soldier loading a boulder to be hurled at the defenders packing the castle ramparts. One defender empties a pot of liquid over the attackers, either boiling water or oil.

The arrival of the Franks in the Middle East resulted in a rash of castle-building, as the crusaders tried to defend their fragile borders against surrounding hostile Muslim states. Taking advantage of the abundance of good fortified sites (including existing Muslim fortifications) and the availability of stone, these structures were far more impressive than the castles of Europe.

When the First Crusade arrived outside Antioch, it proved difficult to encircle because it was so large. It was too soon to have developed an extensive engineering corps to build siege machines, and the crusaders were fortunate that treachery proved a more powerful weapon. At Jerusalem, a train of rudimentary siege towers and trebuchets and mangonels (*see page* 73) was built to enable the crusaders to capture the city

in 1099, after which both sides assigned considerable resources to the creation of engineering cadres.

Sieges took on an almost ritual aspect in Outremer and both sides developed a system of siegecraft that differed from that encountered in the rest of Europe or Asia. A crusader castle had a permanent garrison, which was maintained on a permanent war footing, with mercenaries such as *turcopoles* augmenting the limited manpower. Castles of the military orders were exceptions to this in that they were bases for larger military formations. Although all crusader castles were stripped of their garrisons in times of crisis to create a field army, the permanence of garrison troops led to a professionalism in Outremer not encountered in Europe.

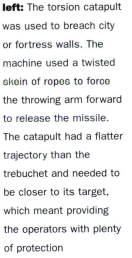

## Engines and towers

Diplomacy rather than force of arms was the usual first recourse when besieging a castle. This took the form of either parleying with the defenders for a free passage to safety if they surrendered, or straightforward attempts at bribery with known elements inside the fortification (both Christians and Muslims had countless spies in each other's camps). If the demand to surrender in return for freedom was rejected, it became the attackers' right to kill the inhabitants if the castle or city should fall.

Muslim generals preferred to begin sieges as soon as possible after winter's recession to gain the longest possible campaigning period before their armies dispersed at harvest-time. Since the simplest way to capture a fortress was by starving its defenders, plenty of time had to be allowed for the besieged to run out of food. The simple method, however, suffered from the drawback that the longer the besiegers sat around the walls, the greater the risk they ran of being attacked from behind by a relief army.

The tougher method was assault on the walls. When available to the commander, siege engines were used to batter at weak sections of walls, or at gates. If a breach opened, it would be stormed, usually with great loss of life on either side. Siege towers were a faster expedient if plenty of wood was available (which was not often the case in many parts of the Holy Land). These tall mobile platforms were designed to permit the attackers to emerge on the same level as the defenders. Hides soaked in water prevented defenders from setting fire to the structures, but they could still be

battered by defensive artillery from the battlements. During the siege of Acre (1189) the crusaders even mounted siege towers on rafts to assault the seaward side of the city.

If the assaulting force gained a foothold within the defenses, weight of numbers usually told—logically, attackers almost always outnumbered defenders. The medieval soldier knew little mercy for the loser—being last into the captured city meant getting the worst of the plunder—so their was no thought of kindness, and in such a situation the defenders were inevitably massacred. The professional aspect of siegecraft in the Holy Land meant that once a breach was made, honor was considered satisfied. If the defenders were given a last opportunity to surrender, it was usually accepted, although the religious military orders fought to the bitter end. These techniques and rituals, developed by crusaders and Muslims alike, eventually came to be standard practice in siegecraft across Europe and Asia.

**left:** The torsion catapult was used to breach city or fortress walls. The machine used a twisted skein of ropes to force the throwing arm forward to release the missile. The catapult had a flatter trajectory than the trebuchet and needed to be closer to its target, which meant providing the operators with plenty of protection

**below:** The traction trebuchet was a counterpoise catapult that used teams of men to haul the throwing arm down by ropes. Another type, the counterweight trebuchet (pictured) used a box filled with earth and rocks. With greater range and higher than the catapult, the trebuchet was better suited to hurling missiles over high walls— sometimes even decapitated heads. Modern experiments have shown the trebuchet to be highly accurate.

The Byzantine Empire in 1203,
on the eve of the Fourth Crusade.

Not all the crusaders taking
part in the Fourth Crusade
disobeyed the pope in
attacking Constantinople.
Simon of Montfort left the
main fleet after Zara and
sailed for Acre, joining
Walter of Autun and John of
Nesle from Europe.

With hindsight, the deaths of Saladin (1193) and King Richard (1199) marked the end of the idealistic period of crusading history when religious belief and codes of chivalry were still important. A mere five years after Richard's death, the Fourth Crusade undertook the most ignoble deed of the entire crusading era: the capture and sack of the Christian city of Constantinople. In 1204, the Byzantines, who had been largely responsible for sponsoring the crusading movement, suffered the effects of a century of religious, economic, and political rivalry with the Crusader States.

The Byzantine Empire had recovered from its disastrous defeat at Manzikert (1071) and gradually regained a portion of its lost territories in Asia Minor, even making inroads into Turkish-held Anatolia, while the Muslims were distracted by events in the Holy Land. During the 12th century a series of Byzantine emperors

maintained a tense working relationship with the rulers of the Crusader States, even offering support when it suited their ends. A half-century of warfare between Byzantines and Turks in Asia Minor ended in 1195 and it seemed the empire would be able to enjoy a period of relative peace and prosperity. Instead, it was divided by a fresh wave of internal disputes and political maneuvering, just as Pope Innocent III called for a fourth crusade in 1199.

Instead of an assault on Islam, the Venetians

# CHAPTER 8

# The Fourth Crusade

and the German emperor urged an assault against their fellow Christians in the East, a decision that owed more to economic and political rivalry than to religion. Although the Fourth Crusade was portrayed as a struggle to reunite the two parts of the Christian church, it was little more than an annexation, encouraged by divisions within the Byzantine state. The loss of Constantinople in 1204 was a mortal blow to the Byzantines, and although the city was recaptured in 1261, the empire remained a shadow of its former self.

# The Decline of Byzantium

**During the 12th century the Byzantine Empire recovered from the disastrous close of the preceding century and regained much of its former status. Although the military situation improved, political divisions and external threats undermined stability.**

**below:** The ruins of a Seljuk bridge span the Eurymedon river near Aspendos in Turkey (see map). Built between the 12th and 13th centuries, its several arches show the skill of medieval Muslim engineering and the emphasis the Seljuks placed on commercial and military communications.

Under Emperor Alexius Comnenus, the Byzantines harnessed participants in the First Crusade, avoided serious confrontations with their Frankish colleagues, and directed them at their Muslim neighbors. A good portion of the lost Byzantine territory in Asia Minor (Anatolia) was recovered, although the interior of the region remained in Turkish hands, becoming the Sultanate of Rum, a semi-independent Turkish state.

The relationship between the Crusader States and the Byzantine Empire was complex, with alliances forged through marriage, trade, and military pact ebbing and flowing to mirror political changes in the courts of Constantinople and Jerusalem. By the mid-11th century—and the fall of the neighboring County of Edessa—the Princes of Antioch needed an ally, and in return for acknowledging the suzerainty of the Byzantine emperor they gained military protection.

Under Emperor John II Comnenus (r.1118–43) further inroads were made into Seljuk Turkish lands in Anatolia and even Syria. His son Manuel Comnenus (r.1143–80) succeeded him and almost immediately faced a potential crusader invasion during the Second Crusade. He rightly determined that the crusaders posed a more serious threat to Byzantine stability than the Turks, so he made a truce with his religious enemy, Sultan Kilij Arslan of Rum, which allowed him to concentrate his efforts on guarding against any crusader threat.

The military disaster of the Second Crusade

and a papal-Byzantine alliance removed any immediate serious crusader threat, but Manuel's campaigns against the king of Sicily increased Italian resentment of the Byzantines. Similar Byzantine advances at the expense of Hungary further alarmed the Europeans, while the emperor's near-constant campaigns to expand the Byzantine frontiers drained the treasury, and nobles at court schemed behind his back.

In 1176, after a period of gains in Anatolia, the Byzantine army was defeated in battle with the Turks. Instead of pushing his advantage home, Sultan Kilij Arslan negotiated a second peace treaty. At war with neighboring Seljuk rivals, he needed more time to defeat them and seized the chance to forge peace.

## From youth to experience

Manuel died four years later. Although the realm was at peace, it was—as usual—divided by political intrigue. Both John and Manuel had increased Byzantine power, but the latter's fascination with the Balkans and Italy had prevented him from improving the political situation in the eastern portion of the empire. Manuel was an accomplished ruler and his loss was sorely felt over the next decades.

The teenage Emperor Alexius II Comnenus (r.1181–3) had been married to a 12-year-old French princess by his Frankish mother, Mary of Antioch. Conservative elements within the Byzantine court feared an increase in "Westernization," so many supported the coup by the late emperor's cousin, Andronicus I Comnenus (r.1183–5). Not only did the 64-year-old Andronicus seize the imperial mantle and kill the emperor and his mother, he also claimed the pubescent bride. The new emperor promptly launched a state-organized persecution and massacre of western foreigners, which caused a flood of refugees to Italy and Hungary, begging for help.

William II of Messina landed at Durazzo on the Adriatic in 1185, hoping to attract opponents of the tyrant Andronicus. Unfortunately for William, the ensuing uprising was all too successful and Andronicus was murdered by a Byzantine mob. His nephew became Emperor Isaac II Angelus (r.1185–95), and a rejuvenated Byzantine army repulsed the Sicilians.

The Angeli family ruled the empire for 19 years, through Isaac, then Alexius III and Alexius IV. During this time, Cyprus was lost to a Byzantine warlord (Isaac Comnenus, *see page 123*), the court and government became rife with corruption, and the empire's weakness was exposed by encounters with Franks of the Third Crusade. While plans were being laid to launch a Fourth Crusade against Egypt, factions in Italy had already decided that Constantinople was a more appealing objective.

**above:** A gold aureus of John II Comnenus. Coinage—rarely used at this time in medieval Europe—had been an oriental standard means of stamping a ruler's authority on everyday life. Byzantine emperors were regarded as incarnations of Christ, seen here blessing John Comnenus.

The major routes of communication on the southern Anatolian coast.

155

# The Venetian Maritime Empire

**During the 11th century the island city of Venice developed into one of the Mediterranean's most prosperous trading centers. It ousted merchant fleets of rival Italian ports and maintained a monopoly of trade with the Byzantines. When the monopoly was revoked, the Venetians sought revenge.**

The city of Venice, on the northern end of the Adriatic Sea, monopolized the rich markets of northern Italy and Germany and sea communications with the Mediterranean world with its access to the Silk Road and the Far East. Venice began life as a Byzantine port and

Pisa and to a lesser extent Genoa also emerged as significant maritime mercantile and naval powers during this period. Pisa gained control of the islands of Sardinia and Corsica, the start of a Mediterranean trading empire that brought the city into direct conflict with Genoa, a struggle for dominance that would continue into the 14th century. This rivalry on the other side of Italy helped Venice to become the leading maritime power in the region.

As well as trading in costly silks and spices, the Venetians also produced ships, glass, and ironwork, making them one of the most

mercantile center but developed into a virtually independent political entity. By the tenth century, Venetian merchants had developed its trading links with the Byzantines and formed the principal maritime link between Byzantium and the Frankish kingdoms.

productive industrial cities in the Mediterranean. By looking toward Byzantium rather than the rest of Italy, they traded freely with eastern European and even Muslim ports, whose markets were closed to Venice's Italian rivals.

Venice was a republic, ruled by the Great

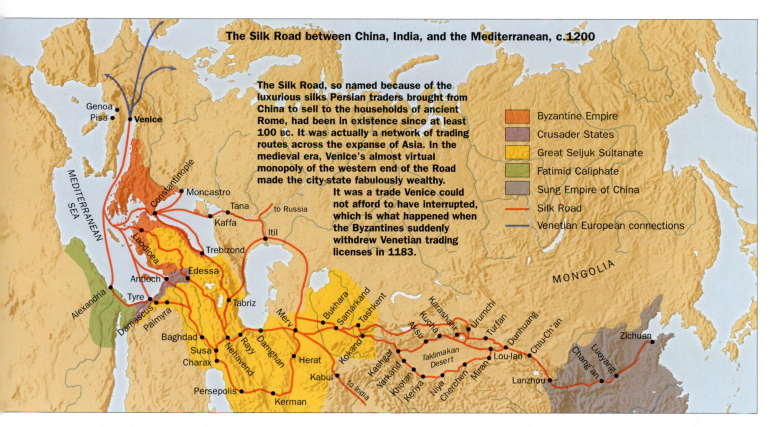

## The Silk Road between China, India, and the Mediterranean, c.1200

The Silk Road, so named because of the luxurious silks Persian traders brought from China to sell to the households of ancient Rome, had been in existence since at least 100 BC. It was actually a network of trading routes across the expanse of Asia. In the medieval era, Venice's almost virtual monopoly of the western end of the Road made the city-state fabulously wealthy.

It was a trade Venice could not afford to have interrupted, which is what happened when the Byzantines suddenly withdrew Venetian trading licenses in 1183.

- Byzantine Empire
- Crusader States
- Great Seljuk Sultanate
- Fatimid Caliphate
- Sung Empire of China
- Silk Road
- Venetian European connections

Council, or the Council of Ten, presided over by a doge (a local variation of the Latin *dux* or duke). Although the doge was elected for life, the remainder of the council was periodically elected, although nominations were restricted to members of a tight oligarchy of rich noblemen. Despite this, Venice was a rarity in Europe—an independent non-feudal state, free of political bonds with either the pope or the German emperor.

## A Venice scorned...

The Great Council supervized the city's administration, mercantile transactions, and systems of justice, and also negotiated trading agreements with other cities and states. For example, during the 12th century the council and the doge maintained trading agreements with the Byzantines, Germans, Outremer, Muslim states of North Africa, and several Italian cities. The island city-state maintained a close relationship with the crusaders, offering freighters, supplies, and warships in exchange for exclusive trading rights with the Kingdom of Jerusalem.

After destroying the power of the Egyptian fleet in 1123, Venice gained a degree of maritime ascendancy in the eastern Mediterranean, a situation enjoyed for the rest of the century, despite competition from Genoa and Pisa. Secret trading agreements with the

Egyptians and emirs of North Africa demonstrated that financial considerations outweighed religious ones for Venetian merchants. As a result, Venice became the European gateway to the Orient. Her ships carried spices and luxury goods while her rivals transported less lucrative pilgrims.

The only limit to Venetian commerce was Byzantium, and although the Venetians enjoyed good relations with the empire, even building and manning their ships, Byzantine merchants were resentful. When Emperor Andronicus Comnenus seized power in 1183, supported by a wave of anti-Western sentiment, he revoked the trading agreement between Venice and the Byzantine Empire. With Venetian ships excluded from Byzantine ports, her maritime supremacy was in jeopardy.

In 1201, when papal envoys approached Doge Enrico Dandolo for assistance in transporting men and supplies for the Fourth Crusade, the Council of Ten considered the proposal and agreed, but at an exorbitant cost. They also demanded half of everything captured on sea or land. The crusaders' objective of Alexandria in Egypt was unacceptable; it would disrupt Venetian trade with the Orient. Instead, the wily doge suggested an alternative. Constantinople would soon encounter the wrath of Venice and the republic's new crusader allies.

**facing:** A 14th-century manuscript illumination depicts the Council of Ten. The doge and nine other council members sit in discussion, while four scribes sitting in front take notes.

# Rogue Crusaders

**The Doge of Venice used the Fourth Crusade as a weapon to further the interests of his city, rather than to benefit Christendom. Despite the pope's disapproval, crusaders joined a struggle against fellow Christians.**

Egypt, but ended up pitting Christian against Christian.

Innocent decided against soliciting help from Europe's princes, to avoid questions over his authority. He wanted this crusade to be carefully controlled. He did so by insisting that Europe's kings devolve their authority to six papal legates. These representatives then negotiated for transport from Venice and called upon the army to gather there, ready for embarkation.

The contract signed by Doge Enrico Dandolo returned a substantial financial benefit for the use of Venetian ships. An escort of 50 Venetian galleys ensured the security of the expedition and also guaranteed that Dandolo could influence the course of the venture. During 1202, some 11,000 crusaders gathered in Venice under the military leadership of marquis Boniface of Montferrat, brother of the crusading Lord Conrad. Unable to pay the Venetians the full contracted sum, the crusaders remained in camp, unable to continue their voyage.

By late summer, Dandolo set a proposal before the envoys. The King of Hungary had recently captured the Venetian city of Zara on the Adriatic coast. Lacking the military muscle to retake it unaided, Dandolo offered to

Pope Innocent III (p.1198–1216) was one of the most successful of the medieval popes in separating the pontiff's office from secular squabbling with the Holy Roman Empire that had plagued the Church for most of the 12th century. He was also responsible for the Fourth Crusade, which was to assault

postpone the crusaders' bill in return for their military help. Many crusaders violently objected to the proposal, particularly since the Hungarian king was a former crusader. Doge Dandolo took the Cross and became a crusader, and after much argument, the legates and leading crusader nobles were forced to acquiesce. As thousands of Venetians joined the expedition, it became clear that the Fourth Crusade would be run by the doge, not the pope.

## Bribed to target Christians

The participants in the Fourth Crusade left Venice in October 1202, and their 200 ships arrived off Zara on November 10. The Abbot of Veaux became the conscience of the crusaders, waving orders from the pope that forbade the attack, "for the people in it are Christians, and you wear the sign of the cross." He was ignored. The boom guarding the harbor was broken and for the next two weeks siege machines bombarded the walls, from land and sea. Eventually the city surrendered, the Venetian flag was raised over its walls, and the plunder was divided.

The crusaders wintered in Zara, where they received news that Innocent had excommunicated everyone in the expedition. Petitions were sent to Rome pleading that the crusaders' hands had been tied by the Venetians. The excommunication was lifted for the crusaders but not for Doge Dandolo and his followers.

Meanwhile, in Constantinople, Emperor Isaac had been blinded and imprisoned by his brother, who took the imperial mantle as Alexius III (r.1195–1204). Isaac's son, another Alexius, traveled to Zara and offered incredible inducements if the crusaders would help him regain his rightful throne. He offered to place the Byzantine Church under the authority of Rome, promised huge financial incentives, and even offered 10,000 soldiers to accompany the crusaders to Egypt, the expedition's declared destination. The Abbot of Veaux raised his objections to another attack on a Christian state, but the majority of the Venetians and crusaders recognized the offer's possibilities. The target was switched, and the crusaders set sail from Zara, bound for the Byzantine capital.

**facing:** Lotario d'Anagni, Pope Innocent III, was a power-broker who came closest to bringing the monarchs of Europe into line. He crowned a German emperor and then tried to depose him. He opposed King Philip II of France's marriage and King John of England's refusal to submit to papal authority. Both countries were excommunicated until the kings submitted to the authority of the Holy See.

**below:** A medieval galley, typical of ships in the Venetian fleet, forms part of a relief on a headstone at the crusader port of Aigues Mortes, France.

# The Sack of Constantinople

**The Byzantine capital of Constantinople was the largest and richest city in Europe and the Near East, a lure too great for the Venetians and their allies to resist. The subsequent storming and sacking of Constantinople was one of the most shameful acts of the crusading era.**

When the crusaders arrived off Constantinople on June 24, 1203, many of them "gazed very intently at the city, having never imagined there could be so fine a place in all the world." The citizens was as stunned by their arrival as the crusaders were by the city's opulence. The usurper Alexius III watched the Venetian galleys row past the walls, displaying Prince Alexius on board, and heard the crew cry out "Here is your natural lord" to the citizens of Constantinople. The crusaders captured the suburb of Galata, breaking the boom that defended the inner harbor, the Golden Horn. On July 17, a simultaneous land and sea assault was launched against the city, but the attack was repulsed by the Varangian Guard. Despite this success, Alexius III was alarmed beyond reason and fled the city that night.

Leading Byzantine elements immediately freed the blinded Isaac and set him on the throne. He deputed his son to co-rule with him in the hope of calming down crusader alarm at this unexpected development. It was an unenviable task. The crusaders were adamant. A papal legate met with Isaac and Alexius and informed Isaac that they were expected to abide by the terms of the agreement negotiated with his son. While the crusaders waited for their money and troops, the Byzantine court tried to raise the funds and Alexius toured the empire soliciting contributions, under the watchful eye of a squadron of crusader knights.

By January 1204, anti-crusade feelings had risen to fever pitch within Constantinople—a

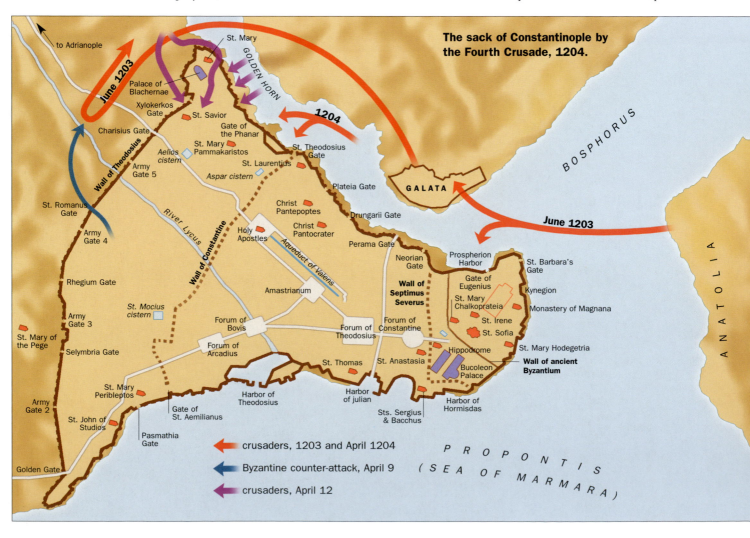

**The sack of Constantinople by the Fourth Crusade, 1204.**

➤ crusaders, 1203 and April 1204

➤ Byzantine counter-attack, April 9

➤ crusaders, April 12

fire started by a French crusader did little to improve relations. The citizens rebelled. Isaac and Alexius were swept from their thrones, murdered, and replaced by the anti-Western figurehead Alexius V Ducas Murzuphlus. Alexius V (r.1204) made it clear that he had no intention of paying the crusaders and began organizing the city's defenses.

## Silent approval

The Venetians had seen enough. Screaming treachery, they persuaded their fellow crusaders that the only recourse remaining was to attack Constantinople. For the crusaders, clerics justified the action by claiming they were unifying the Christian church. Warriors who fell fighting would benefit from forgiveness of sins. As Pope Innocent III failed to oppose an attack, it can be argued that he gave the assault his *de facto* blessing. In March the decision to attack was made and the crusaders laid their plans.

The first attack, on April 9, was a disaster because of an unfavorable wind that kept the attackers from the sea wall, while Byzantine

artillery bombarded the Venetian ships with boulders. The simultaneous land attack was also repulsed. A second attack came on April 12, again a simultaneous assault by land and sea. The Venetians lashed their ships together, protecting them from artillery fire by wooden screens. This time the wind was in the crusaders' favor, and the giant ships *Pilgrim* and *Paradise* slammed against the city's sea wall.

Venetian soldier Pietro Alberti was the first to enter a wall tower, and while he fought the mercenary defenders, two French knights joined him to defend the foothold. A small gate was discovered and opened, and a flood of attackers poured through. By nightfall the emperor had fled and Constantinople was in crusader hands.

The murder, rape, and looting continued for three days. When it was over, the crusaders held a Thanksgiving service. The haul of booty was immense. Holy relics were taken to adorn the churches of western Europe, and the crusaders filled their purses. Many returned home with their booty but thousands more remained to rule their new-found Latin empire.

**below:** The impregnable walls of Theodosius II were never put to the final test, since crusaders found a door left open, which was enough. Constantinople's walls give a good indication of the rapidity of the city's growth in its prime. The wall of the Roman emperor Septimus Severus (see map) was built in about AD 200. Valens extended the precints with his wall in about 370, and Theodosius II added his in about 430.

# Outremer in the Aegean

**Following the sack of Constantinople, the Byzantine Empire crumbled and was replaced by a string of small, semi-autonomous Greek and Latin provinces. The Fourth Crusade not only marked the collapse of the crusading ideal, it also created a political vacuum that would ultimately aid the expansion of Islam into Europe.**

Baldwin of Flanders was elected as leader of the new government in Constantinople, effectively becoming the region's first Latin emperor. His actual title was Emperor of Romania, the new Latin name for the former Byzantine Empire, a term that emphasized the supremacy of the Roman Church over their Orthodox rivals. For the Venetians, who formed the majority of the elective council, he seemed the ideal candidate, lacking the power or influence to oppose their piecemeal appropriation of the best provinces in the Aegean basin. The Venetians coveted a lot more than Byzantine territory.

Over the next few years, European markets were flooded with treasures looted from Constantinople and the rest of the Byzantine Empire. The official tally of plunder was set at 900,000 silver marks, and most of this was claimed by Venetians. Venice also claimed the hinterland of Constantinople, the Adriatic coast of Greece, and almost all of the most productive islands in the Aegean Sea, with a few crusaders

**below:** The Conquest of Trebizond, painting by an unknown Florentine artist, c.1461. The smallest of the split up Byzantine states, Trebizond continued to be a wealthy Christian trading center on the Black Sea until it was finally overwhelmed by Ottoman Turks shortly before the final conquest of Constantinople.

who were willing to become puppet regional administrators. The twinned islands of Andros and Naxos became the Duchy of the Archipelago, province of a Venetian nobleman. Crete also became a Venetian colony and, during the next two decades, over five percent of Venice's population settled there.

While all these new provinces owed their allegiance to the Doge of Venice, in reality most were virtually independent. The new Empire of Romania simply provided an overall forum for this collection of states and a legal and constitutional framework for the region. The Aegean coast of Greece was taken over by crusaders from northwest Europe; the new Duke Otto of Athens was a Burgundian and William de Champlitte became the Prince of Aechea.

## The old empire hangs on

Elsewhere, where traces of the former Byzantine Empire survived, they became focal points for Greek resistance to Latin domination. The Empire of Trebizond on the Black Sea coast of Anatolia, the Empire of Nicaea in western Anatolia, and the Despotate of Epirus in northwestern Greece remained in the hands of provincial Byzantine governors until they were amalgamated into a resurrected Byzantine Empire in the late 13th century. This later resurgence was largely due to the survival of

The division of the Byzantine Empire after the sack of Constantinople in 1204.

**Legend:**
- Byzantine states
- Crusader states
- Byzantine gains, 1224
- Venetian territory
- Muslim territory

these isolated pockets, and by failing to wipe them out, the Latins had sown the seeds of their own destruction.

The Fourth Crusade had not only failed to aid the Christians of Outremer, it also helped drain the Crusader States of their most precious resource—fighting men. Romania became an attractive prospect for the knights and minor nobility of the Crusader States, as well as western Europe, who had hitherto been unable to climb the ladder of feudal society. The Holy Land had enjoyed a period of unprecedented peace after the death of Saladin. At once, this meant there was less for a knight to do and so advance himself. And yet the whole strategic situation was ominous, with a thin coastal strip of crusader strongholds on the edge of an Islamic continent. Romania looked much more stable, so knights abandoned their possessions in the Holy Land and took passage to Greece.

The ultimate weakness of the Latin states in Greece was their structure, based on the European feudal model. Even the republican Venetians adopted feudal structures in Romania, a poor substitute for the old imperial system of regional government. The Latin empire was gradually eroded by the Byzantines, although the resurrected empire remained in pockets and lacked unity, eroding any political influence the Greeks might have had as part of a more homogenous society. The real winners were the Serbs, who expanded their borders southward as far as Thessaly—until they met Ottoman Turks expanding in the other direction.

# Byzantium Survives

**The Frankish rulers of Greece and the Aegean Islands were detested by a local population who longed for the prosperity and stability they had enjoyed as part of the Byzantine Empire. Isolated centers joined forces into a revitalized Byzantium, whose enemies were the Christians who occupied their former capital.**

The three surviving Byzantine provinces of Nicaea and Trebizond in Anatolia and Epirus in Greece served as rallying points for Greeks who resented living under Latin rule.

the rest of the Latin empire. In 1230 the Emperor of Epirus was defeated by Czar John I Asen of Bulgaria, and Thessalonica became a Bulgarian puppet-state. This left the future of Byzantium in the hands of the Empire of Nicaea. In 1208, the imperial title was given to Theodore Lascaris, son-in-law of Emperor Alexius III. Theodore I was attacked by the Latin Emperor Baldwin, but the Franks became distracted by Bulgar attacks and any further Latin expansion was averted.

**above:** Greek lettering and decorative Byzantine patterns are evident in the brickwork of the mid-13th-century Kata Panaghia building in Arta. Arta was one of the major centers of the Despotate of Epirus.

The Empire of Trebizond, founded in 1204, was too remote to have any serious influence on events and did little more than exist on the shores of the Black Sea.

Michael Comnenus Ducas founded the Despotate of Epirus in 1204, and in 1224 his half-brother Theodore conquered Thessaly from the Franks, founding the Empire of Thessalonica. This effectively severed land communications between Constantinople and

In 1214, the Latin and Byzantine emperors signed a peace treaty, leaving the Franks to fight the Bulgars and giving the Byzantines a chance to recover. The first emperor of Nicaea to be dubbed the Byzantine Emperor was John III Ducas Vatatzes (r.1222–54), who began a campaign to win back the old imperial seat.

In 1235, the Bulgars converted to Orthodoxy and signed a peace treaty with the Nicaeans. They needed a secure frontier behind them in order to deal with a serious Mongol invasion. Mongols also invaded Asia Minor but retired after defeating the Turks. With the Mongols gone and the Turks in disarray, the Byzantines were safe from attack from the east and free to concentrate on fighting the Latin occupiers of Greece and Constantinople.

## Byzantines return

By this stage, with the crusading impetus failing, the Latin Empire was crumbling into a mess of local jealousies, although it managed to cling on in isolated pockets around the Aegean. Czar John's death in 1241 proved to be a watershed. The region was freed from further threat of Bulgar expansion, and the Nicaean emperor was recognized as the overlord of Thessalonica. In 1249, Emperor John negotiated a peace treaty with Epirus, which by this time had broken away from Thessalonica.

The Byzantines were ready for their comeback. Founder of a new dynasty, Michael VIII Palaeologus (r.1258–82) was crowned in Nicaea and immediately declared war. The Byzantine and Frankish armies met in Thessaly and the resulting Latin defeat sealed the city's

fate. To discomfit Venice, Michael signed a treaty with Genoa: in return for free trade in the Black Sea the Genoese Fleet would keep the Venetians at bay. With Constantinople cut off from relief, Michael's army captured the city in July 1261. Constantinople was in Byzantine hands once more.

Over the next few years the Byzantines consolidated their gains, although they did come under increasing pressure from a revitalized Turkish power in Anatolia, the Ottomans. The resurgent Byzantine Empire was limited to western Anatolia, northern Greece, and parts of the Balkans. Although it was an amazing political recovery, Byzantium was now a regional power, hardly a Mediterranean superpower.

The empire survived for the next two centuries, an almost forgotten political backwater on the border between the Muslims and the Franks. An empire in name only, it would never regain more than a trace of its former greatness. Its final destruction by Ottoman Turks in 1453 was the unavoidable consequence of the crusaders' sacking of the city two-and-a-half centuries earlier.

**below:** The Predicted Fall of Constantinople, painting by an unknown Turkish artist. Ottoman forces gathered in strength on the finger of land joining Constantinople to Europe in April 1453. The last Byzantine emperor, appropriately named Constantine XI (r.1448–53), faced a genius in Mehmet II (r.1451–81), the Turkish sultan who had finally taken all the Byzantine Empire except for the capital. After a massive assault on the morning of May 29, the Turks took Constantinople and ended an empire that had survived the fall of Rome by a millennium.

# CHAPTER 9

# The Last Crusaders

Attalia

Frederick II 1228–9

Louis IX 1248–54

Damietta

Mansura

Bilbeis

Cairo

Nile

After the Fourth Crusade, the impetus seemed to leave the crusading movement. Ironically, the crusaders had blocked their own land route to the Holy Land by creating an implacable enemy of the Byzantines. Any future crusading expeditions would have to reach the Middle East by sea. This, more than any religious significance, explains why in the 13th century, Egypt became the crusaders' preferred target. As a result, the Crusader States were largely left to fend for themselves.

The Fifth and Sixth Crusades were grand titles for what amounted to little more than a series of raids on the periphery of Muslim power. The Fifth Crusade (1218–21) was a fiasco, as was the naïve Children's Crusade, which achieved nothing other than filling the Arab slave markets.

The century was one of shifting alliances between East and West, as both Islam and Christendom were subjected to attacks by Mongols and were diverted to fighting the "Scourge of God." In the ensuing spirit of co-operation Jerusalem was returned to the crusaders by treaty in 1229 and, following the Mongol invasion of Anatolia and Persia, the

Syrians and the crusaders even forged a military alliance. The Sixth Crusade of Louis IX of France was another invasion of Egypt. It not only ended in failure, it also led to the capture of the French king.

Just as the Mongols were demonstrating their invincibility against Muslim armies, the Egyptian Mamluks who defeated Louis IX were developing into a military force that could stop the invaders from the steppes. In 1260 a climactic battle between Mamluks and Mongols ended in a Muslim victory, and Islam was saved. It was a different story for Christianity in the Holy Land.

Over the next decade, the Mamluks turned their attention on the Crusader States and, despite a last major foreign crusade in 1271–2, the Christians had no way of stopping them. Seljuks and crusaders alike were defeated by the new power in the Middle East until finally, in 1291, the last stronghold in Outremer fell to Islam. The Crusades ended with the fall of Tripoli and Acre, and the Holy Land was left to enjoy the first real peace since Pope Urban II first called on the princes and lords of Europe to take holy vows.

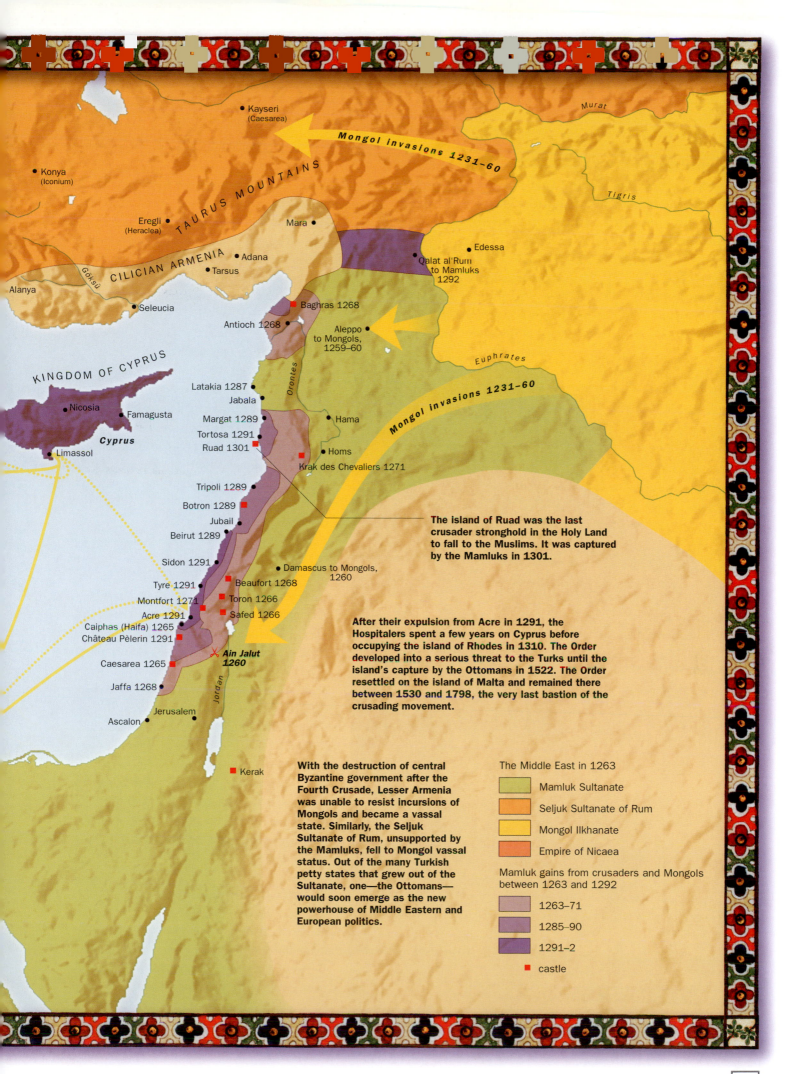

Kayseri
(Caesarea)

**Mongol invasions 1231–60**

Murat

Konya
(Iconium)

Tigris

Eregli
(Heraclea)

TAURUS MOUNTAINS

Mara

Edessa

Qalat al'Rum
to Mamluks
1292

Adana

CILICIAN ARMENIA

Alanya

Göksu

Tarsus

Seleucia

Baghras 1268

Antioch 1268

Aleppo
to Mongols,
1259–60

Euphrates

Orontes

KINGDOM OF CYPRUS

Latakia 1287

Jabala

Nicosia

Famagusta

Margat 1289

Hama

Tortosa 1291

*Cyprus*

Ruad 1301

Limassol

Homs

Krak des Chevaliers 1271

**Mongol invasions 1231–60**

Tripoli 1289

Botron 1289

Jubail

The island of Ruad was the last
crusader stronghold in the Holy Land
to fall to the Muslims. It was captured
by the Mamluks in 1301.

Beirut 1289

Sidon 1291

Damascus to Mongols,
1260

Tyre 1291

Beaufort 1268

Montfort 1271

Toron 1266

Acre 1291

Safed 1266

Caiphas (Haifa) 1265

Château Pèlerin 1291

After their expulsion from Acre in 1291, the
Hospitalers spent a few years on Cyprus before
occupying the island of Rhodes in 1310. The Order
developed into a serious threat to the Turks until the
island's capture by the Ottomans in 1522. The Order
resettled on the island of Malta and remained there
between 1530 and 1798, the very last bastion of the
crusading movement.

Ain Jalut
1260

Caesarea 1265

Jaffa 1268

Jordan

Ascalon

Jerusalem

Kerak

With the destruction of central
Byzantine government after the
Fourth Crusade, Lesser Armenia
was unable to resist incursions of
Mongols and became a vassal
state. Similarly, the Seljuk
Sultanate of Rum, unsupported by
the Mamluks, fell to Mongol vassal
status. Out of the many Turkish
petty states that grew out of the
Sultanate, one—the Ottomans—
would soon emerge as the new
powerhouse of Middle Eastern and
European politics.

The Middle East in 1263

- Mamluk Sultanate
- Seljuk Sultanate of Rum
- Mongol Ilkhanate
- Empire of Nicaea

Mamluk gains from crusaders and Mongols
between 1263 and 1292

- 1263–71
- 1285–90
- 1291–2
- ■ castle

# Crusaders in the 13th Century

**Although Richard the Lionheart saved Outremer and expanded its borders during the Third Crusade, the realm was far from safe. For most of the following century, the Crusader States were divided by political, dynastic, and commercial rivalries.**

**below:** In the 13th century, a new foe—the Mongols—threatened Christians and Muslims.

Under the terms of the peace agreement between Richard the Lionheart and Saladin, the crusaders controlled a strip of coastal land stretching from Tyre to Jaffa,

together with the northern enclaves around Tripoli and Antioch that the Muslims had not been able to conquer. King Guy of Jerusalem lost the support of his nobles and was removed from office and given Cyprus to rule by way of consolation. His sister-in-law, Isabella, became the new titular head of Outremer. Although she had lost her seat in Jerusalem, the remains of her kingdom were relatively secure.

From 1219 onward, the Muslims were placed under increasing pressure from the Mongols to the north and east—it was the year Genghis Khan (1167–1227) conquered the Turkish lands of the Shah of Khwarizm. This vast Muslim state, stretching from the Caspian Sea to Persia, was overrun by the Mongol horde for four years. The Mongols were now the greatest threat to Islam; the crusaders were contained or even placated as the main Ayyubid military effort was directed further east.

In the six decades following the departure of King Richard, no fewer than seven crusades were launched. The death of Holy Roman Emperor Henry VI (r.1191–97) led to the abandonment of another Germanic crusade in 1197. Pope Innocent III's Fourth Crusade never threatened Islam, but his next venture was a "continuous crusade," with successive waves of crusaders reaching the Middle East to batter the Muslims into submission. This Fifth Crusade was a military flop but a diplomatic triumph in that Jerusalem was restored to the Kingdom of Jerusalem through diplomacy rather than assault. Although Saladin's nephew, al-Kamil, was criticized for his actions, the concession allowed him to devote his military resources to the more decisive struggle against the Mongols.

## A patchwork of states

The next foreign crusader, the King of Navarre, also used diplomacy. He restored most of the kingdom's former territory west of the Jordan. In theory, Outremer was capable of defending these newly won possessions. Instead, the same divisive squabbling that had hastened its collapse in the late 12th century once again plagued the realm.

to de mercatatiti reabiator

**left:** 14th-century manuscript illumination of a merchant with weighing scales. It is all too easy to imagine the crusading era as being one of knights and infidel warriors battling over the holy places, but the medieval period was also one of great commercial growth. Trade between Egypt and Europe was already well established before the Fifth and Sixth Crusades. Mercantile relations between Egypt and Italy were only barely disrupted by the great military events, despite the supposed antagonism between Christians and Muslims. Indeed, the Crusader States were not the most important trading partners for European merchants because they were not economic units of any lasting substance.

In 1240 Prince Bohemond V (r.1233–51) ruled over Antioch and Tripoli, now a jointly run independent political state to the north of the Kingdom of Jerusalem. Various members of the Ibelin dynasty ruled over the coastal cities and hinterlands of Jaffa, Caiphas, and Arsuf. The merchant colonies of Venice, Genoa, and Pisa controlled Acre through the rule of elected officials, making it roughly equivalent to the free cities found in northern Italy and Germany during the 13th century. Philip of Montfort ruled in Tyre and was reluctant to acknowledge the suzerainty of Jerusalem. The Knights Templar and the Knights Hospitaler ruled independent domains, including a vast chain of fortresses and castles. Both orders were jealous of each other and of any ruler who threatened to undermine their power.

Outremer was a fragmented patchwork of states and the king of Jerusalem—John of Brienne—was usually absent from his realm and unable to assert his authority. Following the departure of Frederick II for Europe, the lords of Outremer had been left to govern themselves as best they could. Already split by dynastic rivalries, the political division between supporters of the emperor and the pope divided the realm further. Richard, Earl of Cornwall (and brother of England's Henry III), made some progress through diplomacy, but the strategic situation was unchanged.

The real watershed came in 1244 when Jerusalem fell to an Egyptian army and Philip of Montfort and Walter, Count of Jaffa, led a large crusader army to reclaim their lost territories. Sultan as-Salih Ayyub decimated the crusaders at La Forbie, near Gaza, in a battle that has been described as "a second Hattin." From that point Outremer was on the defensive, surviving on borrowed time.

# The Children's Crusade

**A 12-year-old French shepherd boy had a vision: that the Muslims could be shamed into handing over the Holy Land to its rightful Christian owners if they were faced with a crusading movement made up entirely of children. All they had to do was get there.**

Although Peter the Hermit preached that the lower orders of feudal society could participate in the Crusades, since the start of the 12th century no popular movement had occurred, or more correctly had been permitted to occur. The Crusades and the redemption that came with them were the prerogative of the rulers and nobles of Christendom and their retainers.

This changed in 1212 when a 12-year-old French shepherd boy (some sources claim he was 15) from Cloyes near Orléans claimed he had met Christ, who urged the child to lead a "Children's Crusade, which would succeed

where force had failed." Stephen the Shepherd became "The Prophet" and went to Paris to preach his cause. His followers became known as "minor prophets" and soon numbered in the thousands. The king sent the boy away and ordered the children to return to their parents. This proved to be impossible because the mass movement spread into Germany, where a ten-year-old peasant boy from near Cologne named Nicholas served as the rallying point for a German contingent.

It is hard today to begin to understand how such a movement could have reached such proportions. One reason was poverty. As overpopulation, clearance of the woods and forests for cultivation, and the growth of towns increased in pace, the spread of waged labor contributed to the increasing hardship of the rural peasantry. Another reason lay in the growing belief that "the meek shall inherit the earth." For obvious reasons, it was one of the more popular sayings in the Bible among the poor, but it had also become something of a mantra among a clergy desperate to keep the increasingly un-meek in their place. The notion that peasant children, the meekest of all, should take the Cross was a logical conclusion. For the first time since the late 11th century, the poor rose up in their thousands to take holy vows—a result of popular belief rather than papal incentive.

## A calamitous fate

By June 1212, Stephen the Prophet was in Vendôme, close to his birthplace, which became the main assembly point for the juvenile crusaders. When around 9,000 gathered, Stephen led them south toward Marseilles, escorted by priests. Apart from a teenage bodyguard for Stephen, none carried arms—after all, they hoped to convert the Muslims with their innocence, not their skills with the sword. Once they reached the port, it became obvious that Stephen had no clear idea what to do next. It has been suggested that he expected a miracle, such as a parting of the seas.

When local merchants offered to transport the children to the Holy Land in seven ships, it seemed that the children's prayers had been answered. Soon after the fleet departed it encountered a storm. Two vessels were shipwrecked and the children aboard drowned. Once the storm passed, the other ships split into two groups, two vessels sailing to the slave markets of Bougie in North Africa and the remainder carrying on to sell their human cargo to the slavers of Alexandria, Egypt.

While these French children were being paraded in the markets of North Africa, the Germans led by Nicholas arrived in northern Italy, after crossing the Swiss Alps. Most were from the Rhineland, the Low Countries, and Lorraine. A reported "infinite multitude" of these children (in reality there were probably less than 7,000, and less still after many died in the inhospitable Alps) begged for food on the streets of Genoa before drifting south, to Rome and beyond.

Everywhere they were ignored, and while many fell prey to criminals or became a source of cheap labor, most returned home. A few tried to beg an audience with the pope, but Innocent III was preoccupied with arrangements for a real crusade and refused to see them.

By the time the remaining few hundred children reached Brindisi on the southern Italian coast, a Norwegian trader called Friso took them under his wing. Almost inevitably, this meant they were shipped to the brothels and slave markets of the Mediterranean. The few who reached the Holy Land by attaching themselves to groups of pilgrims failed to make any impression on the Muslims who occupied Jerusalem. Like Christian merchants, they saw the children as a commodity.

# The Fifth Crusade: Assault on Egypt

**Pope Innocent III was eager to make amends for the Fourth Crusade, so in 1213 he proclaimed a new venture. This time, the populist zeal that led to the Children's Crusade was harnessed, as well as the military might of the nobility. It would be launched against Egypt.**

*below:* A 15th-century manuscript illumination depicts the papal legate, Pelagius, waiting to disembark at Damietta. as troops prepare to besiege the city.

The sack of Constantinople had been an embarrassment for Pope Innocent II. He now sought to launch a fresh expedition. The princes of Outrmer were less enthusiastic about having a fresh wave of crusaders thrust on them. Harvests had failed, there was starvation in the land, and it was felt that any newcomers should only sail for Acre if their ships were laden with plentiful grain supplies and

everything to make their retinues self-sufficient. Fortunately, the famines had coincided with a period of unusual peace with the Ayyubids. Sultan al-Kamil had encouraged trade with Europe, and over 3,000 Italian merchants were already operating in Alexandria.

However, there was also a widespread belief, after years of stalemate between Christian and Muslim forces, that Damietta on the Nile delta held the key to future success. As William of Chartres, the Templar Master, wrote to the pope: "We have now all decided to undertake an expedition into Egypt by sea and by land, and by destroying the city of Damietta we shall be able to command the road to Jerusalem." In fact Damietta, surrounded by the marshes of the huge river's delta, was the last place in the region European soldiers, unsused to the tropical pestilences rife there, should get bogged down in. And why it should have been so widely thought that Damietta held any key to Jerusalem remains a puzzle. In a sense, though, it was significant to the crusade.

The Holy See agreed, and the target was changed to Egypt. This time the pope extended spiritual benefits to commoners, taking advantage of the widespread populist support for the crusading movement that had been demonstrated. As a result, and unlike earlier crusader armies, this one contained a high proportion of inexperienced peasant infantry.

## A wasted opportunity

There were the high-born as well. In 1215, Frederick II of Germany (r.1211–50) took the Cross, as did numerous French nobles, although the recent war with England necessitated a delay in the departure of the French. By the late summer of 1217, the first contingents had gathered in Acre, and in November a substantial army led by King Andrew II of Hungary, Bohemond IV of Antioch, and Hugh I of Cyprus campaigned in *Oultrejordain*. The Muslim army retreated into Damascus and the crusaders withdrew, unwilling to risk a winter siege. Demoralized, the Hungarian king went home. His sudden defection spread a dismay the length of the Crusader States that was partly alleviated in late April, when the French and German contingents arrived in Acre, although Frederick II himself still had not left Germany.

In May 1218, leaving the Germans stationed in the Holy Land, a large fleet sailed to Damietta. After an early success under King John of Jerusalem in taking a small fortress near the city, the crusaders besieged the city. The pope sent Cardinal Pelagius out as papal legate.

Although no soldier, Pelagius tooks immediate command. Then the delta struck back. The troops began to die of disease. Despite this, the Muslims were ready to make peace and offered to return Jerusalem and the True Cross in return for the abandonment of the assault on Egypt. Pelagius refused, probably because both the pope and the Italian merchants had persuaded him that Egypt was the real key, regardless of earlier crusading objectives.

A second, more generous offer, including a 30-year truce, was rejected when Damietta's citadel fell on August 25, but the cardinal was adamant. The dismal siege continued for another year. The Muslims even demolished the walls of Jerusalem, prior to handing it over. When the deal fell through, they rebuilt them.

Damietta finally fell in November 1219, leaving Pelagius free to advance on Cairo.

In July 1220, the crusaders advanced up the Nile, supported by warships. But the delays had given al-Kamil plenty of time to organize his offensive. The Egyptians encircled the advancing army while overwhelming naval forces cut them off from Damietta. Although Pelagius escaped by boat, the rest of the army was forced to surrender, after negotiating terms. By the following year Damietta was abandoned and the crusaders returned to Acre, their dreams of an easy conquest of Egypt shattered.

**above:** Another manuscript illumination shows Christian soldiers taking Damietta during the Fifth Crusade.

# Stupor Mundi

**The assault on Egypt had been another fiasco. Despondency was dispelled, however, by the eventual arrival of the Sixth Crusade, led by the Holy Roman Emperor. Frederick II's determination to recapture Jerusalem highlighted how far the crusading movement had departed from its original ideals.**

**above:** Front view of a gold aureus of Holy Roman Emperor Frederick II. The man who "stupefied the world" with his feats claimed to be the viceroy on earth of Alexander the Great and Christ. In fact his reign was chaotic, characterized by impulse rather than logic. At his death, his German Hohenstaufen dynasty collapsed.

The city of Damietta and a generous peace offer had been lost through the folly of the papal legate in charge of the Fifth Crusade. By 1220, widespread enthusiasm for the crusading movement had largely been replaced by cynicism. Crusaders felt that they were being exploited for the benefit of the Church rather than fighting for the glory of God.

Frederick II, the new Holy Roman Emperor, seemed to be the last real supporter of the movement. In 1215 he had declared he would take the Cross. Delayed in Germany and forced by illness to break his voyage in Italy, he only arrived in Acre eight years after the Damietta debacle, in late 1228. Newly elected Pope Gregory IX (p.1227–41) had already excommunicated him for his tardy disregard for crusading vows. They were evidently at odds, and the old imperial-papal conflict emerged again in the Holy Land. Frederick ignored Gregory and planned to launch a crusade regardless of the wishes of the Church.

To many contemporaries, Frederick was *stupor mundi* (the amazement of the world), a monarch who claimed to be the viceroy of Christ who wanted to do God's work in the Orient and yet defied the pope at every turn. As soon as he arrived, it became apparent that he would be unlike any crusader who had preceded him. Having married Princess Isabella, daughter of John of Brienne, king of Jerusalem, Frederick quickly made it clear who was now in charge of Outremer. He immediately entered into negotiations with Sultan al-Kamil for control of Jerusalem, a commodity that the Muslims had already demonstrated they were willing to barter.

Both Frederick and al-Kamil were wary of religious extremists within their own camps so the pair arranged a fake campaign to assuage their critics. Frederick marched on Jerusalem at the head of a powerful army and al-Kamil opened formal negotiations, then ceded the city to Frederick on a ten-year lease. On February 18, 1229 the Treaty of Jaffa was signed and Jerusalem returned to Christian control without bloodshed.

## Emperor and antichrist

Frederick should have been the hero of Christendom, but his feud with the pope soured the victory. The Holy Roman Emperor now claimed that he was God's representative on earth, not the pope. In Jerusalem, the patriarch declared that Frederick was the antichrist and Outremer divided into supporters of either pope or emperor. This disunity could have spelled disaster for the Christians were it not for the fact that civil war had broken out in the Muslim world. The careful charade played out between sultan and emperor had fooled few; the loss of Jerusalem was a betrayal by the sultan.

Frederick returned home in late 1229, an excommunicant. Instead of a triumph, he faced war with the Holy See. The pope's anger plunged Germany, Italy, and especially Sicily into a conflict that would last for two decades. Nothing could better illustrate just how much the crusading movement had become a political tool: in effect, the pope had called a crusade against a crusader who had recaptured the Holy Sepulcher in the name of Christendom.

from Rome. Headed by King Tibald of Navarre, the Seventh Crusade arrived in Acre in September 1239, but the renewal of the conflict led to the loss of Jerusalem and the defeat in battle of the Duke of Burgundy near Gaza (1239). Sultan al-Kamil had just died, and a decade of unrest erupted into a civil war of succession between family members in Egypt and Syria. With the Muslim world divided, Tibald was able to negotiate the return of Jerusalem, a fitting end to an otherwise lackluster expedition.

The King of Navarre returned home, leaving Outremer geographically larger but as politically divided as ever. The Fifth, Sixth, and Seventh

below: In the 13th century, both Christians and Muslims spent almost as much time in internecine warfare as in fighting each other. A spate of civil wars debilitated the Ayyubids, and in Outremer frequent territorial bickering led to Christians battling with fellow Christians, as seen in this 14th-century manuscript illumination.

The remainder of Europe and Outremer realized that a once-noble movement had been corrupted, becoming a tool of an intolerant and domineering Church. In 1234, Gregory made one last attempt to launch a crusade controlled

Crusades were a continuous event, a rolling wave of feudal military might. In the end the achievements were won through diplomacy, and the military defeats set a precedent for future disasters.

# Mongols and Mamluks

**In 1219 the Mongol horde invaded the Islamic states south of the Caspian Sea, beginning a wave of conquests that would see their horsemen conquer Baghdad, Damascus, and Aleppo. The only force in the Islamic world capable of stopping them was the Egyptians' elite mamluk troops.**

**facing:** A mamluk horseman killing a boar, from a mid-14th century cavalry training manual. Mounted Muslim warriors differed in several respects from their Christian counterparts. Crusader knights were drawn from the feudal elite; the Muslims were paid professional soldiers. The medieval knight was commonly an irregularly trained fighter, while Muslim cavalry trained continuously, and a part of this was hunting. In Europe, commoners and paid soldiers would be hanged for hunting, since this activity was exclusively reserved for the aristocracy.

The 13th century Mongol invasions of Europe and the Middle East have been described as the "scourge of God." Under the leadership of Timüjin, also known as Genghis Khan (1162–1227), the fierce nomads of the Asiatic steppes became a formidable equestrian army which captured Beijing before carving out a Mongol Empire in China and southwest Asia. In 1219, he led his troops into the empire of the Khwarizm shah and within four years (1219–22) the Mongols had conquered all of the Islamic world east of the Fertile Crescent.

Although Genghis Khan continued into Russia, the Mongols returned to invade eastern Europe in 1238–42, while the Persian territories they captured were incorporated into their empire, becoming the Ilkhanate. The Seljuk Turks and Ayyubid Egyptians joined forces with the remains of the Shah of Khwarizm to confront their common threat, and the Mongols were halted just short of Baghdad. The willingness of Ayyubid sultans to let the crusaders recover Jerusalem indicated the seriousness of the Mongolian threat. They understood that all the resources of Islam would be needed to prevent further Mongol onslaught.

In 1231, Shah Jalal ad-Din was defeated and Islam lost its buffer. Azerbaijan was occupied by the Mongols but no further westward expansion occurred until 1242, when the Mongols invaded Armenia and defeated the Seljuk army sent to stop them. The Seljuk Sultanate of Rum became a client state of the Ilkhanate, as did the Byzantine Empire of Trebizond and the Kingdom of Armenia.

## Ruled by ex-slaves

It took a decade for the Mongols to fully assimilate their new territories but in 1255 they renewed their attack on the Muslim world. Mongol Prince Hulagu overran the strongholds of the Assassins that had survived in the mountains south of the Caspian Sea for centuries, then moved against the Abbasid Caliphate, which still controlled the hinterland of Baghdad and the Arabian peninsula. Baghdad fell in 1258, and the caliph and most of the city's population were slaughtered, sending shockwaves through the Islamic world.

**right:** Mongols and Turks originated from the same geographic region of the steppes north of China, but the two races had little love for each other. As they made their westward migration, the Mongols absorbed many legends of those they conquered. This Mongol illumination of c.1310 depicts Alexander battling a dragon.

As every Turkish army sent against the Mongols had been destroyed, there was only one force in the Islamic world capable of halting the onslaught. The *mamluks* of Egypt were Islam's last hope. The freedmen corps of *mamluks* had long been the military core of the Egyptian army. By the 13th century, *mamluks* had risen to positions of great power, but the *mamluk* system still relied on fresh recruits of boy slaves rather than conscripting indigenous Muslim.

Sultan al-Salih Ayyub (r.1240–49) was the last effective Ayyubid ruler of Egypt, the dynasty founded by Saladin. Faced with the prospect of an invasion by King Louis IX (*see following two pages*), he greatly expanded the *mamluk* force. They were given so much control over their own organization that the sultan effectively turned them into an army in their own right. His brief successor, Turanshah, tried reining in the *mamluks*, but only succeeded in arousing the ire of the brilliant young *mamluk* commander, the emir Rukn ad-Din Baibars. Just after the capture of King Louis IX, Baibars slew Turanshah and a military coup overthrew the Ayyubids. Now an extraordinary new power emerged—the Mamluk Sultanate. Mamluk rulers were slave-recruited soldiers, men from the lowest rung of medieval society, but who became mighty princes. It was a Muslim version of the "meek inheriting the earth."

Emir Baibars, as one of the ringleaders in the coup, controlled the Mamluk war machine, but the army elected the Mamluk emir Kutuz ibn Abdullah as their new sultan. This was not a dynasty in the family sense because the throne was not hereditary, although for the next 130 years new sultans tended to be chosen from among the leading emirs of the Mamluk army, perpetuating the rule of Egypt by a military elite. This Islamic army would soon be pitted against the Mongol horde in a battle to the death.

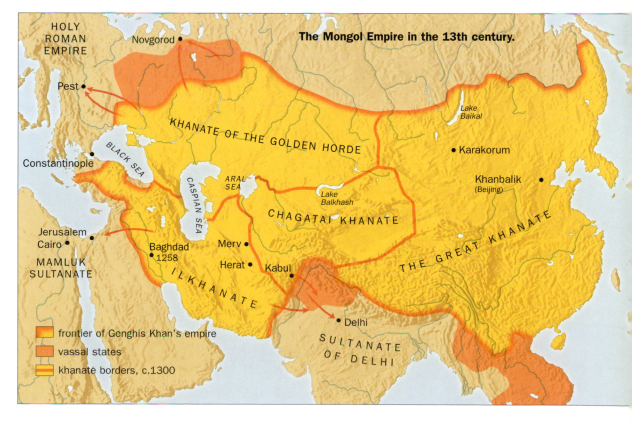

The Mongol Empire in the 13th century.

HOLY ROMAN EMPIRE

Novgorod

Pest

BLACK SEA

Constantinople

Jerusalem
Cairo

MAMLUK SULTANATE

Baghdad
1258

ILKHANATE

ARAL SEA

CASPIAN SEA

Merv

Herat  Kabul

KHANATE OF THE GOLDEN HORDE

Lake Baikal

Karakorum

Khanbalik
(Beijing)

Lake Balkhash

CHAGATAI KHANATE

THE GREAT KHANATE

Delhi

SULTANATE OF DELHI

frontier of Genghis Khan's empire

vassal states

khanate borders, c.1300

# The Crusade of St. Louis

**The recapture of Jerusalem by the Muslims made King Louis IX of France take the Cross. He landed at Damietta in 1248 and marched an army to Cairo, following the route of the disastrous Fifth Crusade. His venture was a still bigger fiasco.**

**facing:** The 15th-century manuscript *Speculum Majus* shows the conquest of Damietta by Louis IX. In this illumination, the French king triumphantly accepts the obeissance of the Egyptians as his army prepares to enter the city, which he took in a matter of days after Ayyubid resistance collapsed.

Louis IX of France (r.1226–70) was a pious man. Although he was aware that the crusading movement had lost its way, he regarded it as his duty to punish the Muslims for their actions. He had already increased the power of the French crown by increasing the royal demesne. By the time he went on crusade his realm stretched from the English Channel to the Mediterranean Sea. It took Louis four years to plan and equip his expedition—he was only ready to sail in August 1248.

Although Pope Innocent IV (p.1243–54) supported his efforts, the papacy was too preoccupied in its struggle with the Holy Roman Emperor to offer more than vocal support for Louis's enterprise, which he organized virtually singlehanded. He discounted a direct assault on the Holy City because Outremer was still reeling from the disaster of La Forbie (1144). After much deliberation, he decided the best objective was Egypt, the heartland of the Ayyubid dynasty. By seizing control of significant cities in Egypt, Louis anticipated having something to bargain with to get Jerusalem back through diplomacy.

The crusader fleet wintered in Cyprus. Unwilling to repeat the mistakes of the Fifth Crusade, Louis had his 15,000 men build a flotilla of invasion barges, ready for use on the Nile. However, he also decided to make Damietta his first objective.

The highly organized amphibious landing worked smoothly, allowing Louis to land his cavalry and siege equipment in safety. After a brief skirmish, the crusaders had only just begun to invest the city when the defenders abandoned it on June 6, 1249. The vital port that had defied the crusaders in 1219–20 for over a year had fallen in a matter of days.

## A fatal error

They remained at Damietta for another two months, waiting for the Nile's floodwaters to recede. The crusaders eventually marched south toward Cairo in late November, supported by a flotilla carrying supplies. To the north of the

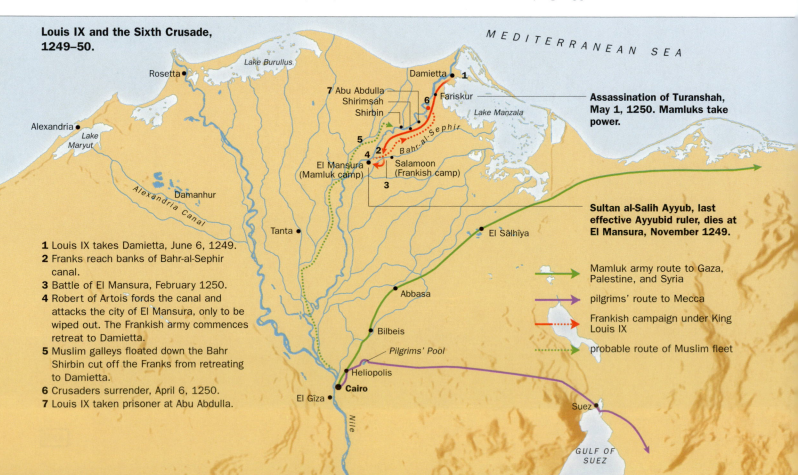

**Louis IX and the Sixth Crusade, 1249–50.**

MEDITERRANEAN SEA

Lake Burullus
Rosetta
Damietta 1
7 Abu Abdulla Shirimsah Shirbin
6 Fariskur
Lake Manzala
Alexandria
Lake Maryut
5
Bahr-al-Sephir
4 2
El Mansura (Mamluk camp)
Salamoon (Frankish camp)
3
Alexandria Canal
Damanhur
Tanta
El Sâlhîya
Abbasa
Bilbeis
Pilgrims' Pool
Heliopolis
Cairo
El Gîza
Nile
Suez
GULF OF SUEZ

**Assassination of Turanshah, May 1, 1250. Mamluks take power.**

**Sultan al-Salih Ayyub, last effective Ayyubid ruler, dies at El Mansura, November 1249.**

1 Louis IX takes Damietta, June 6, 1249.
2 Franks reach banks of Bahr-al-Sephir canal.
3 Battle of El Mansura, February 1250.
4 Robert of Artois fords the canal and attacks the city of El Mansura, only to be wiped out. The Frankish army commences retreat to Damietta.
5 Muslim galleys floated down the Bahr Shirbin cut off the Franks from retreating to Damietta.
6 Crusaders surrender, April 6, 1250.
7 Louis IX taken prisoner at Abu Abdulla.

→ Mamluk army route to Gaza, Palestine, and Syria
→ pilgrims' route to Mecca
→ Frankish campaign under King Louis IX
⋯ probable route of Muslim fleet

fortress city of El Mansura was a formidable obstacle, the Bahr-al-Sephir canal. An Egyptian force led by former Damietta governor Fakhr al-Din prevented any further advance for two months, until a local told the Franks of a ford.

A vanguard led by the king's brother, Robert of Artois, crossed the ford and was meant to attack the defenses facing the main army. Instead they attacked El Mansura. As the Franks reached the walls they were assailed by arrows then attacked by two *mamluk* regiments. The vanguard was slaughtered and the king's brother killed.

Meanwhile, Louis led the main army across the canal in an assault on the Egyptian defenses. He gained a bridgehead on the far bank but was eventually forced to retreat. Rather than return to Damietta, Louis elected to remain at the canal, hoping to reverse his fortunes. Instead, the Egyptians sent a powerful flotilla downstream to secure the Nile and cut the crusaders off from their supplies.

As disease raged in the Frankish camp, Louis at last decided to retreat north. Although seriously weakened by dysentery, he commanded the rearguard, but was unable to prevent the isolation and capture of his army. In April 1250, King Louis IX surrendered to the Egyptians. He was not the only ruler suffering. At about the same time, the young Sultan Turanshah was murdered by his own *mamluk* bodyguard. Louis witnessed the act, which left the French king fearing for his own life.

On the next day he was released along with the few companions left to him, to begin the discussions that would lead to a treaty with the new power, the Mumluk rulers Rukn ad-Din Baibars and Kutuz ibn Abdullah. The deal allowed Louis, his knights, captive men-at-arms, siege equipment, supplies, and all the French still holding Damietta to sail for Acre. In return Louis agreed to surrender Damietta and pay a large ransom. Early in May 1250, the still unwell French king set sail for Acre.

**below:** After defeat at Mansura, a treaty with the new Mamluk rulers allowed Louis to sail away from Damietta with his surviving ships and men bound for Acre. Illumination from *Vie et Miracles de Saint Louis* by Guillaume de Saint Pathus, c.1330.

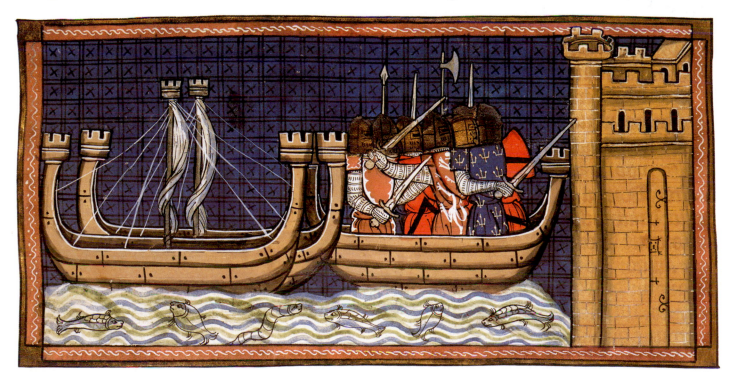

# Ain Jalut: Battle for the Holy Land

**The Mongol invasion of the Middle East threatened to engulf Islam. The barbarian onslaught decimated the Muslim population and destroyed Syria and the Fertile Crescent before reaching the borders of the new Mamluk Sultanate. A climactic battle would decide the fate of Islam and seal the fate of the Crusader States.**

**below:** Landscape near Nazareth, scene of one of the bloodiest battles of the 13th century, when the Mamluk army of Baibars defeated the Mongol horde at Ain Jalut.

When the Mongols destroyed the strongholds of the Assassins in 1255, it seemed unthinkable that these nomadic horsemen could pose a threat to Baghdad, the greatest city in the Middle East. In 1257, a Mongol horde rode eastward toward the fertile Tigris and besieged Baghdad. The nomads showed that they had absorbed the lessons of siege warfare and, after a week's bombardment,

the city fell under Mongol assault in January 1258. The slaughter lasted for 40 days; contemporary Muslim chroniclers put the death toll at over 80,000. According to Arab legend, the caliph was locked in his treasury and starved to death amid his gold.

The news of the sack of Baghdad shocked the Muslim world, but in Outremer the crusaders viewed the Mongols as saviors, and even quoted the legend of Prester John, where a lost Christian people would come to the rescue of their co-religionists. The Mongols were no lost Christians but they inadvertently relieved pressure on the crusaders at a time when the realm was virtually defenseless. Locked in a struggle for power between Venice and Genoa and the followers of emperor or pope, the nobles and merchants of Outremer had little option but to hope the Mongol scourge would pass them by. The Mongols realized the importance of this potential Christian ally in a Muslim world and left the Armenian Christian churches in Baghdad undisturbed.

Impressed, the King of Armenia formed an alliance with the Mongols, his logic being that any enemy of Islam was an ally. The Mongol horde stormed Mosul in the Fertile Crescent between the Tigris and Euphrates, then the Armenian-Mongol army besieged Aleppo in late 1259. An offer to surrender was ignored. After another week-long bombardment by Mongol siege engines, the city was stormed, prompting a massacre that reputedly continued for six days. Once again, the Christian centers in the city were spared, and the Armenians occupied the city. They were now a subject state of the Mongol Ilkhanate, as was the Sultanate of Rum to the north.

## Bow down or be destroyed

The Mongols headed south into Syria. Faced with what seemed like certain destruction, the population of Homs and Damascus fled south into Egypt—even Sultan Nasir of Damascus sought the protection of the Mamluks. Ominously, on their way south the Mongols visited Antioch, the one great crusader city spared the wrath of Saladin. Realizing that

**above:** Mongol warriors fighting, painting from the Persian School, early 15th century.

resistance was futile, Prince Bohemond offered his submission to the Mongol warlord, Prince Hulagu, ending exclusive Latin rule in the first city the crusaders ever captured.

With the capture of Damascus in 1260, Syria became a Mongol province. Only the Mamluks stood between the nomadic horsemen and the riches of Egypt. The Mamluk sultan was ordered to "bow down to the Khan or be destroyed." In fact, Mongke Khan (r.1241–59) had just died, so the Mongols were in need of a successor. At that moment the Mamluk army caught up with the horde.

The two armies met near Nazareth on September 3, 1260 at Ain Jalut (Goliath's Spring, the traditional site of David's victory over the Philistines). The Mongol army consisted of about 10,000 horsemen, supported by their Armenian allies. The army of 12,000 Mamluks commanded by Baibars divided their forces and lured the Mongols into an ambush by means of a feigned retreat. The Mongols were decisively defeated, ending the Mongol threat to Islam for good.

As Baibars and his Mamluks pursued their enemy they recaptured Damascus and Aleppo and pushed the Mongols back beyond the Euphrates. On the strength of his victory, Baibars also seized power, killing the Mamluk Sultan Kutuz and claiming control of an empire that surrounded Outremer. Like Saladin before him, Baibars was now the master of a united Muslim realm and the collapse of the Crusader States was just a matter of time.

# The Collapse of Outremer

**From 1260, Outremer was surrounded by a powerful and hostile Islamic state. The Mamluk sultan began a systematic campaign of conquest in 1263, while the crusaders seemed unable to set aside their quarrels long enough to defend themselves. By 1291 only Acre and a handful of smaller towns remained of the once-proud crusader Kingdom of Jerusalem.**

Following his defeat of the Mongols, Mamluk Sultan Rukn ad-Din Baibars spent two years strengthening his hold over his new Muslim realm. The link between the Mongols and the Christian Armenians had been broken following the Battle of Ain Jalut and the Mongols were no longer a serious threat.

Indeed, over the next few decades, many of the Mongol overlords of Armenia, Persia, and Iraq converted to Islam.

In 1263, Baibars launched his first attack against Outremer, a probe toward Acre. He captured Caesarea in 1265, slighting the city defenses before repeating the process at Caiphas. In each city, the surviving population was massacred, which prompted Arsuf's defenders to seek quarter. It was denied, and once again the Latin population was put to the sword.

The following year Mamluks captured the strategic Templar castle of Safed, north of Lake Tiberias (Galilee), and executed their prisoners. Meanwhile another Mamluk army launched a punitive expedition into Cilician Armenia, where it defeated an Armenian army before capturing and razing the Armenian capital. Some 40,000 inhabitants were led south in chains. By the end of the year, only Jaffa remained in crusader hands south of Acre.

In the face of this onslaught the limited military resources of Outremer had difficulty defending themselves because the coastal cities were still gripped in a power struggle between Venice and Genoa. A Mamluk assault on Acre in the following year failed because the Muslims lacked the siege equipment to capture the port. Christian peace overtures were rejected and the remorseless Muslim conquests continued.

## Acre falls

Baibars seemed to be everywhere in 1268. Following the death of John of Ibelin, Lord of Beirut, a treaty between the Mamluks and the Latin ruler of Jaffa ended. The Mamluks stormed the city, then dismantled the castle to

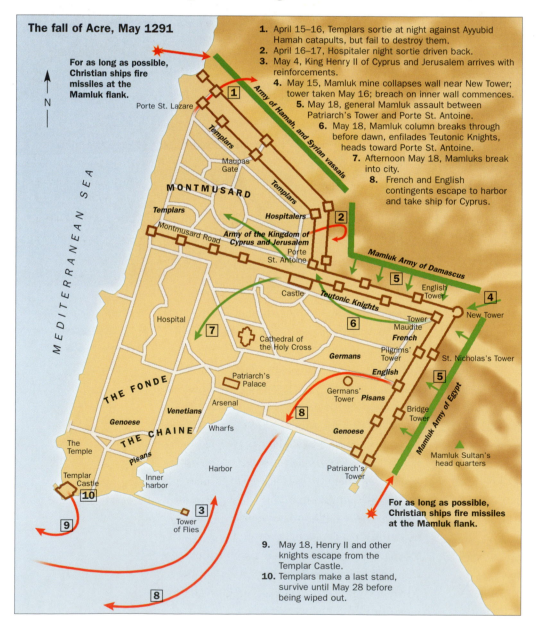

**The fall of Acre, May 1291**

For as long as possible, Christian ships fire missiles at the Mamluk flank.

1. April 15–16, Templars sortie at night against Ayyubid Hamah catapults, but fail to destroy them.
2. April 16–17, Hospitaler night sortie driven back.
3. May 4, King Henry II of Cyprus and Jerusalem arrives with reinforcements.
4. May 15, Mamluk mine collapses wall near New Tower; tower taken May 16; breach on inner wall commences.
5. May 18, general Mamluk assault between Patriarch's Tower and Porte St. Antoine.
6. May 18, Mamluk column breaks through before dawn, enfilades Teutonic Knights, heads toward Porte St. Antoine.
7. Afternoon May 18, Mamluks break into city.
8. French and English contingents escape to harbor and take ship for Cyprus.

Porte St. Lazare

Templars

Maupas Gate

MONTMUSARD

Templars

Montmusard Road

Templars

Hospitalers

Army of Hamah, and Syrian vassals

Army of the Kingdom of Cyprus and Jerusalem

Porte St. Antoine

Mamluk Army of Damascus

Castle

Teutonic Knights

English Tower

New Tower

Tower Maudite

Hospital

Cathedral of the Holy Cross

French

Pilgrims' Tower

St. Nicholas's Tower

Germans

English

Patriarch's Palace

Germans' Tower

Pisans

Mamluk Army of Egypt

THE FONDE

Arsenal

Venetians

Genoese

Wharfs

Genoese

Bridge Tower

Mamluk Sultan's head quarters

THE CHAINE

The Temple

Pisans

Harbor

Patriarch's Tower

Templar Castle

Inner harbor

MEDITERRANEAN SEA

N

For as long as possible, Christian ships fire missiles at the Mamluk flank.

Tower of Flies

9. May 18, Henry II and other knights escape from the Templar Castle.
10. Templars make a last stand, survive until May 28 before being wiped out.

form part of a celebratory mosque in Cairo. Next he besieged and captured the Templar stronghold of Beaufort, before marching north to Antioch. Revenge on the Christians who had allied themselves with the Mongols was within Baibars' grasp. When the city fell the entire population was killed or enslaved. The richest city in Outremer was plundered and "coins were so plentiful they were handed out in bowlfuls."

King Louis IX had arrived in Acre after the disaster in Egypt, and even though there were pressing reasons for his return to France, he decided to remain as long as he could be useful. He was joined in the defense of Acre by Prince Edward of England. The arrival of fresh English crusaders in Acre prompted Baibars to offer a ten-year truce, so at least the crusaders postponed the inevitable. In 1254, unable to put it off any longer, Louis set sail for France, having been able to offer little assistance to Outremer. He was the last European monarch to go on crusade and his failure marked the end of a series of large-scale and high-profile crusading ventures, sent from Europe to the Middle East. Louis was killed 20 years later, still crusading, in a raid on Tunis. He was canonized as St. Louis in 1297.

While support for a fresh crusade waned, the nobles of Outremer continued to bicker. In 1277 Charles of Anjou, King of Sicily, became the new King of Acre, a man with powerful allies in Europe. Baibars died in the same year and the Mamluks bided their time. On Charles' death in 1285, Henry II, King of Cyprus (r.1285–1324), succeeded him, a ruler with little support in either Europe or Outremer. The Italian merchants in Outremer continued to feud, so the new Mamluk Sultan Qalawun seized the moment. He gathered an overwhelming army and in 1287 captured Latakia.

Tripoli fell two years later. By 1291 his 100,000-man army was outside Acre. Pleas for help from Europe fell on deaf ears. On May 18, 1291, Acre fell after six weeks of bombardment and two assaults. The defenders bought time for the population to flee in boats, but in the end, anyone remaining in the city was slaughtered.

Tyre, Sidon, Beirut, and the few remaining crusader cities fell in quick succession, ending two centuries of crusader rule in the Holy Land. Although crusader enclaves remained for several decades in remote outposts in the eastern Mediterranean, the Crusades ended on the quayside of Acre.

**above:** Acre today, seen from the air, still reveals the shape of the old crusader city, with the site of the Templar Castle in the foreground and the distant line of the old walls running along Montmusard Road.

# The Crusading Aftermath

**What did the Crusades achieve? Did they produce any legacy, apart from the simmering religious intolerance?**

In the course of world history, the Crusades achieved relatively little. The cost of the crusading movement in manpower and financial resources was high, but in the end the Crusaders had little to show for their efforts. Probably the only people to benefit from the venture were the Italians, whose city-states gathered the profits in trade and transportation as long as the Frankish states of Outremer survived, but then continued to trade with the Orient in the years that followed. Some historians accuse the Crusades for hindering the cultural and social development of Europe by locking its people in a futile struggle for religious dominance on another continent. Others point to the expansion of European consciousness after a period of stagnation during the so-called Dark Ages as a beneficial side effect. Certainly, the after effects have survived for a long time, and even today the battle for the Holy Land between rival faiths continues.

The crusading movement continued even after the fall of Acre, but it was no longer the cause of princes. The military orders recuperated and regrouped on Aegean and Mediterranean islands. The devastated Templars managed to hold onto their lands in Cyprus, but failed to find a proper military role, although they still functioned as bankers throughout Europe. That is, until the Order's demise at the hands of envious prelates and princes in 1302–12.

## Decline of the Hospitallers

The Hospitallers took temporary refuge on Cyprus in their strongholds at Colos and Limassol. Unlike their brother Order, they had no financial business to fall back on and determined to change into an island-based sea power. In 1301 a new official position appeared — that of Admiral. Expansion to the island of Rhodes began in 1306 and the expulsion of Muslims was complete by 1307 with the exception of the city of Rhodes itself, which fell two years later.

From their new stronghold, the Hospitallers battled with Muslim corsairs throughout the Aegean. The island of Smyrna was taken in 1345 and held until it fell to the Mongol invasion of 1402. The Order supported Cypriot campaigns against Egypt in the 1390s, but otherwise concerned itself mainly with sorties against the Ottoman Turks.

Rhodes became the last outpost of Christianity in the East after the fall of Constantinople in 1453. Relations between the Hospitallers and the Ottoman sultans worsened, and Rhodes came under siege in 1480. On this occasion, the Christians managed to drive off the Muslims, but the second siege in 1522 ended after months of assaults and attrition. The Hospitallers accepting the inevitable and surrendering the island. They resettled on the island of Malta and became the scourge of the Barbary Coast corsairs. The Ottomans struck again in July 1565. The great siege lasted until a Spanish relief army chased off the Turks at the beginning of September.

From this point on, the Order began to lose its military meaning. Opulence, decadence and internecine strife between different arms drained the Hospitallers until the Order finally surrendered to Napoleon Bonaparte after a two-day siege in 1798.

Outremer lasted a mere two centuries, but other claimants on the Holy Land also suffered for their temerity. The Ottoman Turks reunited the Islamic world under a state that defied the might of Napoleon Bonaparte, before it succumbed during the bloody hell of the First World War. The British and the French became temporary guardians of the region, until the withdrawal from their empires prompted a reappraisal of the role of colonial guardians.

In 1948 the new State of Israel emerged and the Israelis immediately found themselves surrounded by hostile Islamic neighbours. Clear parallels can be drawn between Israel and Outremer, but only time will tell how closely the modern Jewish state mirrors the historical development of the earlier Christian realm. If the Crusades' only lasting legacy is religious hatred, we have learned little from the mistakes of our forebears.

**facing:** The east gate of the Crusader fortress of Caesarea at sunset.

# Crusades Chronology

**64 BC** The collapse of the Hellenistic Seleucid Empire creates a power vacuum in the Middle East

**AD 6** Palestine is annexed by the Romans

**50** Christian faith begins to spread

**66** Jews in Judea revolt against the Romans

**313** Christianity becomes the religion of the Roman Empire

**527** Byzantine Empire formed under Roman Emperor Justinian in Constantinople

**622** Mohammed and his followers are forced from Mecca

**628** Mohammed captures Mecca

**634** Caliph Abu Bakr's Arabian army captures Jerusalem

**c.634** The Byzantine Empire loses most of its Middle Eastern territory to Muslim armies

**640** The Arabs reach North Africa

**644** Caliph Uthman gains power, founding the Umayyad dynasty

**661** On the murder of Caliph Ali, son-in-law of Mohammed, Islam is divided into Shi'ite and Sunni sects

**692** The Muslim Dome of the Rock is completed in Jerusalem

**c.715** Muslim armies take Spain from the Visigoths

**732** The Moors' planned invasion of the Frankish kingdom ends after defeat at Tours

**c.750** Peace between Christians and Muslims in Asia Minor

**750** Umayyad dynasty collapses after an Abbasid caliph is enthroned

**777** The first Arabian regional dynasty is established

**823** Arabs take Sicily from the Byzantines

**969** Shi'ite Fatimids gain power in Egypt

**974** Byzantine Empire controls northern Palestine and Syria

**987** Capetian dynasty established in France with the election of Hugh

**1009** Al-Hakim destroys the Holy Sepulchre in Jerusalem

**1051** Abbasid secular rule is replaced by Seljuk Turks

**1054** Catholic and Orthodox Churches are divided in the Great Schism

**1055** Seljuk Turks capture Baghdad and expand their territory westwards

**1059** The Fatimid caliphate gains control of Baghdad

**1070** Spanish Christians, including Raymond of Toulouse, drive away Moors in the *Reconquista*

**1071** Byzantine defeat by Seljuk Turks at Manzikert leads to collapse of its rule in Anatolia

**1075** Pope Gregory VII excommunicates German Emperor Henry IV

**1081** Trade agreement established between Venice and the Byzantines

**1088** Urban II becomes Pope

**1091** Normans, including Prince Bohemond of Taranto, conquer Moorish Sicily

**1094–5** Byzantine Emperor Alexius appeals for help against the Seljuk Turks

**1095** On 27 November Pope Urban II calls for a crusade to the Holy Land

**1096** The Peasants' Crusade, led by Peter the Hermit, ends with the pilgrims' slaughter

**1096–7** Crusading armies arrive at Constantinople

**1098** The Crusaders take Antioch, gateway to the Holy Land

**1099** The Crusaders arrive at Montjoie, the hill overlooking Jerusalem, on 7 June

**1099** The siege of Jerusalem begins on 8 June; the Crusaders take the Holy City on 15 July

**1099** In August a Fatimid army is driven away at the Battle of Ascalon

**c.1100** Feudal system established in France, the model for the Crusader states

**1100** Baldwin of Edessa becomes King of Jerusalem, leader of the Crusader states

**1113** The Knights Hospitaller are founded as the Order of the Hospital of St John

**1115** The Knights Templar are founded, originally known as 'the poor knights'

**1119** Roger of Salerno is killed while defending Antioch in the Field of Blood battle

**1119** A combined Aleppo and Damascus army massacre the Franks in the Battle of Ager Sanguinus, Antioch

**1122** A rebellion led by Count Pons of Tripoli against the feudal overlordship of King Baldwin II is defeated

**1123–4** Baldwin II is held by Seljuk Turks led by Balak

**1126** A union between Antioch and Jerusalem is formed when Baldwin II forces Prince Bohemond II of Antioch to marry his daughter

**1137** Turkish Emir Zengi wins a

ransom after besieging King Fulk V of Jerusalem in Montferrand castle, near Tripoli

**1144** Joscelin II, Count of Edessa, loses the city to Seljuk Turks led by Zengi

**1146** Bernard, Abbot of Clairvaux, boosts Pope Eugenius III's call for the Second Crusade

**1148** French and German Crusaders arrive at Constantinople, others group at Acre

**1148** Crusaders led by Louis IV of France fail to take Damascus and retreat to Outremer

**1154** Nur ed-Din conquers Damascus

**1161–75** Reynald of Châtillon is held by Turks, losing his principality of Antioch but gaining *Oultrejordain* through marriage on his release

**1163** Baldwin III dies and is succeeded by younger brother Almaric

**1164** Nur ed-Din invades Antioch to draw King Almaric from the invasion of Egypt

**1167** A combined Seljuk-Fatimid force defends Egypt from Crusaders in the Day of Al-Babein

**1169** Saladin becomes *wazir* of Egypt on the death of General Shirkuh

**1174** Nur ed-Din and King Almaric die; Saladin seizes power in Damascus

**1180** Baldwin IV makes peace with Saladin

**1181–83** Reynald of Châtillon targets Muslims, breaking the peace

**1186** Baldwin V is succeeded by his mother's new husband, Guy of Lusignan

**1187** The crusading army is devastated at Hattin; Saladin immediately begins to conquer Crusader States

**1187** Saladin takes Jerusalem on 2 October

**1190** Richard I the Lionheart and Philip II Augustus of France prepare for the Third Crusade

**1190** Frederick I Barbarossa of the Holy Roman Empire drowns on 10 July while travelling to Antioch

**1191** Richard aids King Guy in the capture of Muslim Acre

**1192** Saladin is thwarted by Richard at Jaffa (5 August); on 2 September a three-year truce is signed

**1193** Saladin dies in March

**1199** Pope Innocent III calls for the Fourth Crusade

**1201** After supplying ships, the Venetians redirect the Fourth Crusade from Alexandria to Constantinople

**1202** The Crusaders sail from Venice to Zara; the Venetians are excommunicated by the Pope

**1203** The Crusaders' land and sea assault on Constantinople is repulsed (July)

**1204** The Crusaders take Constantinople (April); Baldwin of Flanders becomes Emperor of Romania

**1212** Stephen the Prophet leads the Children's Crusade

**1217** Members of the Fifth Crusade gather at Acre and campaign in *Oultrejordain*

**1218** Crusaders besiege Damietta but Cardinal Pelagius refuses the Muslims' offer of peace

**1219** Muslim territories come under threat from the Mongols

**1220** Crusaders' assault on the Nile ends with their surrender to the Egyptian navy

**1221** The Crusaders abandon Damietta and retreat to Acre

**1228** Excommunicated Holy Roman Emperor Frederick II arrives in Acre

**1229** On 18 February al-Kamil cedes Jerusalem to Frederick II for ten years

**1231** Armenia and Iran are invaded by Mongols

**1239** A Crusade led by King Tibald of Navarre ends in the death of the Duke of Burgundy and the temporary loss of Jerusalem

**1244** Jerusalem falls to an Egyptian army

**1249** Damietta is taken in the Sixth Crusade by King Louis IX

**1250** A ransom is paid to release King Louis IX after his failed assault on Egypt

**1258** The caliph of Baghdad and his people are slaughtered by the invading Mongols

**1260** The Mongols are defeated at Ain Jalut by the Egyptian Mamluks commanded by Baibars

**1261** Emperor Michael VIII Palaeologus and his army restore Constantinople to the Byzantine Empire

**1263** The Mamluks begin taking the Crusader States

**1268** The Eighth Crusade is called after the Mamluks conquer Antioch; Baibars offers a truce

**1291** Mamluks led by Sultan Qalawun take Acre, followed by other Crusader cities; Outremer ceases to exist

# Glossary and Genealogy Tables

**Abbasid:** Sunni dynasty of caliphs based in Baghdad (750–1262), later in Cairo (1262–1517).

**Advocate of the Holy Sepulchre:** leader of Christian Jerusalem; the title was replaced by King with the election of Baldwin I.

**Almoravid:** Berber dynasty of rulers based in northwest Africa (1056–1147).

**amir:** *see* emir.

**Anatolia:** Asia Minor, now Turkey.

**antipope:** a rival Pope set up by Holy Roman Emperor Henry IV during the investiture crisis between Church and State.

**atabeg:** Middle Eastern autonomous governor of an Islamic state who owes allegiance only to the Great Seljuk Sultan.

**Ayyubid:** dynasty of rulers descended from Saladin (1169–1252, based in Egypt and Mesopotamia).

**benefice system:** granting of land in return for military support; forerunner of the feudal system.

**Byzantium:** original name of the capital of the Byzantine Empire, Constantinople (now Istanbul).

**caliph:** head of the Islamic world, usually religious; successor to Mohammed.

**Cilicia:** an Armenian kingdom in Asia Minor (Anatolia).

**Druze:** a follower of a Middle Eastern religion based on Islam, but rejected by true Muslims.

**Eastern Roman Empire:** surviving section of the empire, which became the Byzantine Empire under Emperor Justinian.

**emir:** secular ruler of an Islamic state or emirate.

**Fatimid:** Shi'ite dynasty of caliphs based in Cairo.

**Fertile Crescent:** a region running from southern Palestine, through Jordan and Syria then across to Mesopotamia (southeastern Turkey and Iraq) and the Persian Gulf, named for its favourable growing conditions.

**fief:** land given to a knight by a king to generate income for himself and his retinue.

**ghulams:** slaves recruited into an army; see *mamluks*.

**Holy Lance:** the weapon said to have pierced Christ's side on the Cross.

**Holy Roman Empire:** Christian European empire based around Germany, its emperor elected by German princes.

**Hospitaller:** *see* Knights Hospitaller.

**Holy See:** the seat of the Roman Catholic Church; also called the 'papal see' or the 'Apostolic See'; *see* Papal States.

**ifranj:** Arabic term for foreigners or Europeans, literally 'franks'.

**Ilkhanate:** Mongol dynasty of Persia (1256–1353).

**imam:** a Muslim leader, initially the title of the chosen interpreter of the Koran and Mohammed's successor.

**jihad:** a conflict with evil, a term often linked with 'holy war'.

**jizyah:** a tax payable by non-Muslims in Jerusalem.

**Khwarizm:** region around the mouth of the River Oxus, Central Asia.

**Knights Hospitaller:** religious soldiers of the Order of St John's Hospital.

**Knights Templar:** religious soldiers of the Order of the Temple.

**mamluk:** professional slave-recruited soldier, notably in Egypt.

**Mamluk:** ruling dynasty in Egypt and Syria (1252–1517), usually headed by a mamluk soldier.

**mangonel:** stone-throwing siege machine.

**Mongols:** tribes of nomads from south central Asia, united under Genghis Khan.

**Moors:** generic term covering Umayyad Arab-Berber Muslims from northwest Africa who invaded Spain and later generations of Almoravid and Almohad dynasties.

**mutatawi'ah:** religiously motivated volunteer soldiers in Muslim armies.

**Ottomans:** Turkish people named after Sultan Osman.

**Outremer:** (Fr.) 'overseas' — the Crusader States in the Middle East.

**papal legate:** a representative of the Pope.

**Papal States:** territory in central Italy governed by the Holy See and subject to variation in size and position over the centuries; now effectively the Vatican State, Rome.

**Patriarch of Jerusalem:** the senior Orthodox cleric in the Holy Land.

**Peasants' Crusade:** Peter the Hermit's unsanctioned Crusade of French non-nobles.

**Reconquista:** campaign by Spanish Christians to drive the Moors from the Iberian Peninsula.

**Rum:** the part of Anatolia Seljuk Turks took from the Byzantines, a derivation of 'Roman', since this was once part of the Roman Empire.

**Saracens:** generic term for Arabs and Muslims; originally a term for tribesmen of the Syria region.

**Seljuks:** Turkish people and dynasty that conquered the Islamic world (1040–1194; 1048–1307 for the Seljuks of Rum).

**serjeant/segeant:** non-professional soldier, either infantry or mounted.

**Shi'ite:** sect of Islam that believes Ali, Mohammed's son-in-law, and his descendants are the prophet's true successors.

**siege engine:** generic name for various types of catapult used to assault the walls of castles.

**sultan:** a Muslim ruler.

**Sunni:** sect of Islam that believes Mohammed's successors should be elected by the Muslim community.

**Templar:** *see* Knights Templar.

**Teutonic Knight:** member of the military order of the Knights of the Hospital of St Mary in Jerusalem, originally established to care for wounded German soldiers, but later combat knights in the Crusades. The Order later operated extensively in northern Europe.

**trebuchet:** a catapult designed like a large seesaw, the weighted end released to throw a missile from the other.

**turcopoles:** Muslim light cavalrymen who fought in Crusader armies after conversion to Christianity. (Grk.) 'Turkish people."

**Umayyad:** Arab dynasty of caliphs, also known as the Caliphs of Damascus.

**Varangian Guard:** Imperial Byzantine military unit comprised of foreigners, invariably of Viking stock.

**vizir** or **vizier:** senior Muslim government minister; *wazir* in the original Arabic.

## Simplified Ayyubid dynasty

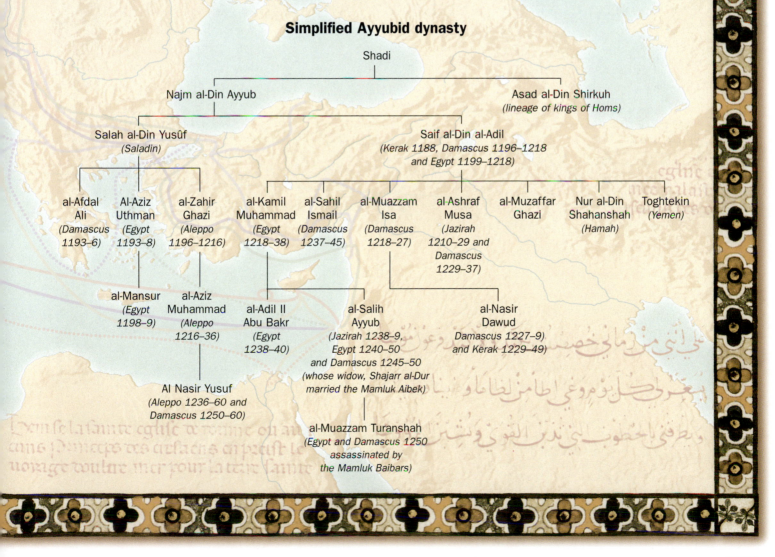

Shadi

Najm al-Din Ayyub — Asad al-Din Shirkuh (lineage of kings of Homs)

Salah al-Din Yusûf (Saladin)

Saif al-Din al-Adil (Kerak 1188, Damascus 1196–1218 and Egypt 1199–1218)

al-Afdal Ali (Damascus 1193–6) — Al-Aziz Uthman (Egypt 1193–8) — al-Zahir Ghazi (Aleppo 1196–1216) — al-Kamil Muhammad (Egypt 1218–38) — al-Sahil Ismail (Damascus 1237–45) — al-Muazzam Isa (Damascus 1218–27) — al-Ashraf Musa (Jazirah 1210–29 and Damascus 1229–37) — al-Muzaffar Ghazi — Nur al-Din Shahanshah (Hamah) — Toghtekin (Yemen)

al-Mansur (Egypt 1198–9)

al-Aziz Muhammad (Aleppo 1216–36)

al-Adil II Abu Bakr (Egypt 1238–40)

al-Salih Ayyub (Jazirah 1238–9, Egypt 1240–50 and Damascus 1245–50 (whose widow, Shajarr al-Dur married the Mamluk Aibek))

al-Nasir Dawud Damascus 1227–9) and Kerak 1229–49)

Al Nasir Yusuf (Aleppo 1236–60 and Damascus 1250–60)

al-Muazzam Turanshah (Egypt and Damascus 1250 assassinated by the Mamluk Baibars)

## Princes of Antioch
*Princes who occupied the throne in bold*

## The Throne of Jerusalem
*Ruling kings in bold*

### Princes of Antioch

Robert Guiscard

**Bohemond**

Emma
*m. Eudes the Good*

**Bohemond II**
*m. Alice of Jerusalem*

**Tancred**
*m. Cecily of France*

Richard 'of the Principality"

Constance
*m. 1 **Raymond of Poitiers***
*m. 2 **Reynald of Châtillon***

**Roger of Salerno**

**Bohemond III**
*m. 2 Orguilleuse of Harenc*

Maria
*m. Manuel Comnenus*

Raymond
*m. 1 Alice of Armenia*

**Bohemond IV**
*Count of Tripoli*
*m. Melisende of Lusignan*

**Raymond Roupen**

Maria
*m. Philip of Montfort*

Raymond

Philip
*m. Isabella of Armenia*

Maria
*pretender to the throne of Jerusalem*

**Bohemond V**
*m. 1 Alice of Champagne*
*m. 2 Lucia of Segni*

Henry 'du Prince"
*m. Isabella of Lusignan*

Hugh III

**Bohemond VI**
*m. Sibylla of Armenia*

**Bohemond VII**

Lucia

### The Throne of Jerusalem

Eustace, Count of Boulogne
*m. Ida of Lower Lorraine*

Melisende
*m. Hugh I of Rethel*

**Godfrey**  **Baldwin I**  Eustace

**Baldwin II of Bourg**

Melisende
*m. **Fulk of Anjou***

Alice
*m. Bohemond II*

Hodierna
*m. Raymond II*

Joetta
*Abbess*

**Baldwin III**

**Almaric**
*m. 1 Agnes of Courtenay*
*m. 2 Maria Comnena*

**Baldwin IV**

Sibylla
*m. 1 William of Montfort*
*m. 2 Guy of Lusignan*

Isabella
*m. 1 Humphrey of Toron*
*m. 2 **Conrad of Montferrat***
*m. 3 **Henry of Champagne***
*m. 4 **Aimery of Lusignan***

**Baldwin V**

Maria
*m. John of Brienne*

Alice
*m. 1 Hugh I of Lusignan*
*m. 2 Ralph of Soissons*

Melisende
*m. Bohemond IV*

Isabella
*m. **Frederick II***

Maria
*(ceded her rights to* **Charles of Anjou**)

**Conrad IV**

Henry I

Isabella
*m. Henry 'du Prince"*

Conradin

Hugh II

**Hugh III**

John  **Henry II**  Guy  Almaric  Aimery

### Counts of Tripoli (of the Toulouse dynasty)
*Counts who occupied the throne in bold*

Pons, Count of Toulouse  m.  Almodis  Raingarde

William IV

**Raymond of St Giles**

Adelaide
*m. William Raymond, Count of Cerdagne*

**Bertrand**

Alphonse Jordan

**Pons**
*m. Cecily of France*

Bertrand
*(illegitimate)*

**William Jordan**

**Raymond II**
*m. Hodierna of Jerusalem*

**Raymond III**
*m. Eschiva of Tiberias*
*adopted son of Bohemond III*

Melisende

# INDEX